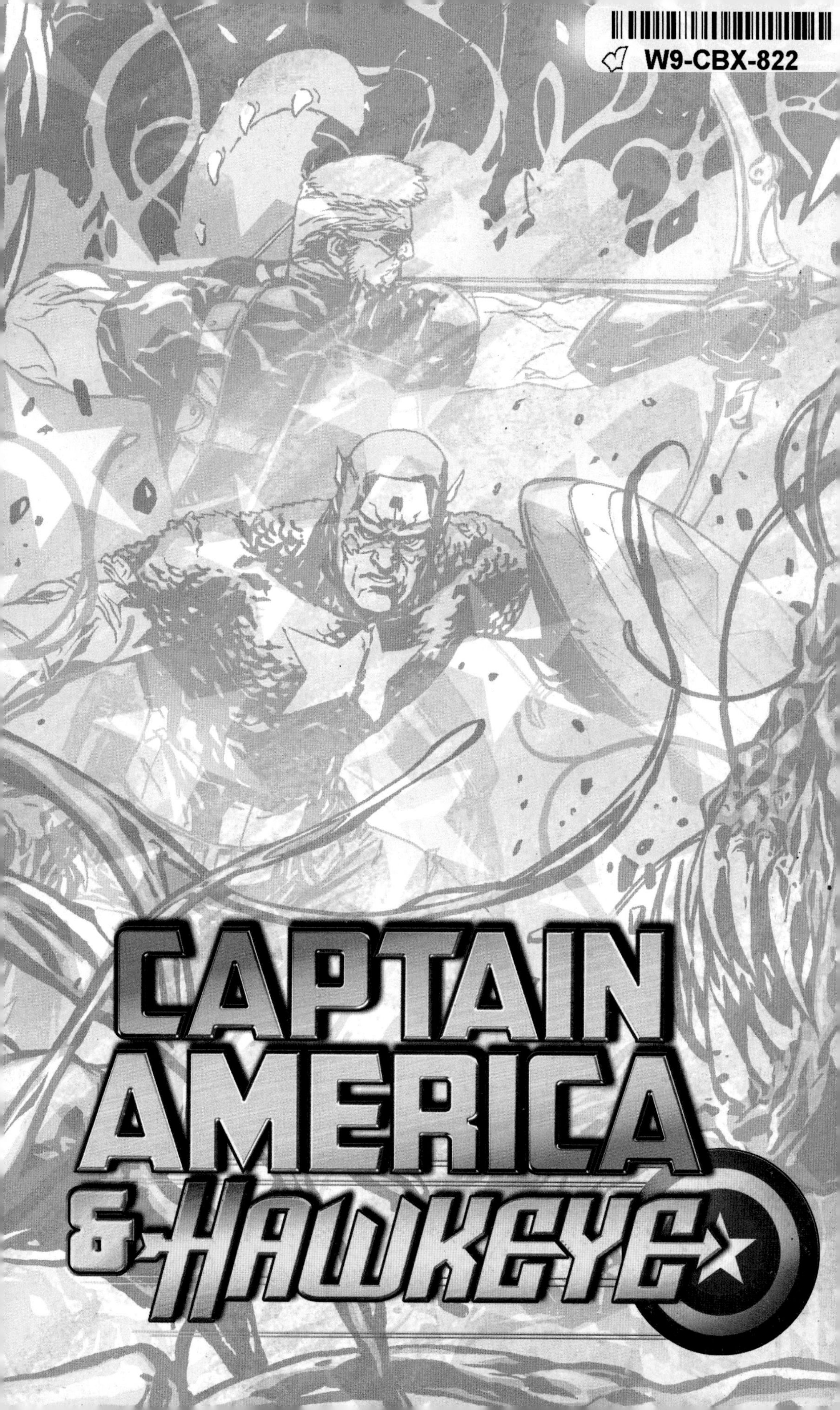
CAPTAIN
AMERICA
& HAWKEYE

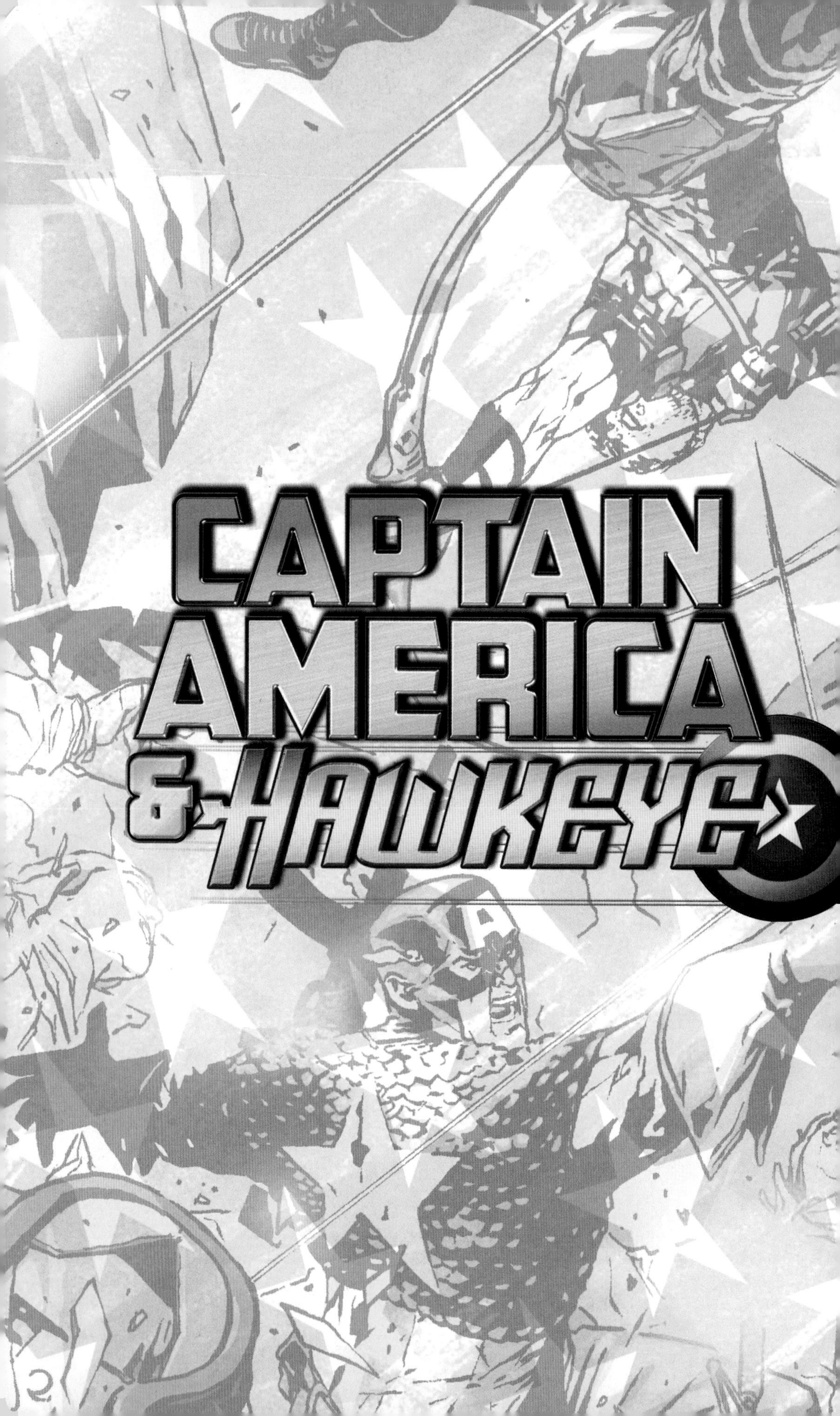
CAPTAIN AMERICA
& HAWKEYE

WRITER
CULLEN BUNN
ARTIST
ALESSANDRO VITTI
WITH **MATTEO BUFFAGNI**
(ISSUE #631)
COLOR ARTIST
JAVIER TARTAGLIA
LETTERER
VC'S JOE CARAMAGNA
COVER ARTISTS
GABRIELE DELL'OTTO
(ISSUE #629);
AND **PATCH ZIRCHER**
& **MATT HOLLINGSWORTH**
(ISSUES #630-632)
ASSISTANT EDITOR
JOHN DENNING
EDITOR
LAUREN SANKOVITCH
CAPTAIN AMERICA CREATED BY
JOE SIMON & JACK KIRBY

COLLECTION EDITOR
CORY LEVINE
ASSISTANT EDITORS
ALEX STARBUCK & NELSON RIBEIRO
EDITORS, SPECIAL PROJECTS
JENNIFER GRÜNWALD & MARK D. BEAZLEY
SENIOR EDITOR, SPECIAL PROJECTS
JEFF YOUNGQUIST
SENIOR VICE PRESIDENT OF SALES
DAVID GABRIEL
SVP OF BRAND PLANNING & COMMUNICATIONS
MICHAEL PASCIULLO
BOOK DESIGN
JEFF POWELL

EDITOR IN CHIEF
AXEL ALONSO
CHIEF CREATIVE OFFICER
JOE QUESADA

PUBLISHER
DAN BUCKLEY
EXECUTIVE PRODUCER
ALAN FINE

CAPTAIN AMERICA AND HAWKEYE. Contains material originally published in magazine form
as CAPTAIN AMERICA AND HAWKEYE #629-632. First printing 2012. ISBN# 978-0-7851-
6086-1. Published by MARVEL WORLDWIDE, INC., a subsidiary of MARVEL ENTERTAINMENT,
LLC. OFFICE OF PUBLICATION: 135 West 50th Street, New York, NY 10020. Copyright © 2012
Marvel Characters, Inc. All rights reserved. $12.99 per copy in the U.S. and $13.99 in Canada
(GST #R127032852); Canadian Agreement #40668537. All characters featured in this issue
and the distinctive names and likenesses thereof, and all related indicia are trademarks of
Marvel Characters, Inc. No similarity between any of the names, characters, persons, and/or
institutions in this magazine with those of any living or dead person or institution is intended,
and any such similarity which may exist is purely coincidental. **Printed in the U.S.A.** ALAN
FINE, EVP - Office of the President, Marvel Worldwide, Inc. and EVP & CMO Marvel Characters
B.V.; DAN BUCKLEY, Publisher & President - Print, Animation & Digital Divisions; JOE QUESADA,
Chief Creative Officer; TOM BREVOORT, SVP of Publishing; DAVID BOGART, SVP of Operations
& Procurement, Publishing; RUWAN JAYATILLEKE, SVP & Associate Publisher, Publishing; C.B.
CEBULSKI, SVP of Creator & Content Development; DAVID GABRIEL, SVP of Publishing Sales
& Circulation; MICHAEL PASCIULLO, SVP of Brand Planning & Communications; JIM O'KEEFE,
VP of Operations & Logistics; DAN CARR, Executive Director of Publishing Technology; SUSAN
CRESPI, Editorial Operations Manager; ALEX MORALES, Publishing Operations Manager; STAN
LEE, Chairman Emeritus. For information regarding advertising in Marvel Comics or on Marvel.
com, please contact Niza Disla, Director of Marvel Partnerships, at ndisla@marvel.com. For
Marvel subscription inquiries, please call 800-217-9158. **Manufactured between 8/2/2012
and 9/4/2012 by QUAD/GRAPHICS, DUBUQUE, IA, USA.**

10 9 8 7 6 5 4 3 2 1

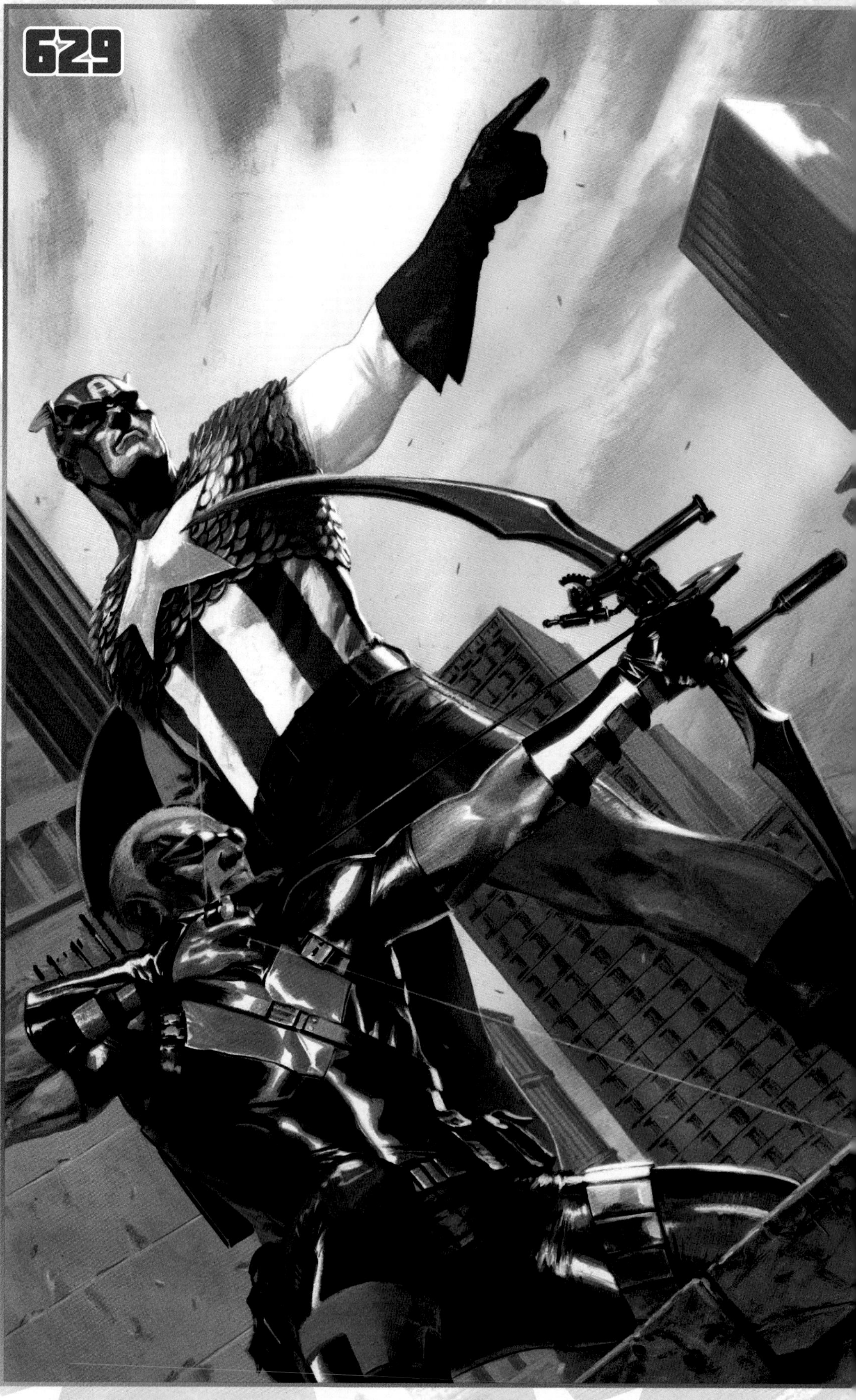
629

CAPTAIN AMERICA

STEVE ROGERS
PEAK STRENGTH, REFLEXES AND ENDURANCE. TACTICAL GENIUS.
THE SUPER-SOLDIER OF WORLD WAR II. LEADER OF THE AVENGERS.

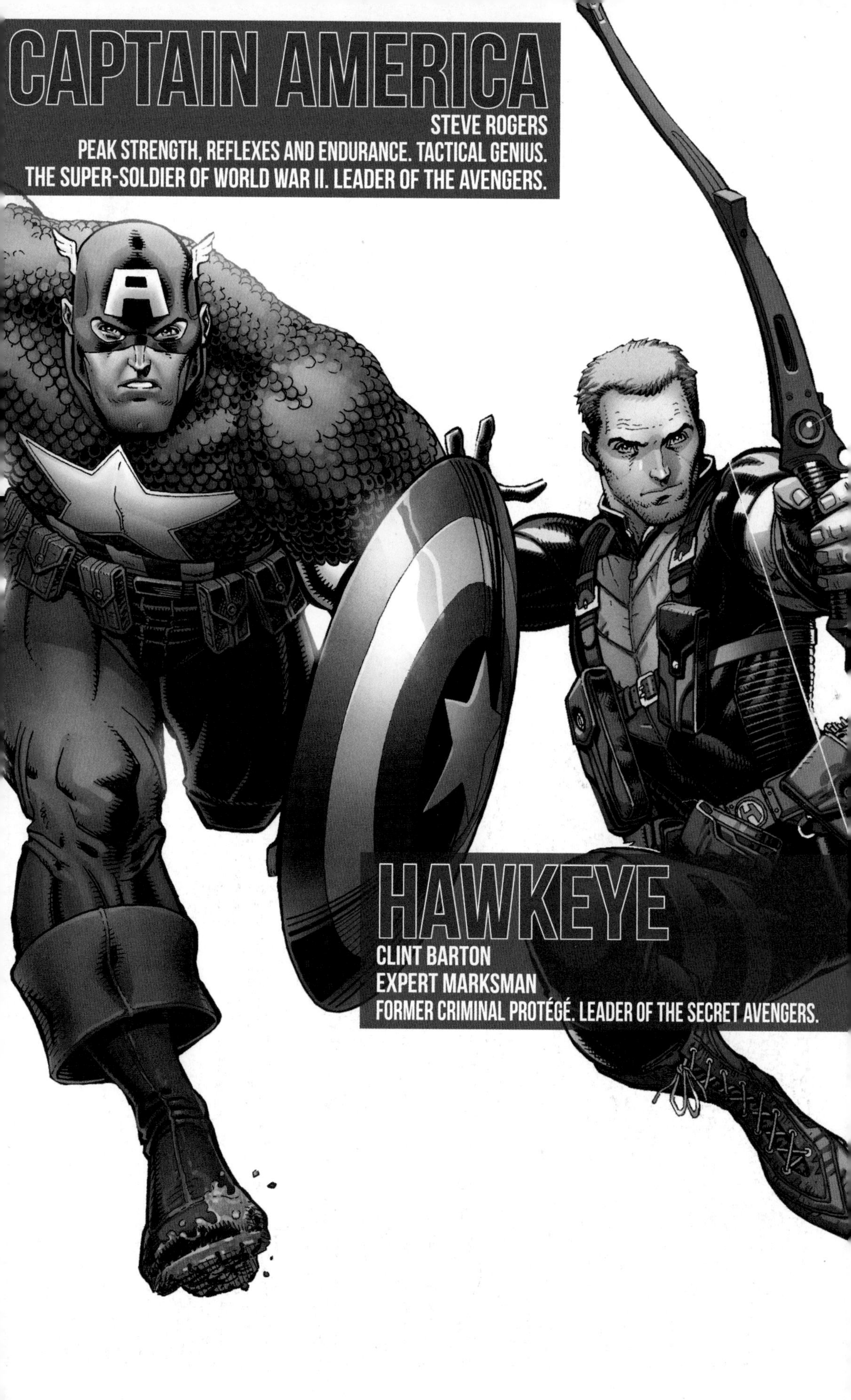

HAWKEYE

CLINT BARTON
EXPERT MARKSMAN
FORMER CRIMINAL PROTÉGÉ. LEADER OF THE SECRET AVENGERS.

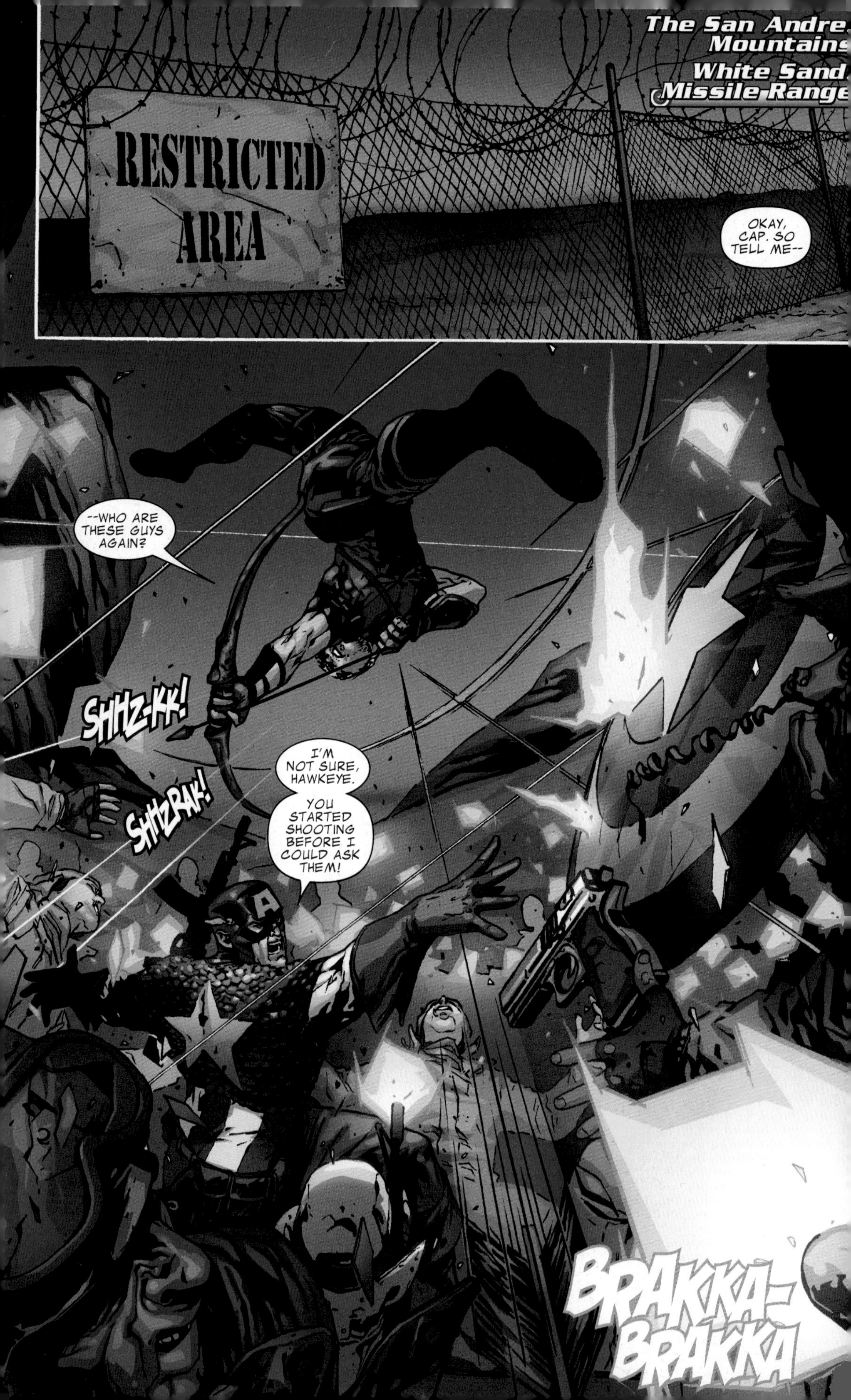

The San Andre
Mountains
White Sand
Missile Range
RESTRICTED AREA
OKAY, CAP. SO TELL ME--
--WHO ARE THESE GUYS AGAIN?
SHHZ-KK!
SHHZRAK!
I'M NOT SURE, HAWKEYE.
YOU STARTED SHOOTING BEFORE I COULD ASK THEM!
BRAKKA-BRAKKA

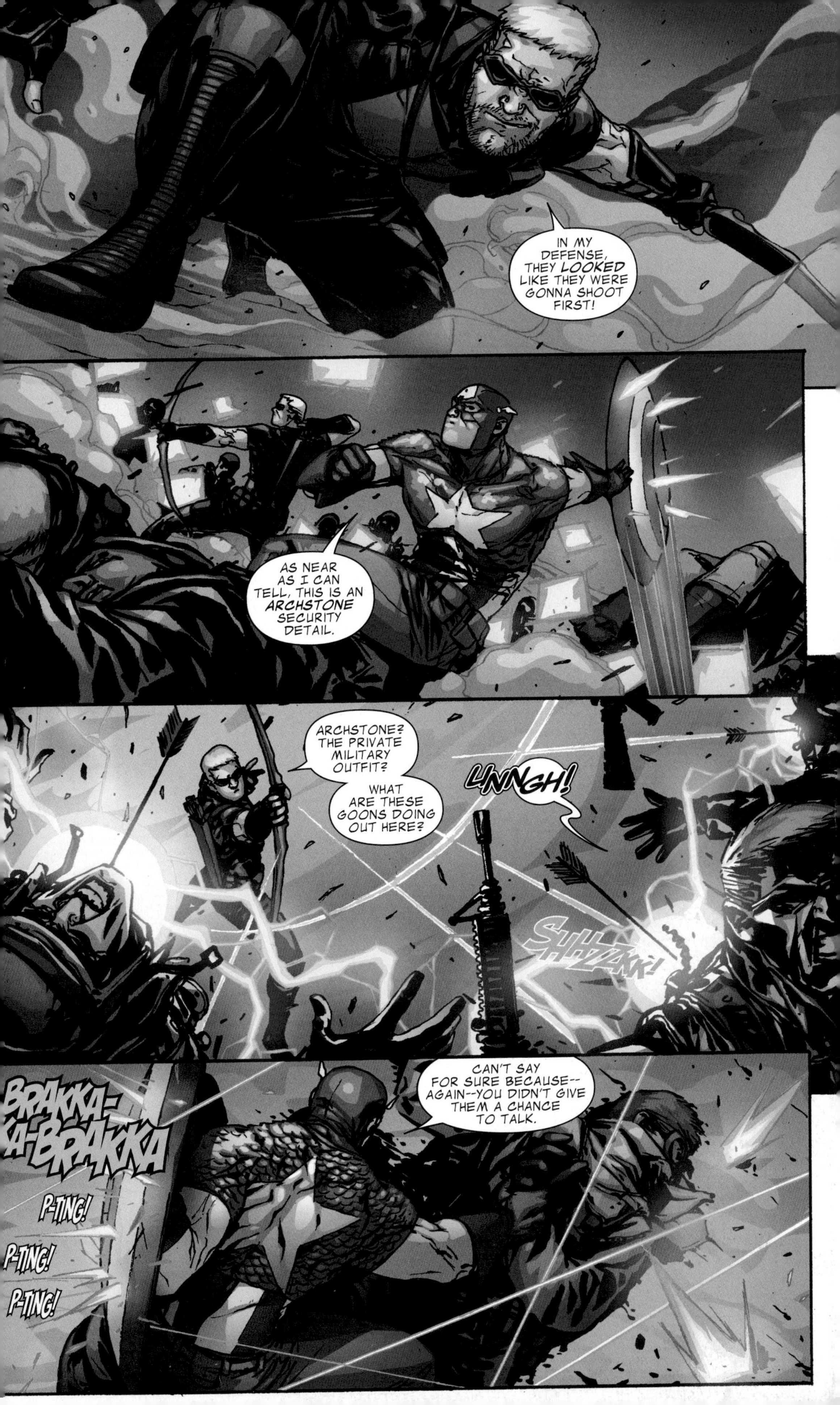
IN MY DEFENSE, THEY LOOKED LIKE THEY WERE GONNA SHOOT FIRST!
AS NEAR AS I CAN TELL, THIS IS AN ARCHSTONE SECURITY DETAIL.
ARCHSTONE? THE PRIVATE MILITARY OUTFIT?
WHAT ARE THESE GOONS DOING OUT HERE?
UNNGH!
SHHZAKK!
BRAKKA-KA-BRAKKA
CAN'T SAY FOR SURE BECAUSE--AGAIN--YOU DIDN'T GIVE THEM A CHANCE TO TALK.
P-TING!
P-TING!
P-TING!

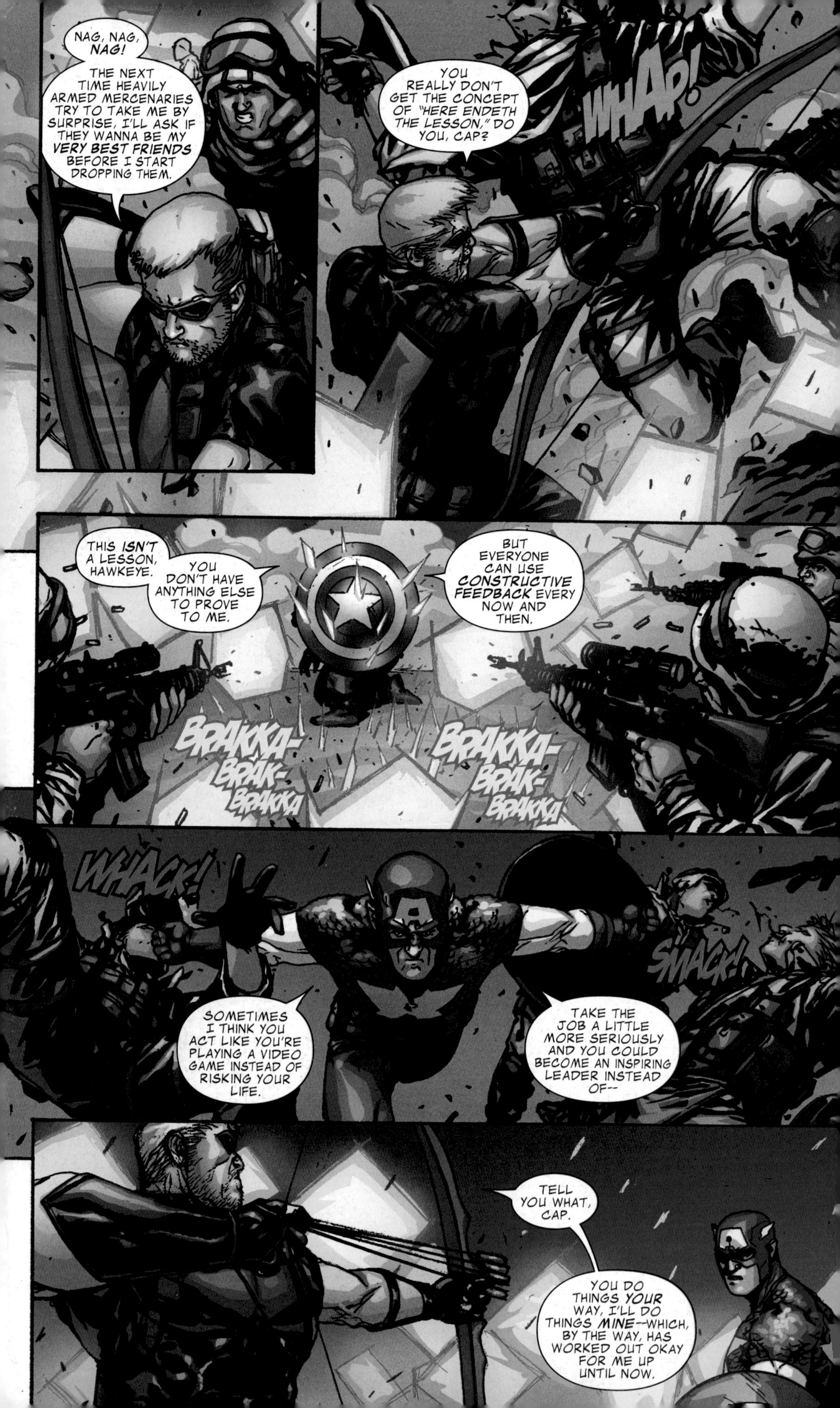
NAG, NAG, NAG!
THE NEXT TIME HEAVILY ARMED MERCENARIES TRY TO TAKE ME BY SURPRISE, I'LL ASK IF THEY WANNA BE MY VERY BEST FRIENDS BEFORE I START DROPPING THEM.
YOU REALLY DON'T GET THE CONCEPT OF "HERE ENDETH THE LESSON," DO YOU, CAP?
WHAP!
THIS ISN'T A LESSON, HAWKEYE.
YOU DON'T HAVE ANYTHING ELSE TO PROVE TO ME.
BUT EVERYONE CAN USE CONSTRUCTIVE FEEDBACK EVERY NOW AND THEN.
BRAKKA-BRAK-BRAKKA
BRAKKA-BRAK-BRAKKA
WHACK!
SMACK!
SOMETIMES I THINK YOU ACT LIKE YOU'RE PLAYING A VIDEO GAME INSTEAD OF RISKING YOUR LIFE.
TAKE THE JOB A LITTLE MORE SERIOUSLY AND YOU COULD BECOME AN INSPIRING LEADER INSTEAD OF--
TELL YOU WHAT, CAP.
YOU DO THINGS YOUR WAY, I'LL DO THINGS MINE--WHICH, BY THE WAY, HAS WORKED OUT OKAY FOR ME UP UNTIL NOW.

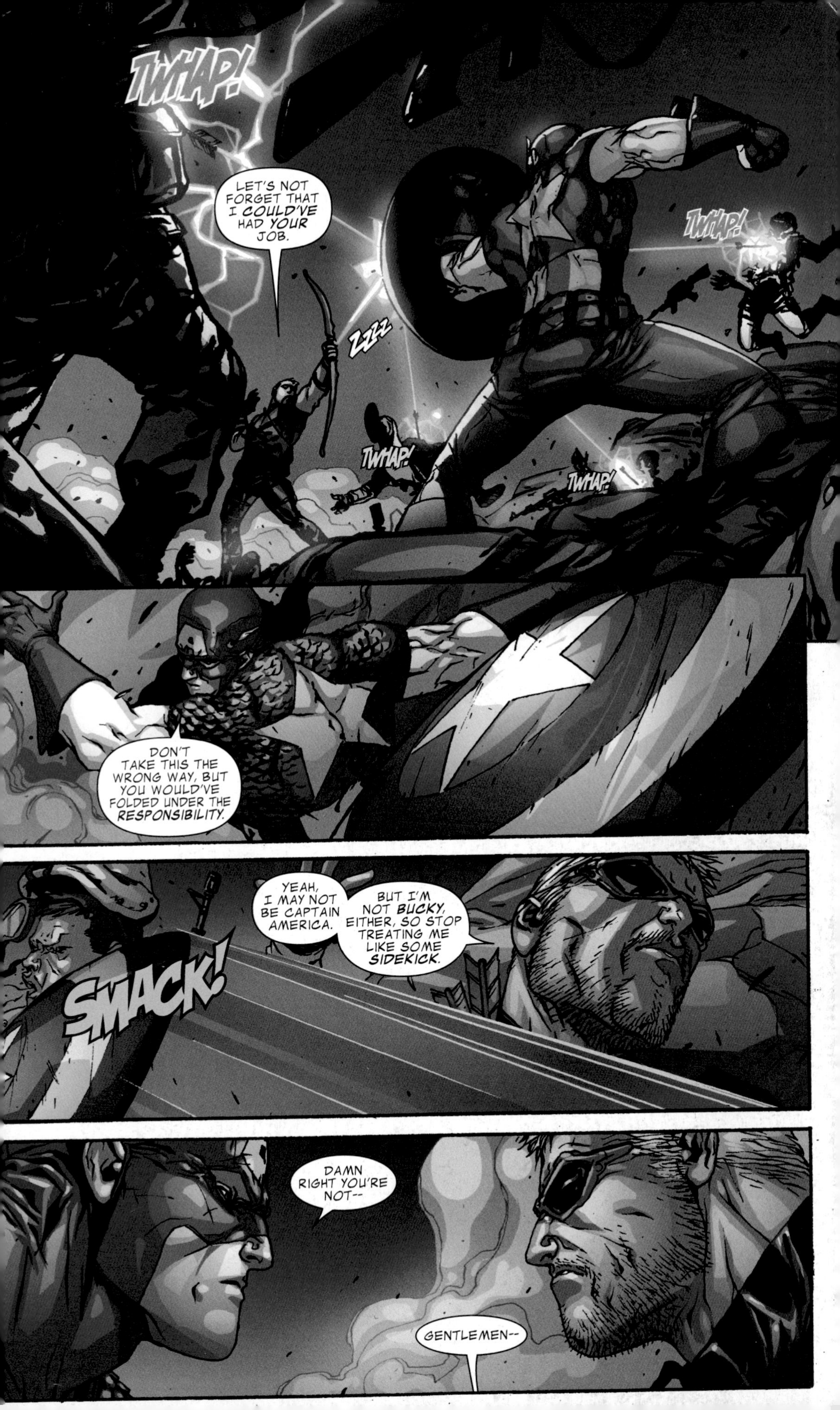
TWHAP!
LET'S NOT FORGET THAT I COULD'VE HAD YOUR JOB.
ZZZZ
TWHAP!
TWHAP!
TWHAP!
DON'T TAKE THIS THE WRONG WAY, BUT YOU WOULD'VE FOLDED UNDER THE RESPONSIBILITY.
YEAH, I MAY NOT BE CAPTAIN AMERICA.
BUT I'M NOT BUCKY, EITHER, SO STOP TREATING ME LIKE SOME SIDEKICK.
SMACK!
DAMN RIGHT YOU'RE NOT--
GENTLEMEN--

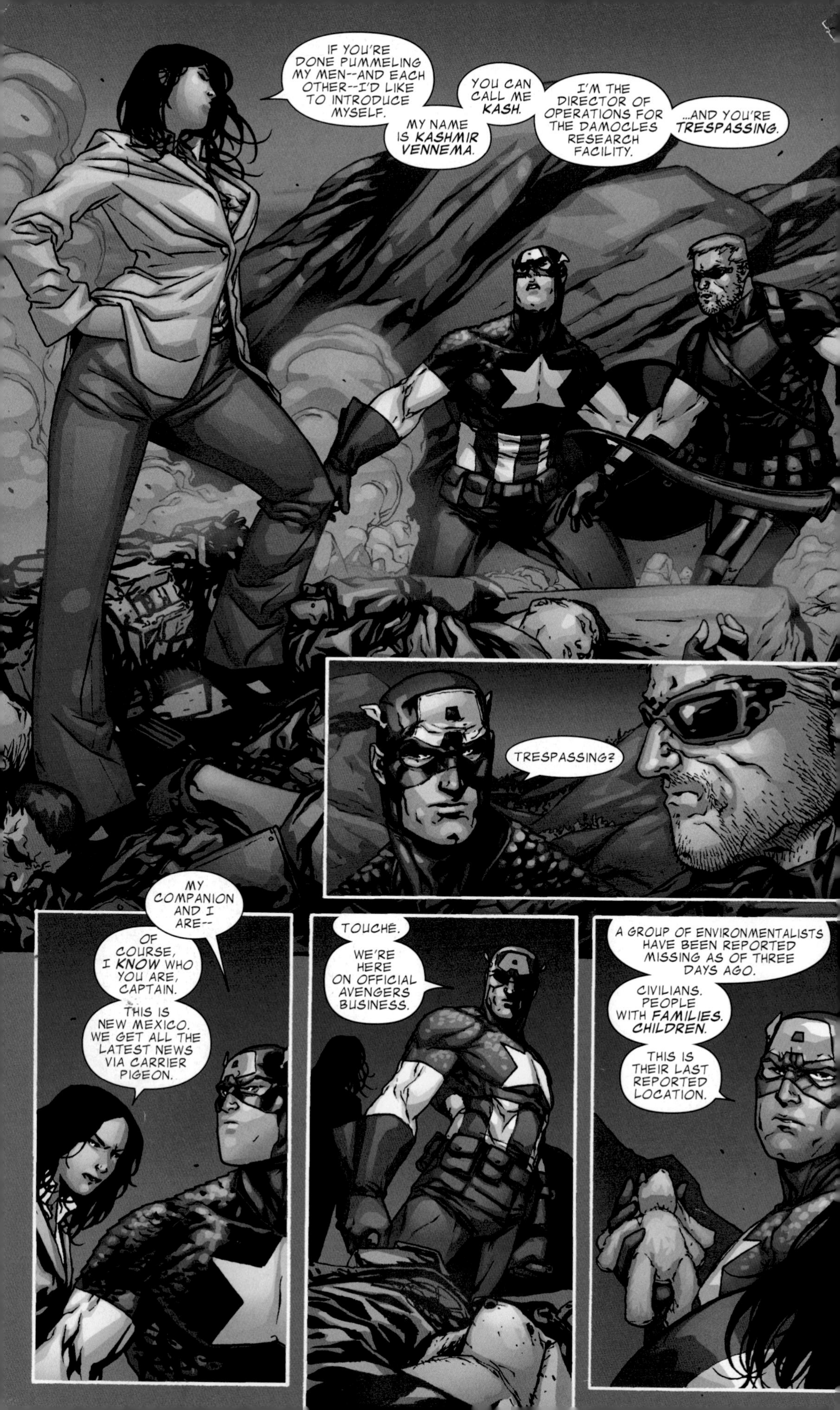

IF YOU'RE DONE PUMMELING MY MEN--AND EACH OTHER--I'D LIKE TO INTRODUCE MYSELF.
MY NAME IS KASHMIR VENNEMA.
YOU CAN CALL ME KASH.
I'M THE DIRECTOR OF OPERATIONS FOR THE DAMOCLES RESEARCH FACILITY.
...AND YOU'RE TRESPASSING.
TRESPASSING?
MY COMPANION AND I ARE--
OF COURSE, I KNOW WHO YOU ARE, CAPTAIN.
THIS IS NEW MEXICO. WE GET ALL THE LATEST NEWS VIA CARRIER PIGEON.
TOUCHÉ.
WE'RE HERE ON OFFICIAL AVENGERS BUSINESS.
A GROUP OF ENVIRONMENTALISTS HAVE BEEN REPORTED MISSING AS OF THREE DAYS AGO.
CIVILIANS. PEOPLE WITH FAMILIES. CHILDREN.
THIS IS THEIR LAST REPORTED LOCATION.

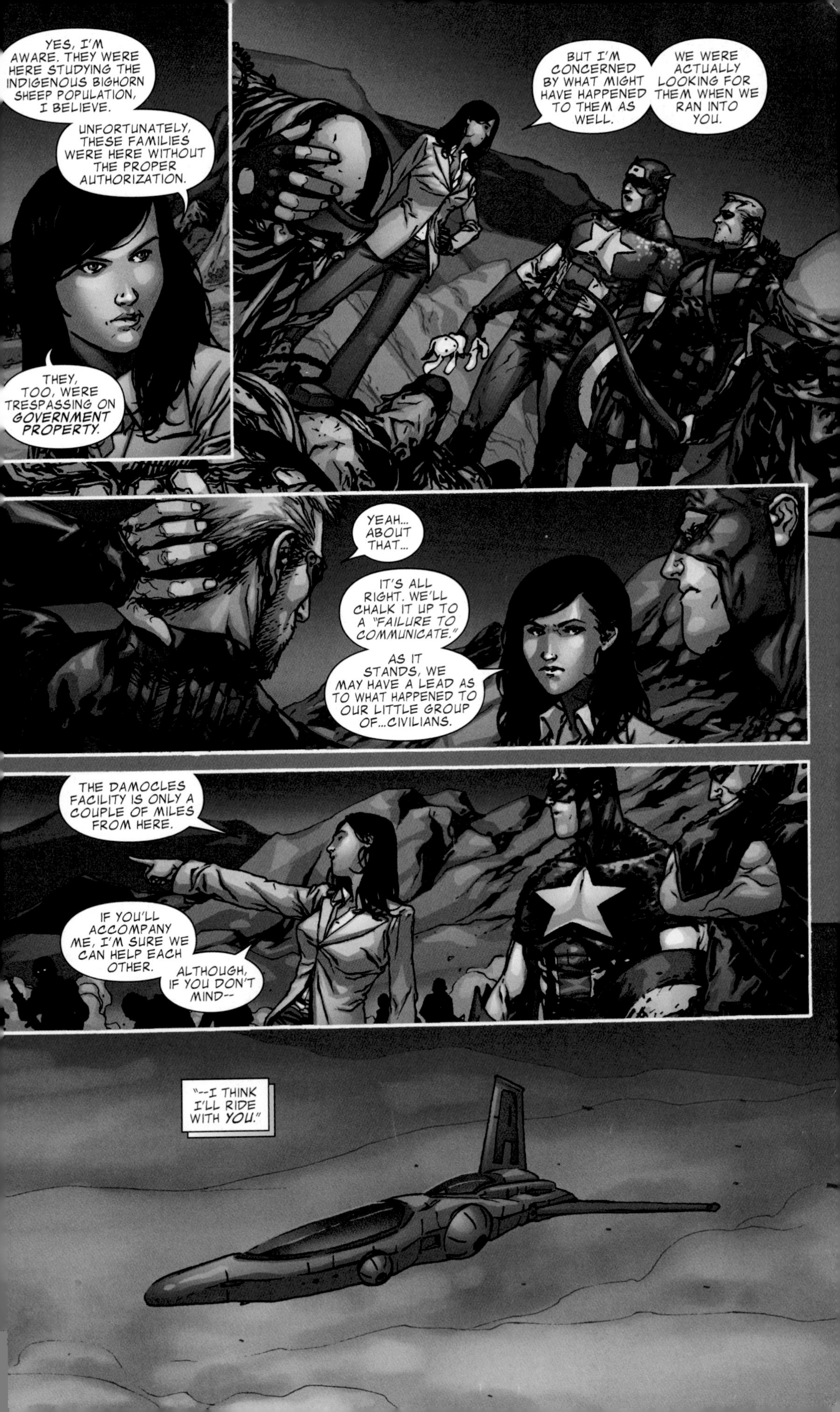
YES, I'M AWARE. THEY WERE HERE STUDYING THE INDIGENOUS BIGHORN SHEEP POPULATION, I BELIEVE.
UNFORTUNATELY, THESE FAMILIES WERE HERE WITHOUT THE PROPER AUTHORIZATION.
THEY, TOO, WERE TRESPASSING ON GOVERNMENT PROPERTY.
BUT I'M CONCERNED BY WHAT MIGHT HAVE HAPPENED TO THEM AS WELL.
WE WERE ACTUALLY LOOKING FOR THEM WHEN WE RAN INTO YOU.
YEAH... ABOUT THAT...
IT'S ALL RIGHT. WE'LL CHALK IT UP TO A "FAILURE TO COMMUNICATE."
AS IT STANDS, WE MAY HAVE A LEAD AS TO WHAT HAPPENED TO OUR LITTLE GROUP OF...CIVILIANS.
THE DAMOCLES FACILITY IS ONLY A COUPLE OF MILES FROM HERE.
IF YOU'LL ACCOMPANY ME, I'M SURE WE CAN HELP EACH OTHER.
ALTHOUGH, IF YOU DON'T MIND--
"--I THINK I'LL RIDE WITH YOU."

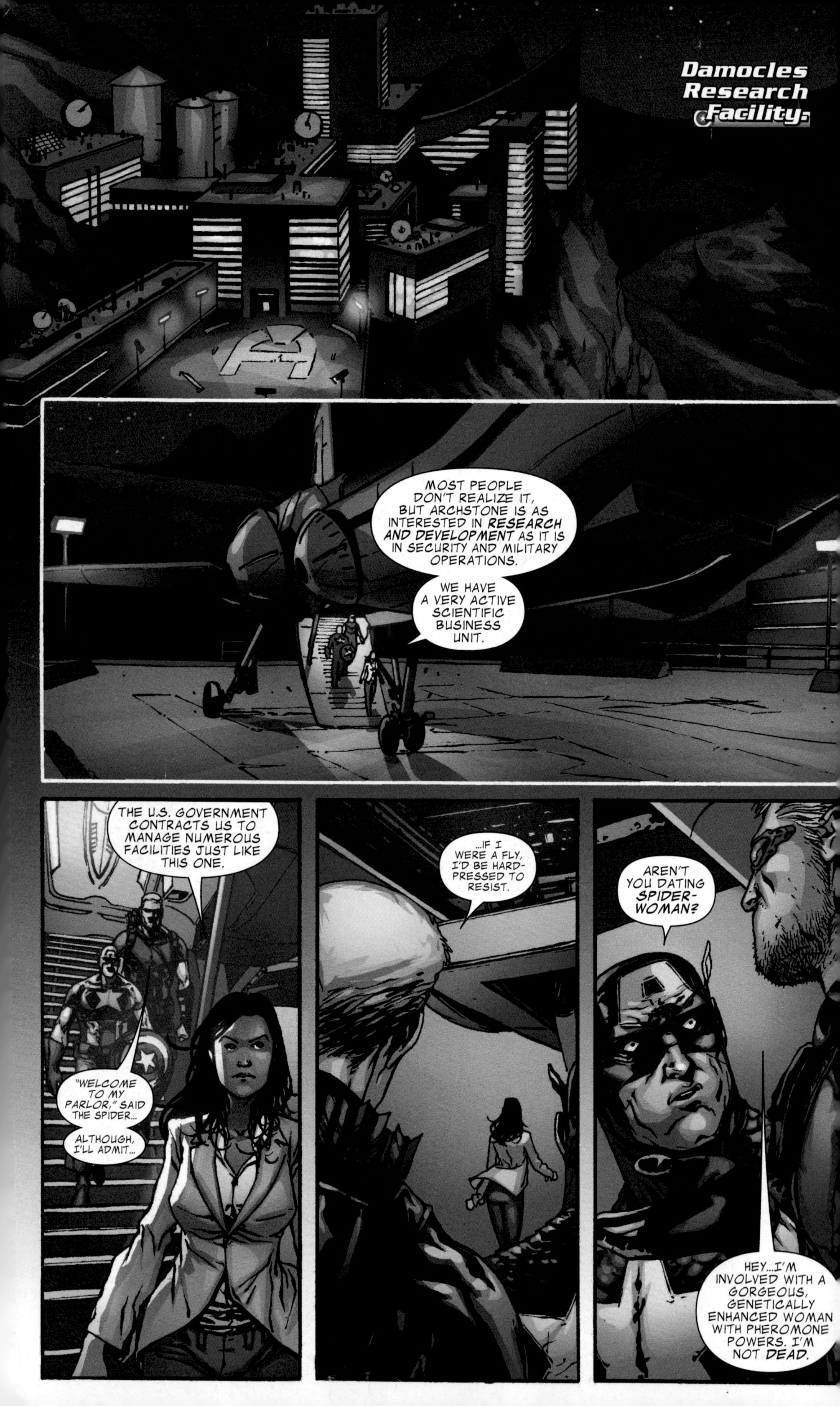

Damocles Research Facility.
MOST PEOPLE DON'T REALIZE IT, BUT ARCHSTONE IS AS INTERESTED IN RESEARCH AND DEVELOPMENT AS IT IS IN SECURITY AND MILITARY OPERATIONS.
WE HAVE A VERY ACTIVE SCIENTIFIC BUSINESS UNIT.
THE U.S. GOVERNMENT CONTRACTS US TO MANAGE NUMEROUS FACILITIES JUST LIKE THIS ONE.
"WELCOME TO MY PARLOR," SAID THE SPIDER...
ALTHOUGH, I'LL ADMIT...
...IF I WERE A FLY, I'D BE HARD-PRESSED TO RESIST.
AREN'T YOU DATING SPIDER-WOMAN?
HEY...I'M INVOLVED WITH A GORGEOUS, GENETICALLY ENHANCED WOMAN WITH PHEROMONE POWERS. I'M NOT DEAD.

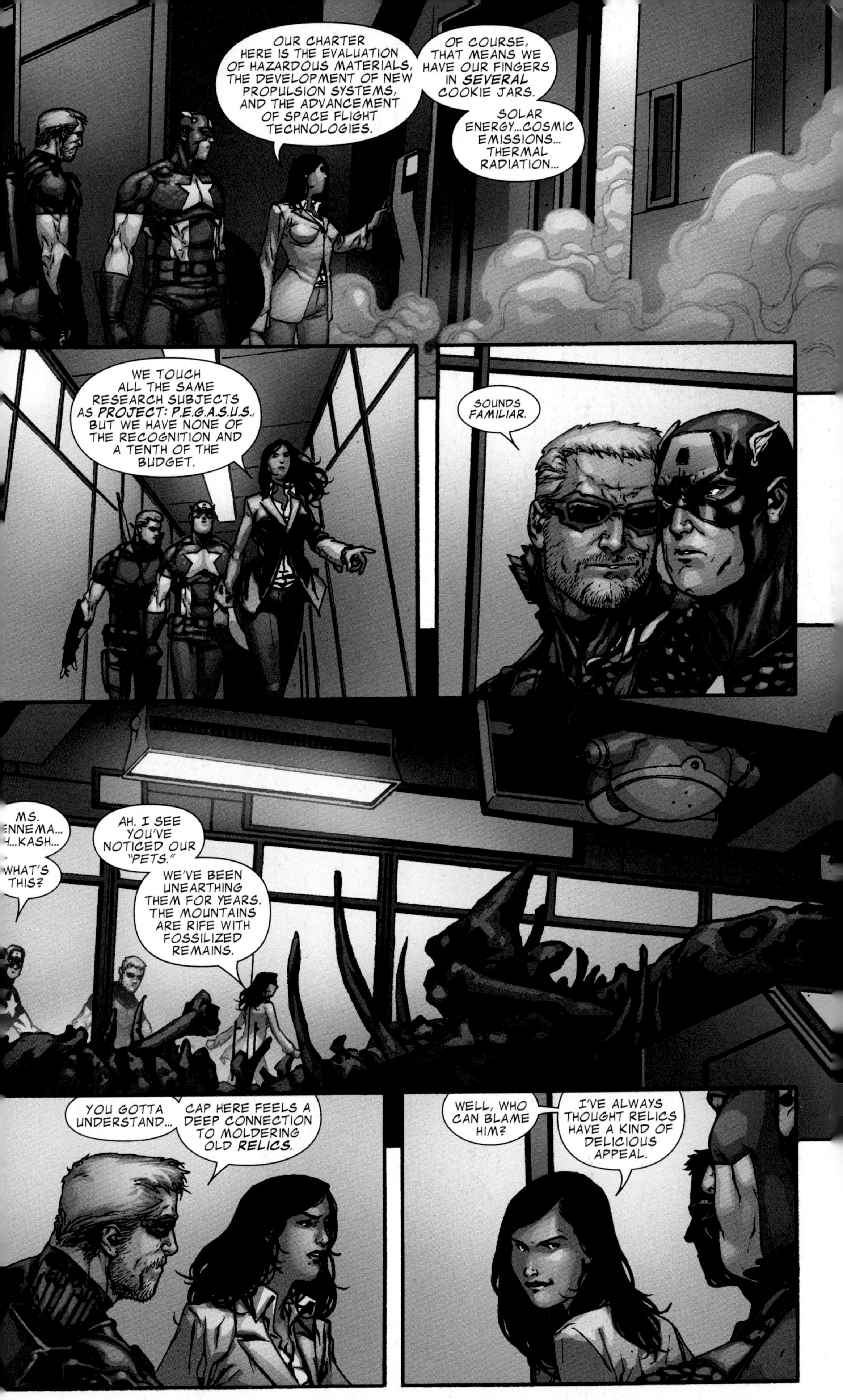

OUR CHARTER HERE IS THE EVALUATION OF HAZARDOUS MATERIALS, THE DEVELOPMENT OF NEW PROPULSION SYSTEMS, AND THE ADVANCEMENT OF SPACE FLIGHT TECHNOLOGIES.
OF COURSE, THAT MEANS WE HAVE OUR FINGERS IN SEVERAL COOKIE JARS.
SOLAR ENERGY...COSMIC EMISSIONS... THERMAL RADIATION...
WE TOUCH ALL THE SAME RESEARCH SUBJECTS AS PROJECT: P.E.G.A.S.U.S., BUT WE HAVE NONE OF THE RECOGNITION AND A TENTH OF THE BUDGET.
SOUNDS FAMILIAR.
MS.
WHAT'S THIS?
AH. I SEE YOU'VE NOTICED OUR "PETS."
WE'VE BEEN UNEARTHING THEM FOR YEARS. THE MOUNTAINS ARE RIFE WITH FOSSILIZED REMAINS.
YOU GOTTA UNDERSTAND...
CAP HERE FEELS A DEEP CONNECTION TO MOLDERING OLD RELICS.
WELL, WHO CAN BLAME HIM?
I'VE ALWAYS THOUGHT RELICS HAVE A KIND OF DELICIOUS APPEAL.

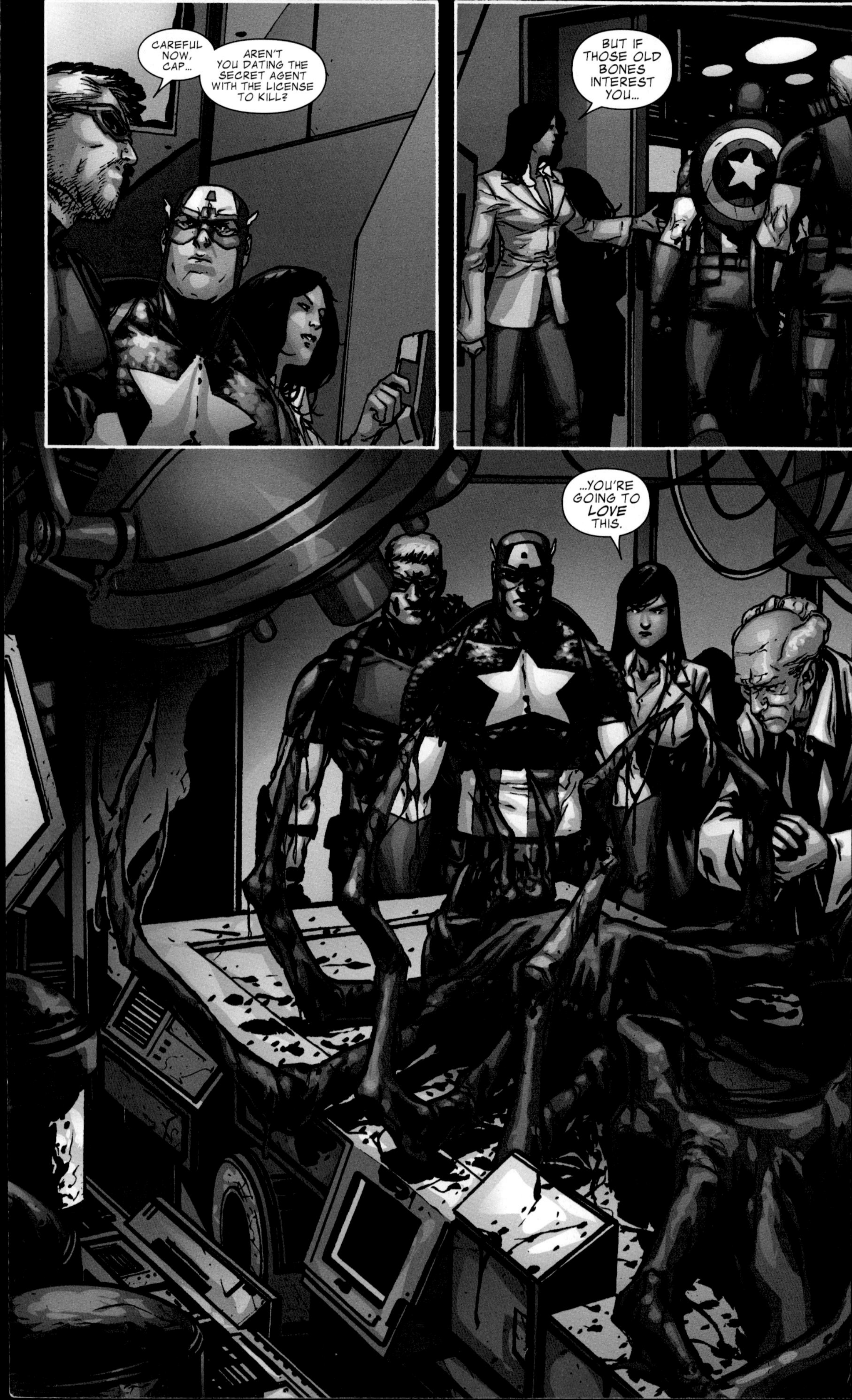
CAREFUL NOW, CAP...
AREN'T YOU DATING THE SECRET AGENT WITH THE LICENSE TO KILL?
BUT IF THOSE OLD BONES INTEREST YOU...
...YOU'RE GOING TO LOVE THIS.

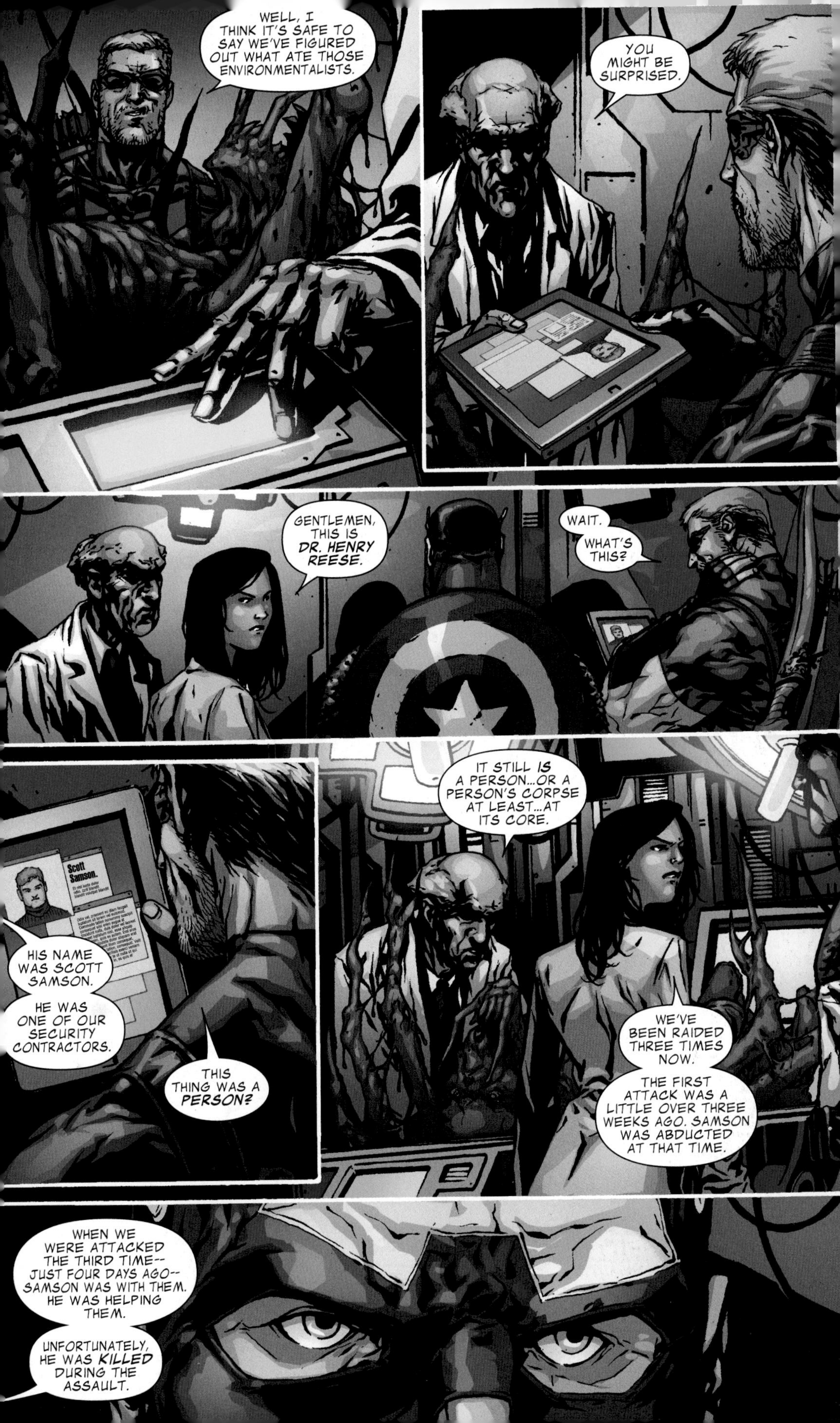
WELL, I THINK IT'S SAFE TO SAY WE'VE FIGURED OUT WHAT ATE THOSE ENVIRONMENTALISTS.
YOU MIGHT BE SURPRISED.
GENTLEMEN, THIS IS ***DR. HENRY REESE.***
WAIT.
WHAT'S THIS?
Scott Samson.
HIS NAME WAS SCOTT SAMSON.
HE WAS ONE OF OUR SECURITY CONTRACTORS.
THIS THING WAS A ***PERSON?***
IT STILL ***IS*** A PERSON...OR A PERSON'S CORPSE AT LEAST...AT ITS CORE.
WE'VE BEEN RAIDED THREE TIMES NOW.
THE FIRST ATTACK WAS A LITTLE OVER THREE WEEKS AGO. SAMSON WAS ABDUCTED AT THAT TIME.
WHEN WE WERE ATTACKED THE THIRD TIME--JUST FOUR DAYS AGO--SAMSON WAS WITH THEM. HE WAS HELPING THEM.
UNFORTUNATELY, HE WAS ***KILLED*** DURING THE ASSAULT.

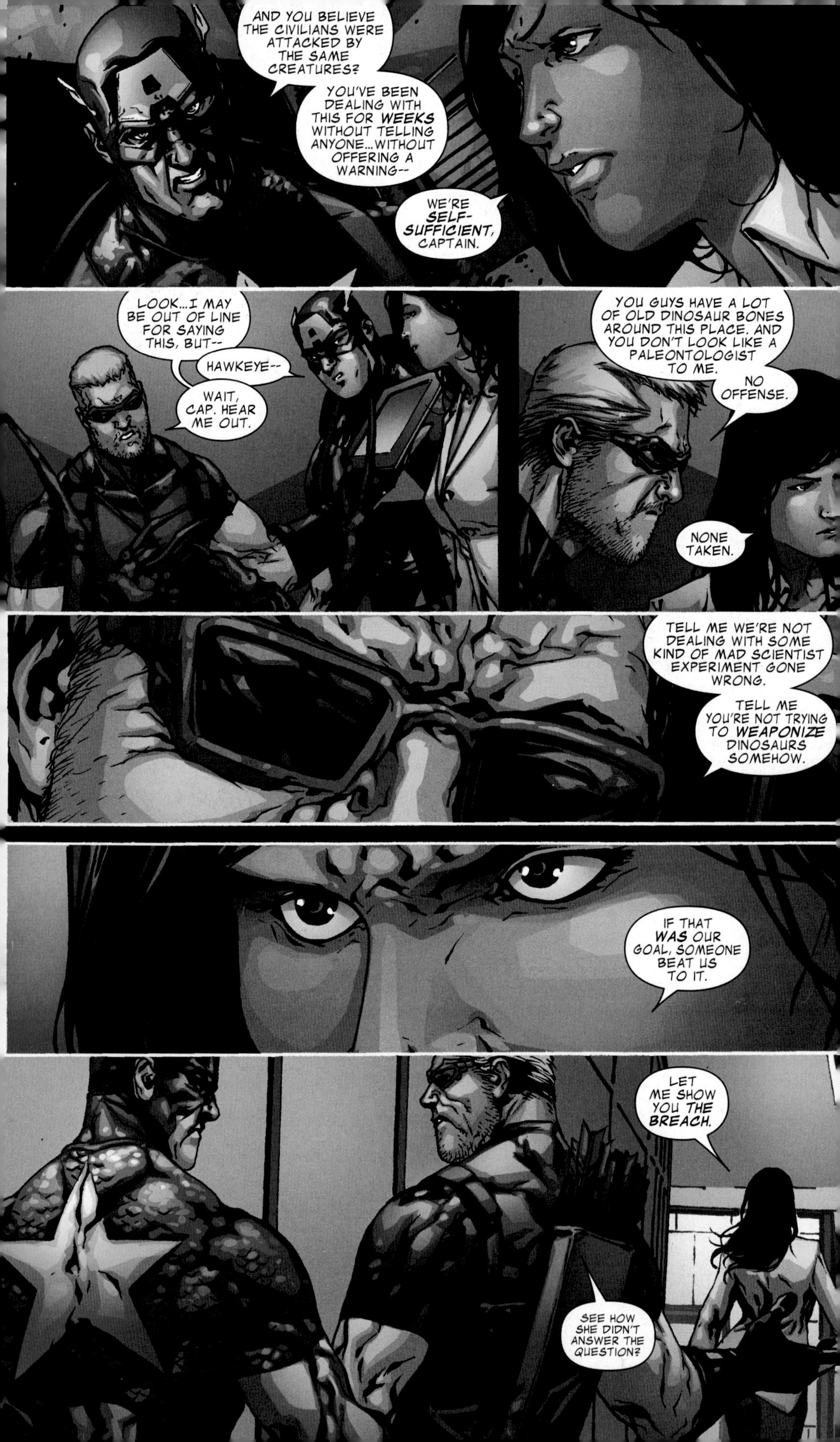
AND YOU BELIEVE THE CIVILIANS WERE ATTACKED BY THE SAME CREATURES?
YOU'VE BEEN DEALING WITH THIS FOR WEEKS WITHOUT TELLING ANYONE...WITHOUT OFFERING A WARNING--
WE'RE SELF-SUFFICIENT, CAPTAIN.
LOOK...I MAY BE OUT OF LINE FOR SAYING THIS, BUT--
HAWKEYE--
WAIT, CAP. HEAR ME OUT.
YOU GUYS HAVE A LOT OF OLD DINOSAUR BONES AROUND THIS PLACE. AND YOU DON'T LOOK LIKE A PALEONTOLOGIST TO ME.
NO OFFENSE.
NONE TAKEN.
TELL ME WE'RE NOT DEALING WITH SOME KIND OF MAD SCIENTIST EXPERIMENT GONE WRONG.
TELL ME YOU'RE NOT TRYING TO WEAPONIZE DINOSAURS SOMEHOW.
IF THAT WAS OUR GOAL, SOMEONE BEAT US TO IT.
LET ME SHOW YOU THE BREACH.
SEE HOW SHE DIDN'T ANSWER THE QUESTION?

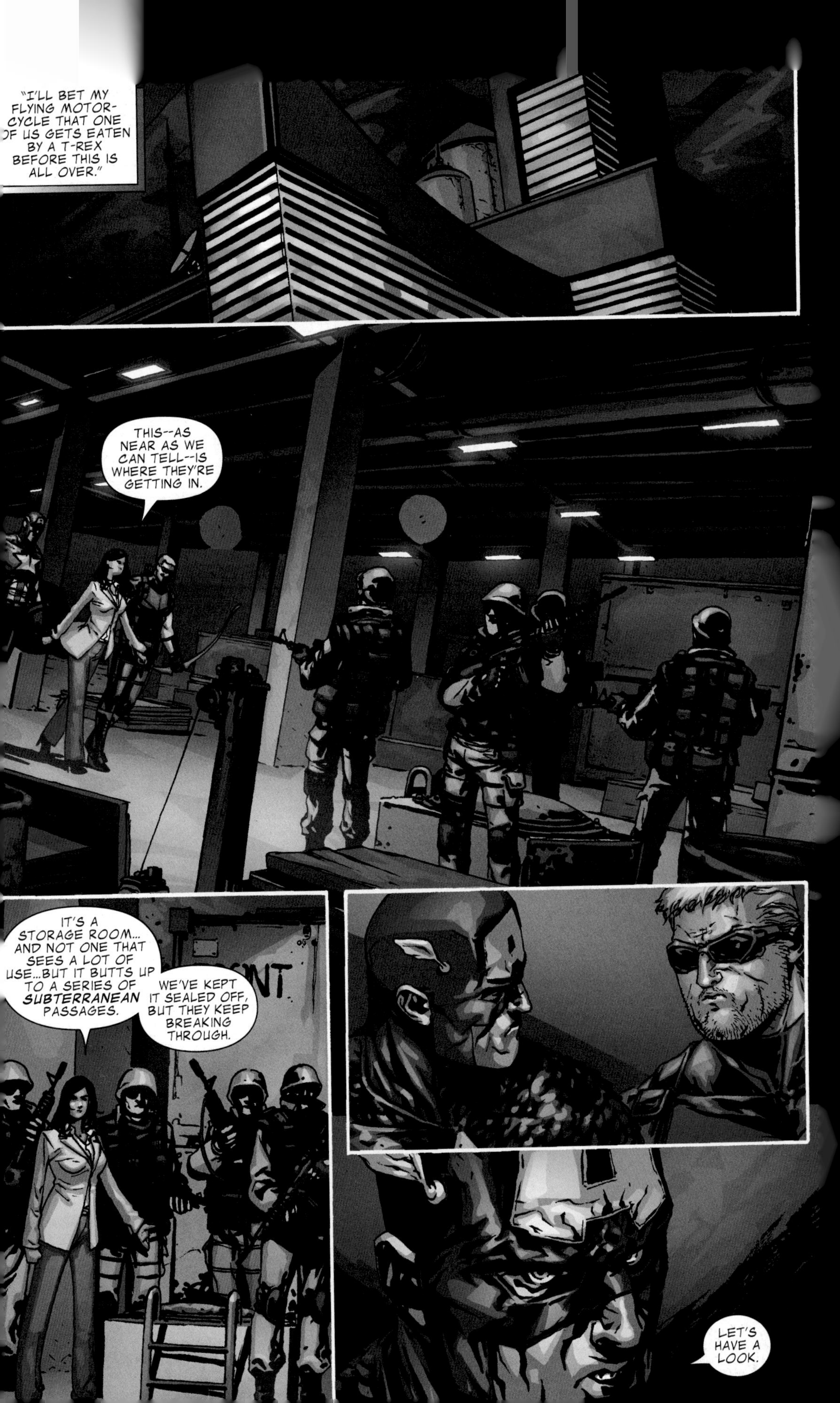

"I'LL BET MY FLYING MOTOR-CYCLE THAT ONE OF US GETS EATEN BY A T-REX BEFORE THIS IS ALL OVER."
THIS--AS NEAR AS WE CAN TELL--IS WHERE THEY'RE GETTING IN.
IT'S A STORAGE ROOM... AND NOT ONE THAT SEES A LOT OF USE...BUT IT BUTTS UP TO A SERIES OF SUBTERRANEAN PASSAGES.
WE'VE KEPT IT SEALED OFF, BUT THEY KEEP BREAKING THROUGH.
LET'S HAVE A LOOK.

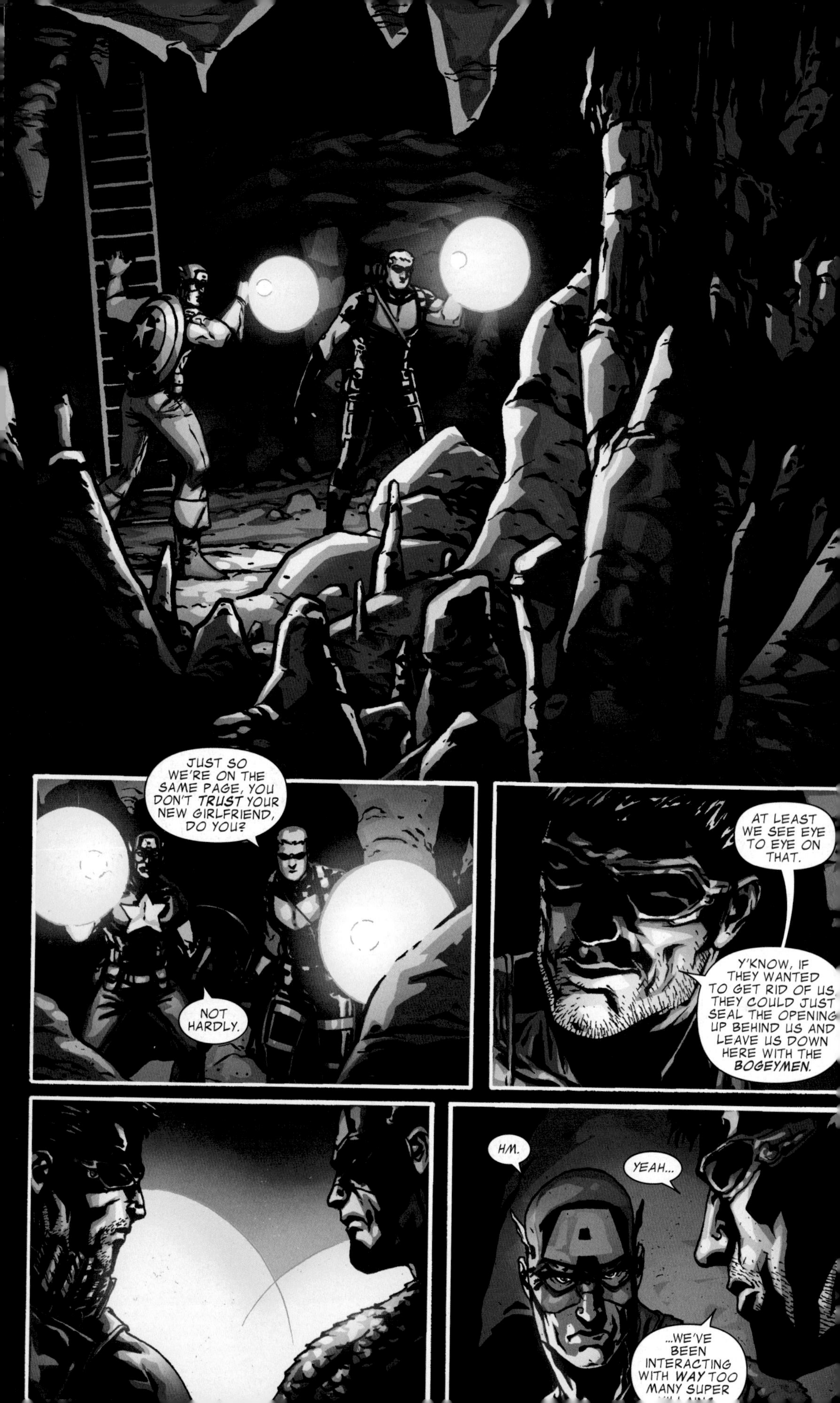
JUST SO WE'RE ON THE SAME PAGE, YOU DON'T TRUST YOUR NEW GIRLFRIEND, DO YOU?
NOT HARDLY.
AT LEAST WE SEE EYE TO EYE ON THAT.
Y'KNOW, IF THEY WANTED TO GET RID OF US THEY COULD JUST SEAL THE OPENING UP BEHIND US AND LEAVE US DOWN HERE WITH THE BOGEYMEN.
HM.
YEAH...
...WE'VE BEEN INTERACTING WITH WAY TOO MANY SUPER

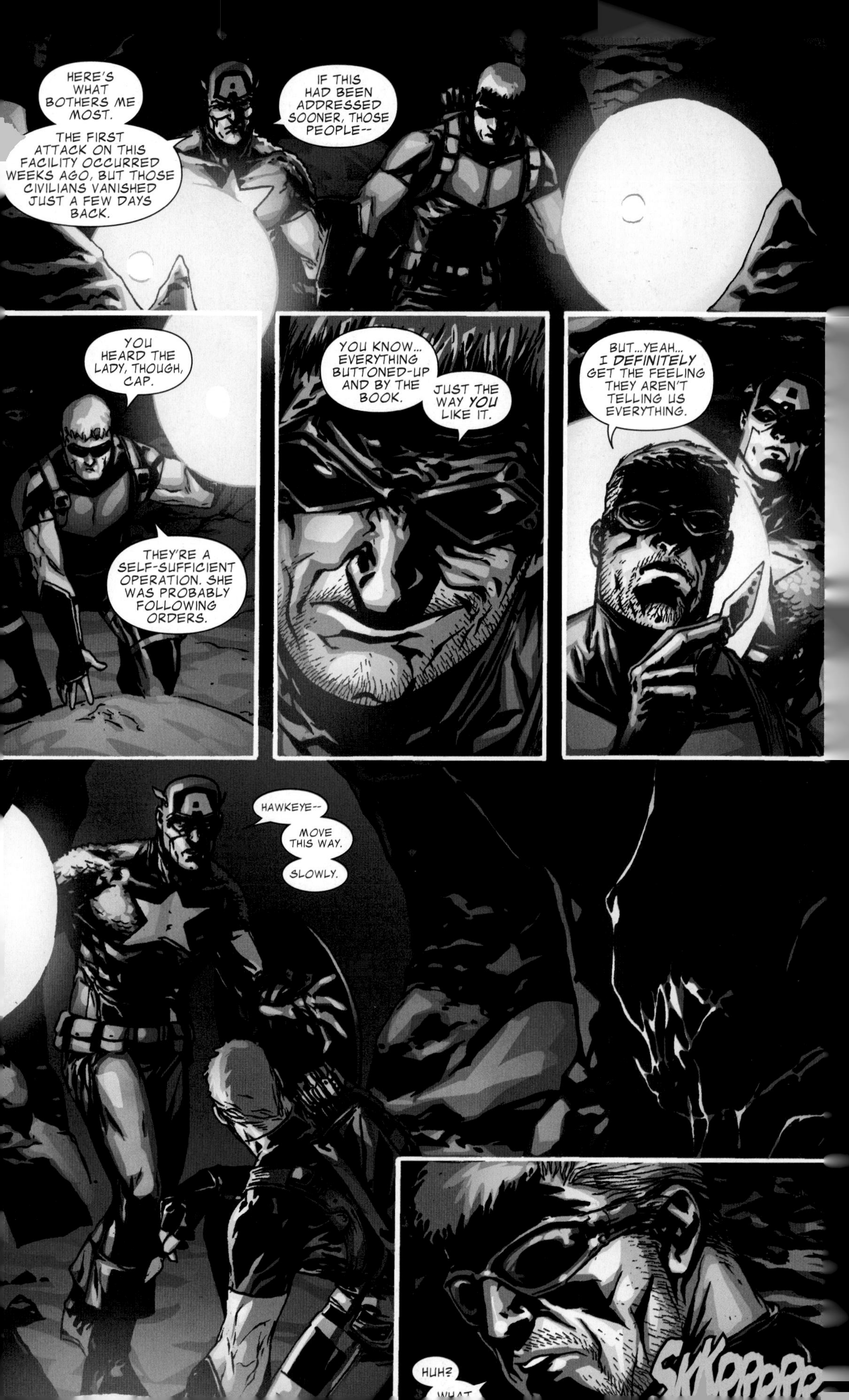
HERE'S WHAT BOTHERS ME MOST.
THE FIRST ATTACK ON THIS FACILITY OCCURRED WEEKS AGO, BUT THOSE CIVILIANS VANISHED JUST A FEW DAYS BACK.
IF THIS HAD BEEN ADDRESSED SOONER, THOSE PEOPLE--
YOU HEARD THE LADY, THOUGH, CAP.
THEY'RE A SELF-SUFFICIENT OPERATION. SHE WAS PROBABLY FOLLOWING ORDERS.
YOU KNOW... EVERYTHING BUTTONED-UP AND BY THE BOOK.
JUST THE WAY *YOU* LIKE IT.
BUT...YEAH... I *DEFINITELY* GET THE FEELING THEY AREN'T TELLING US EVERYTHING.
HAWKEYE--
MOVE THIS WAY.
SLOWLY.
HUH?
SKKRRRR

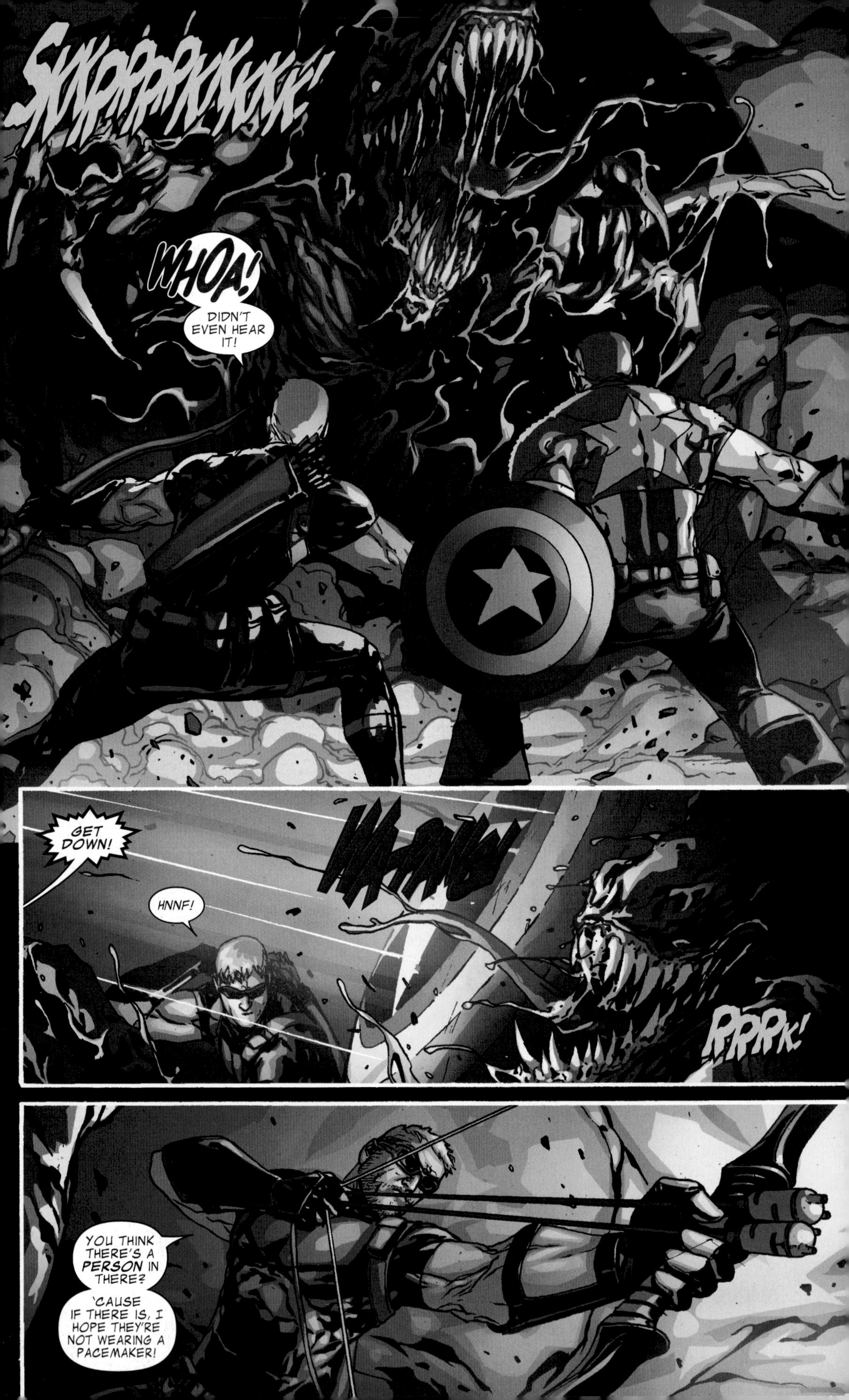
WHOA!
DIDN'T EVEN HEAR IT!
GET DOWN!
HNNF!
RRRK!
YOU THINK THERE'S A ***PERSON*** IN THERE?
'CAUSE IF THERE IS, I HOPE THEY'RE NOT WEARING A PACEMAKER!

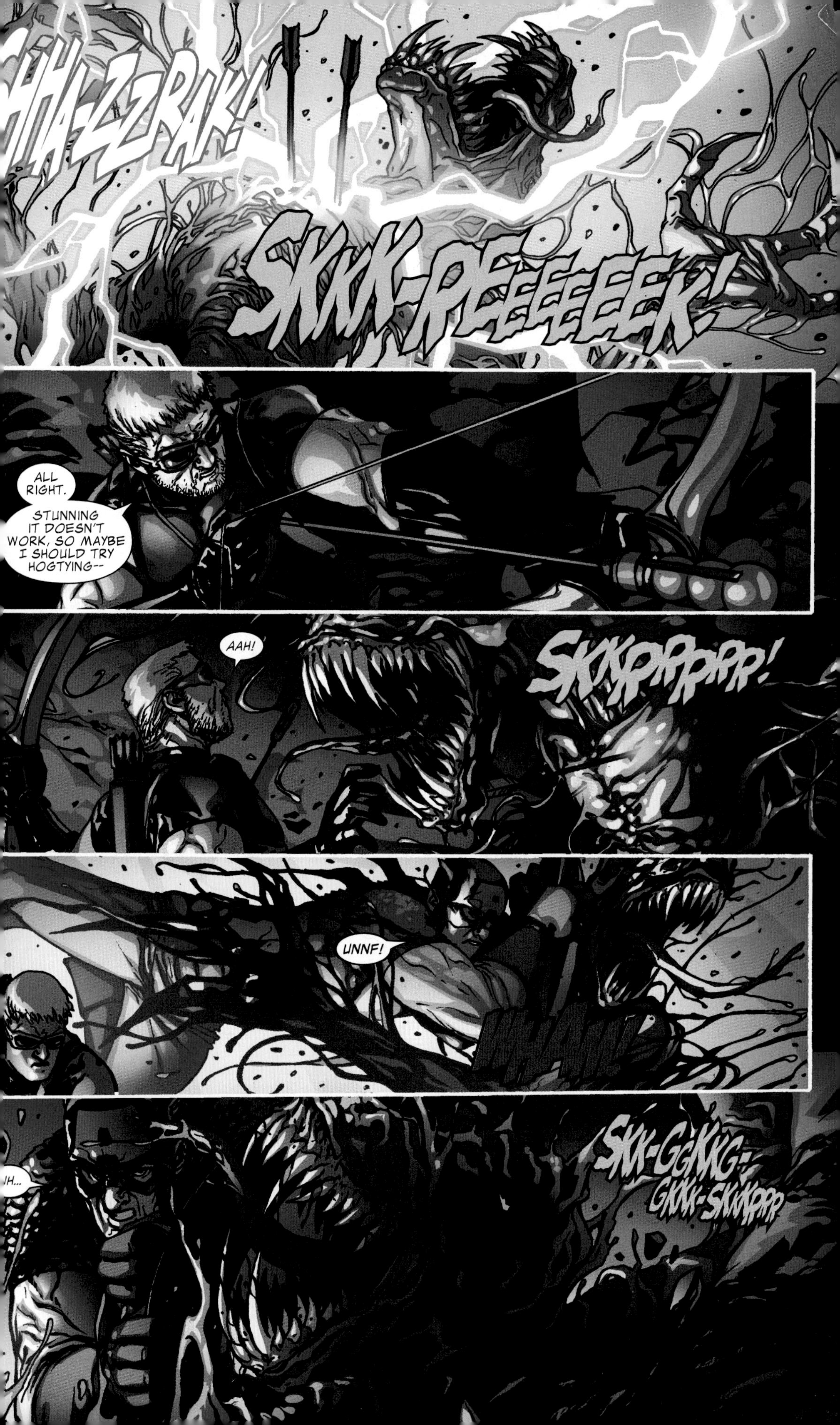
HA-ZZRAK!
SKKK-REEEEEEK!
ALL RIGHT.
STUNNING IT DOESN'T WORK, SO MAYBE I SHOULD TRY HOGTYING--
AAH!
SKKRRRRR!
UNNF!
SKK-GGKKG-
GKKK-SKKKRRR

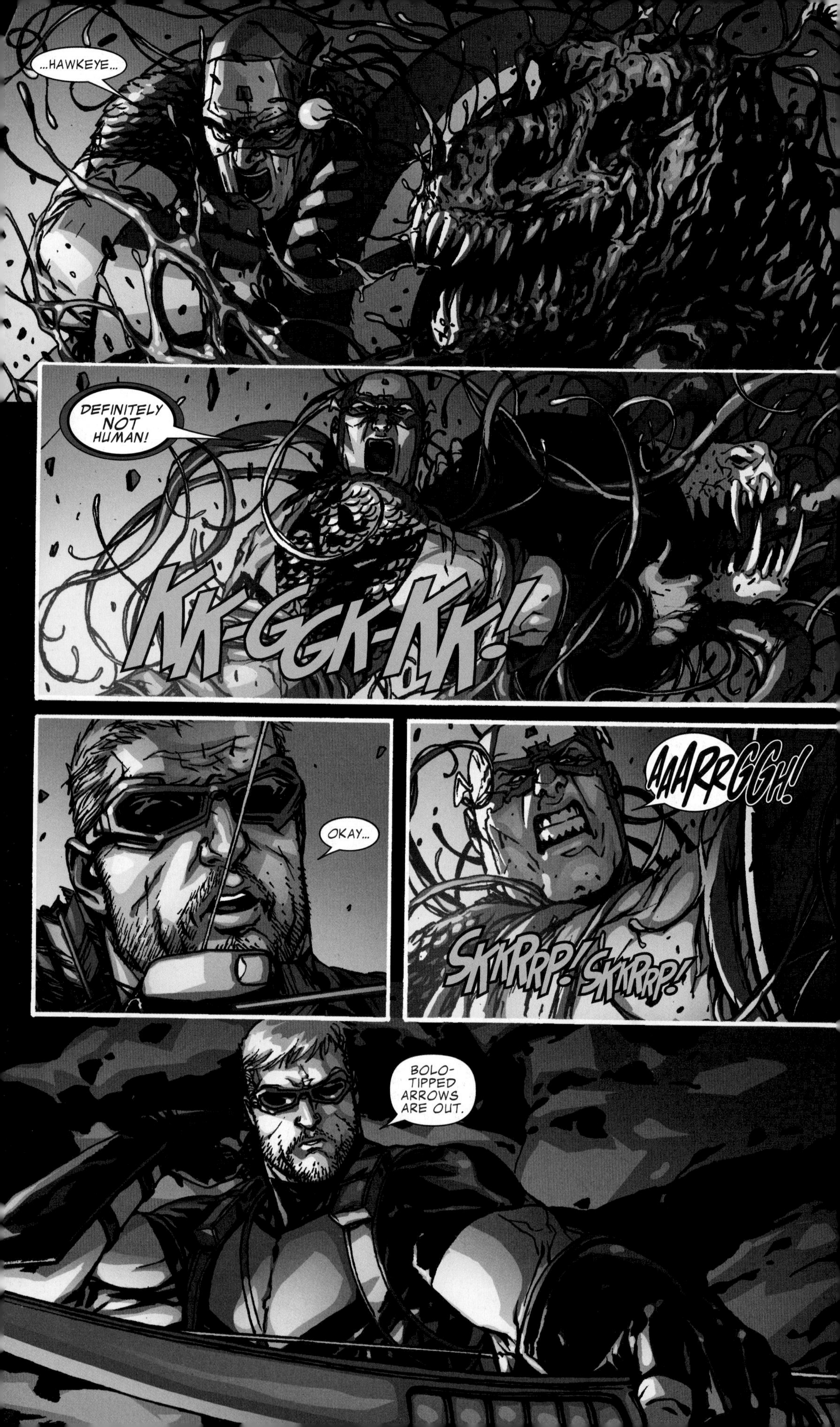
...HAWKEYE...
DEFINITELY NOT HUMAN!
KK-GGK-KK!
OKAY...
AAARRGGH!
SKKRRP! SKKRRP!
BOLO-TIPPED ARROWS ARE OUT.

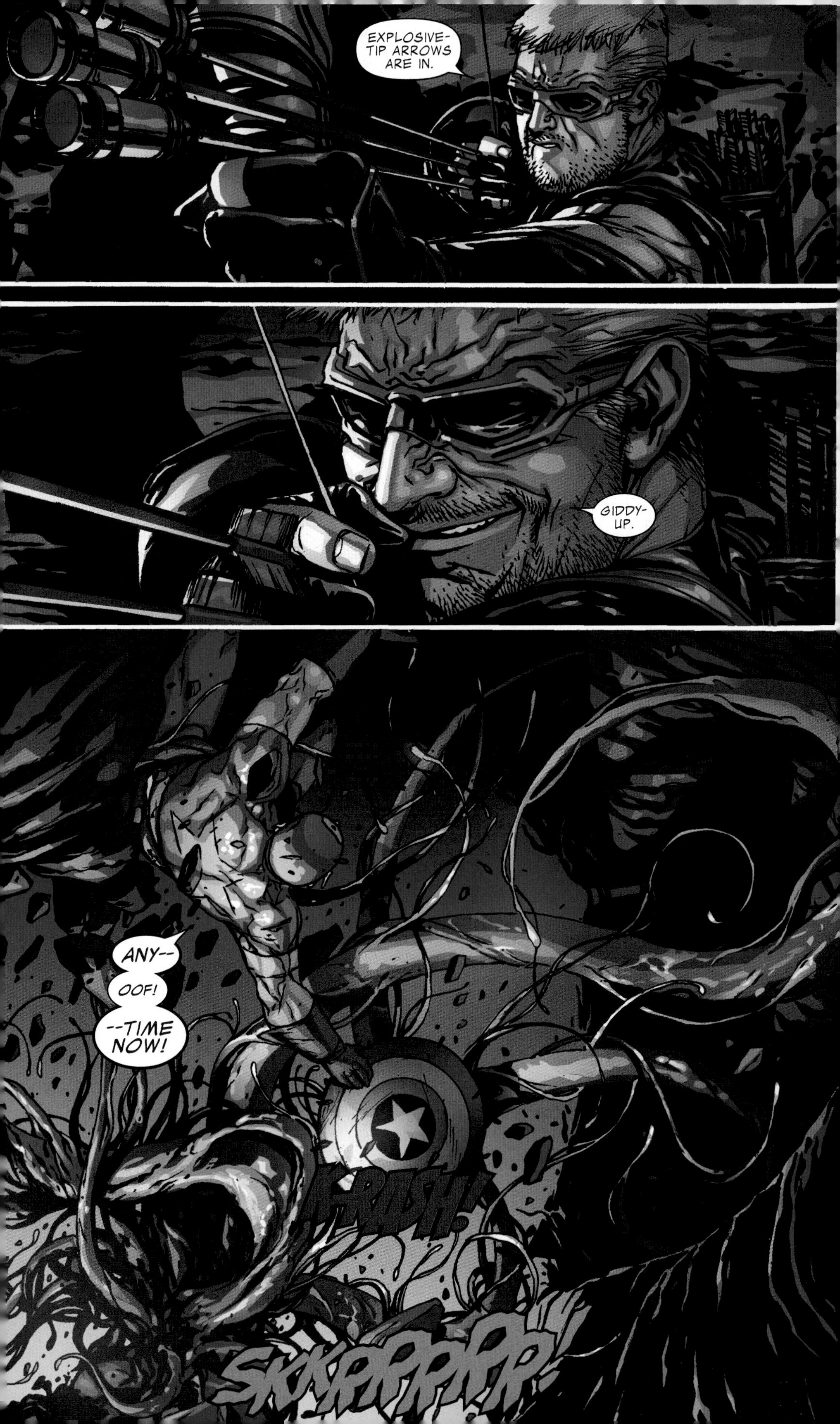
EXPLOSIVE-TIP ARROWS ARE IN.
GIDDY-UP.
ANY--
OOF!
--TIME NOW!

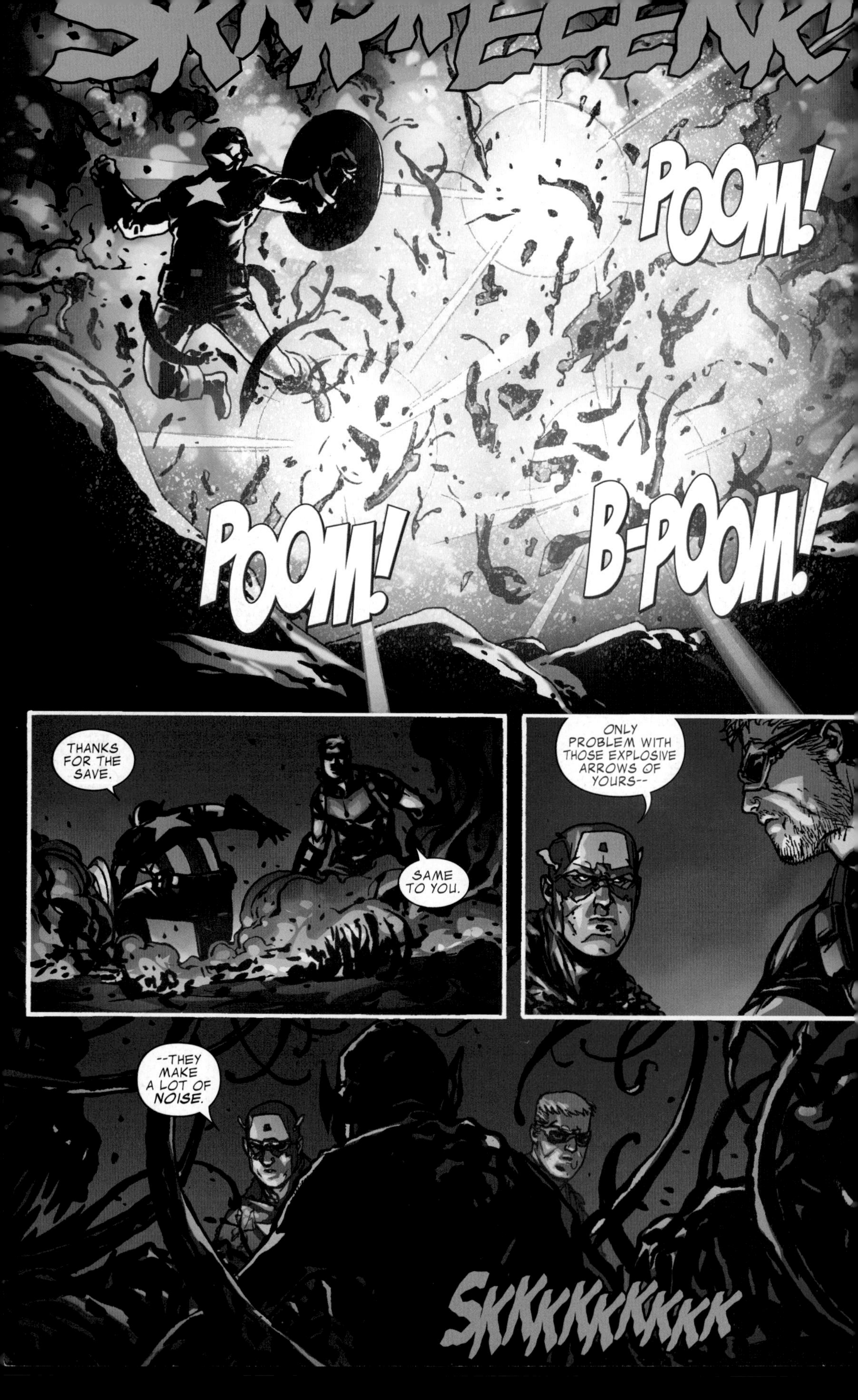
POOM!
POOM!
B-POOM!
THANKS FOR THE SAVE.
SAME TO YOU.
ONLY PROBLEM WITH THOSE EXPLOSIVE ARROWS OF YOURS--
--THEY MAKE A LOT OF NOISE.
SKKKKKKKKK

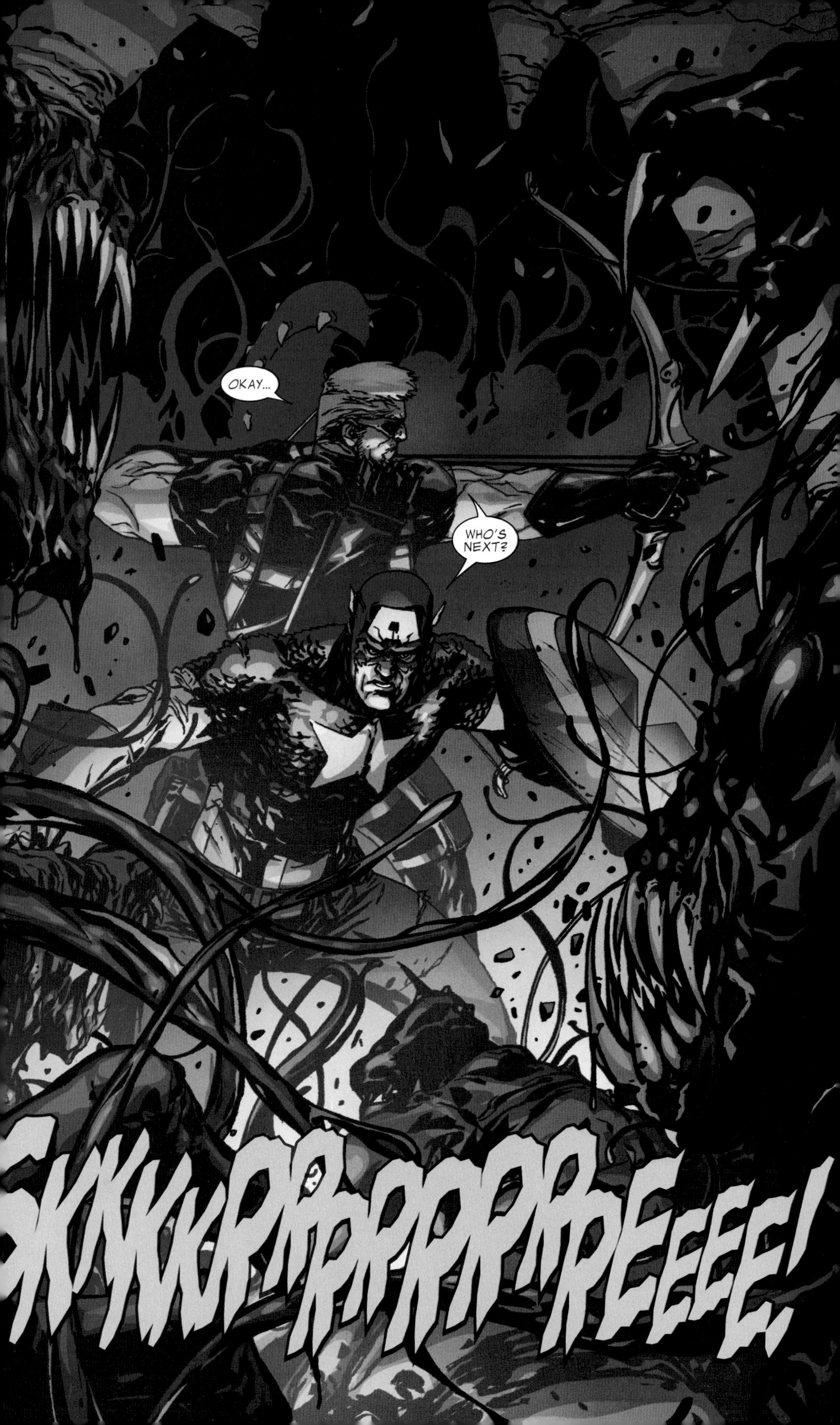
OKAY...
WHO'S NEXT?
SKKKRRRRRRRREEEE!

630

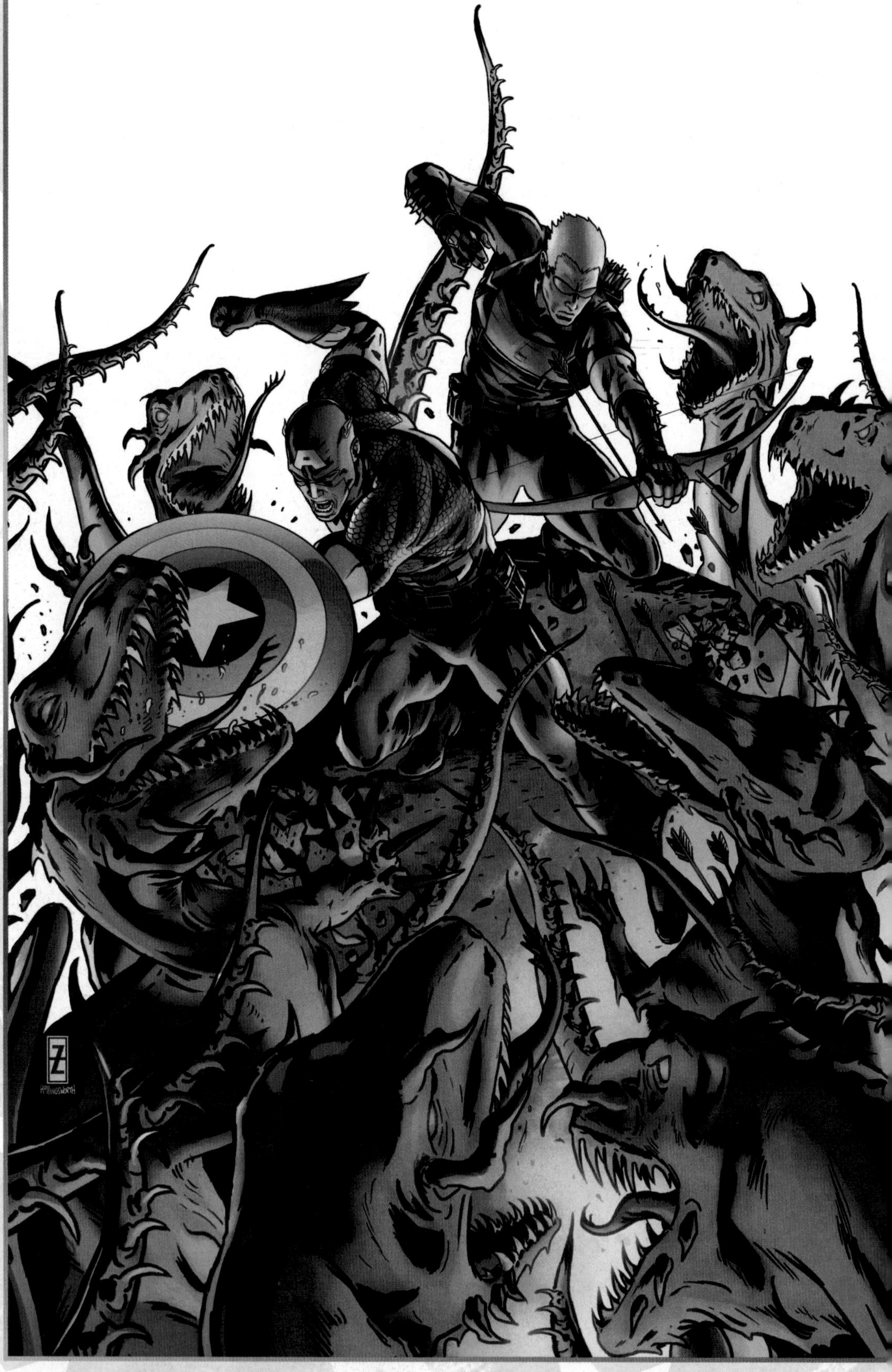

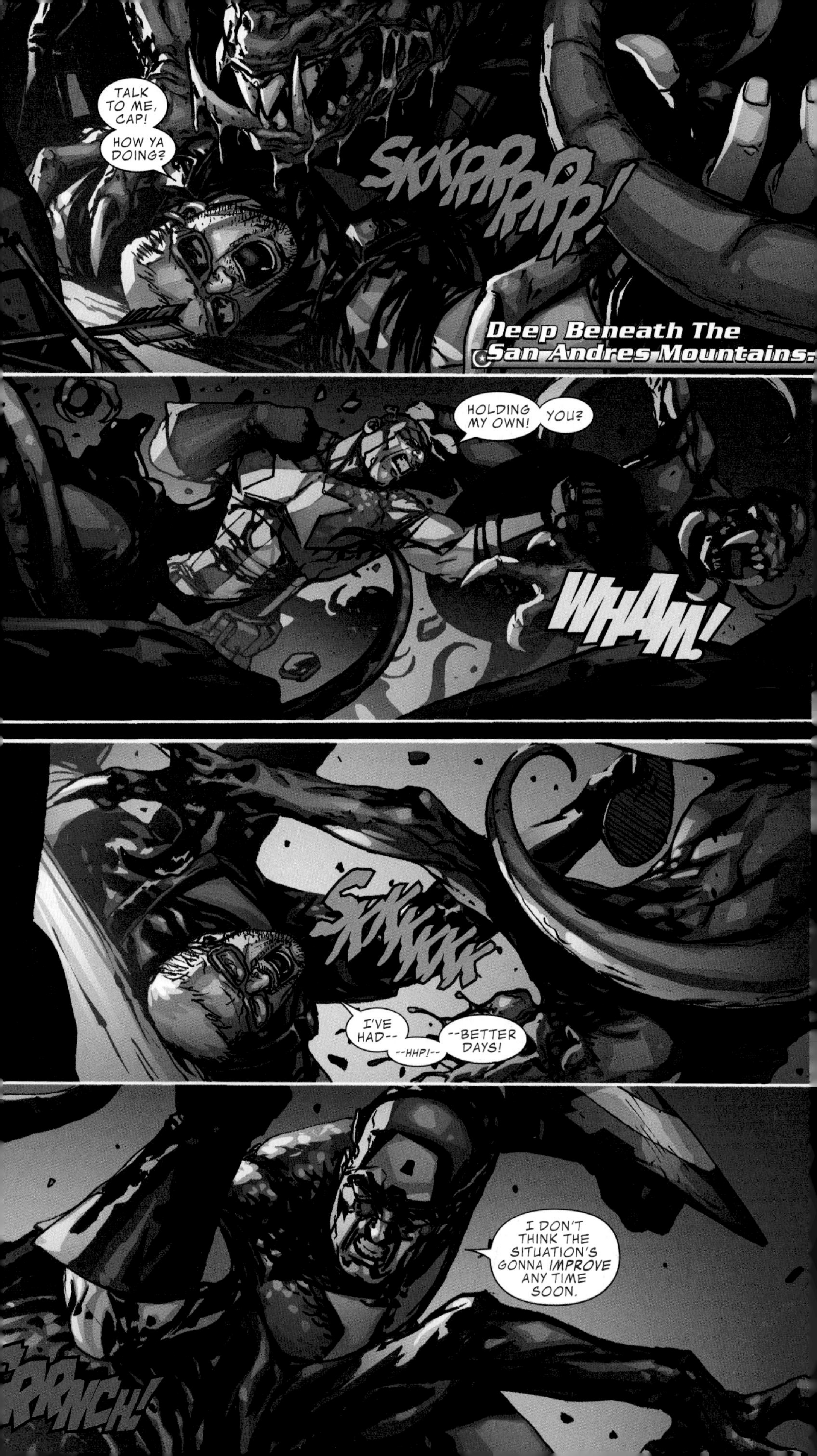
TALK TO ME, CAP!
HOW YA DOING?
SKKRRRRRR!
Deep Beneath The San Andres Mountains.
HOLDING MY OWN!
YOU?
WHAM!
SKKKKK
I'VE HAD--
--HHP!--
--BETTER DAYS!
I DON'T THINK THE SITUATION'S GONNA IMPROVE ANY TIME SOON.
RRNCH!

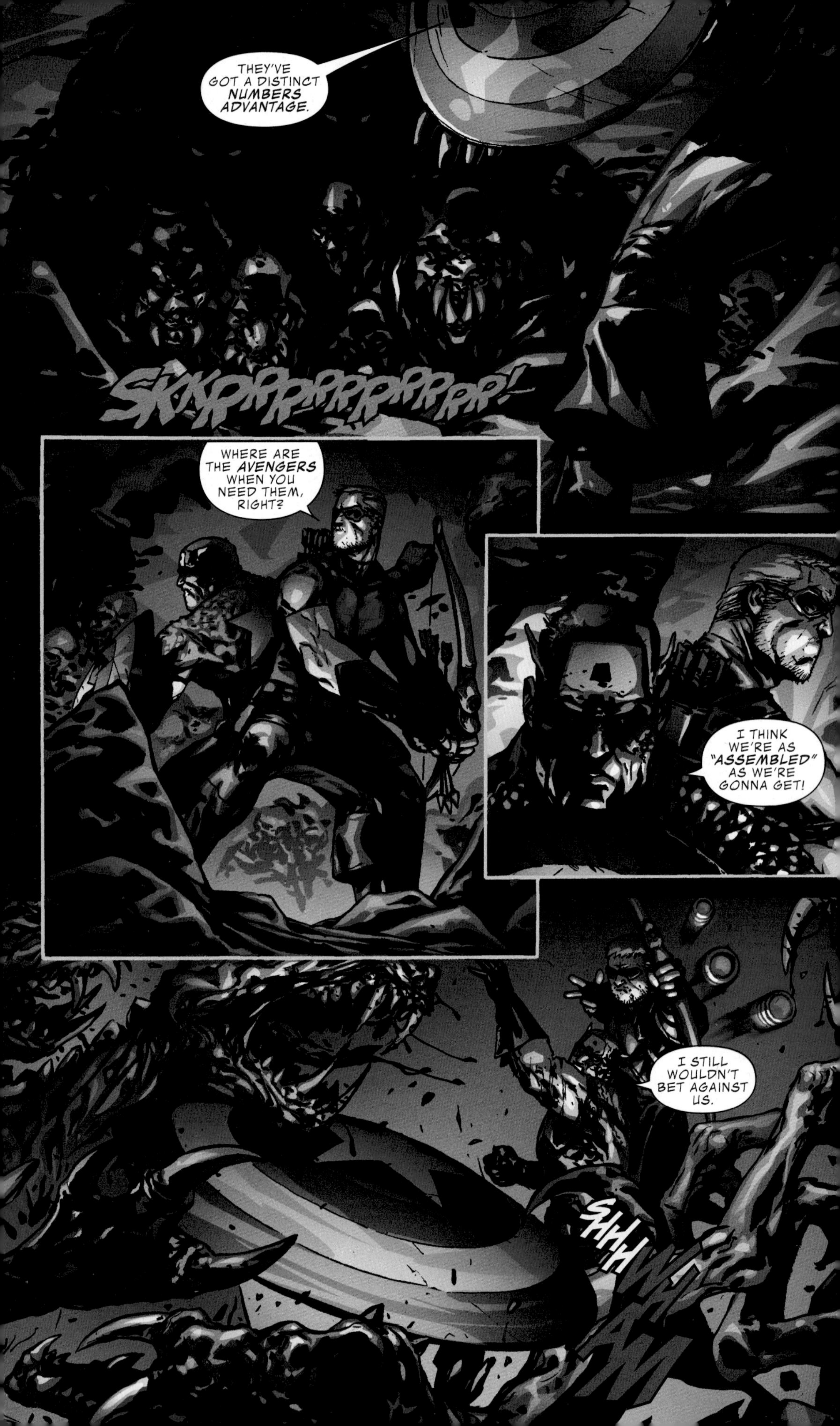
THEY'VE GOT A DISTINCT NUMBERS ADVANTAGE.
SKKRRRRRRRRRRRRRR!
WHERE ARE THE AVENGERS WHEN YOU NEED THEM, RIGHT?
I THINK WE'RE AS "ASSEMBLED" AS WE'RE GONNA GET!
I STILL WOULDN'T BET AGAINST US.
SHHHWAM

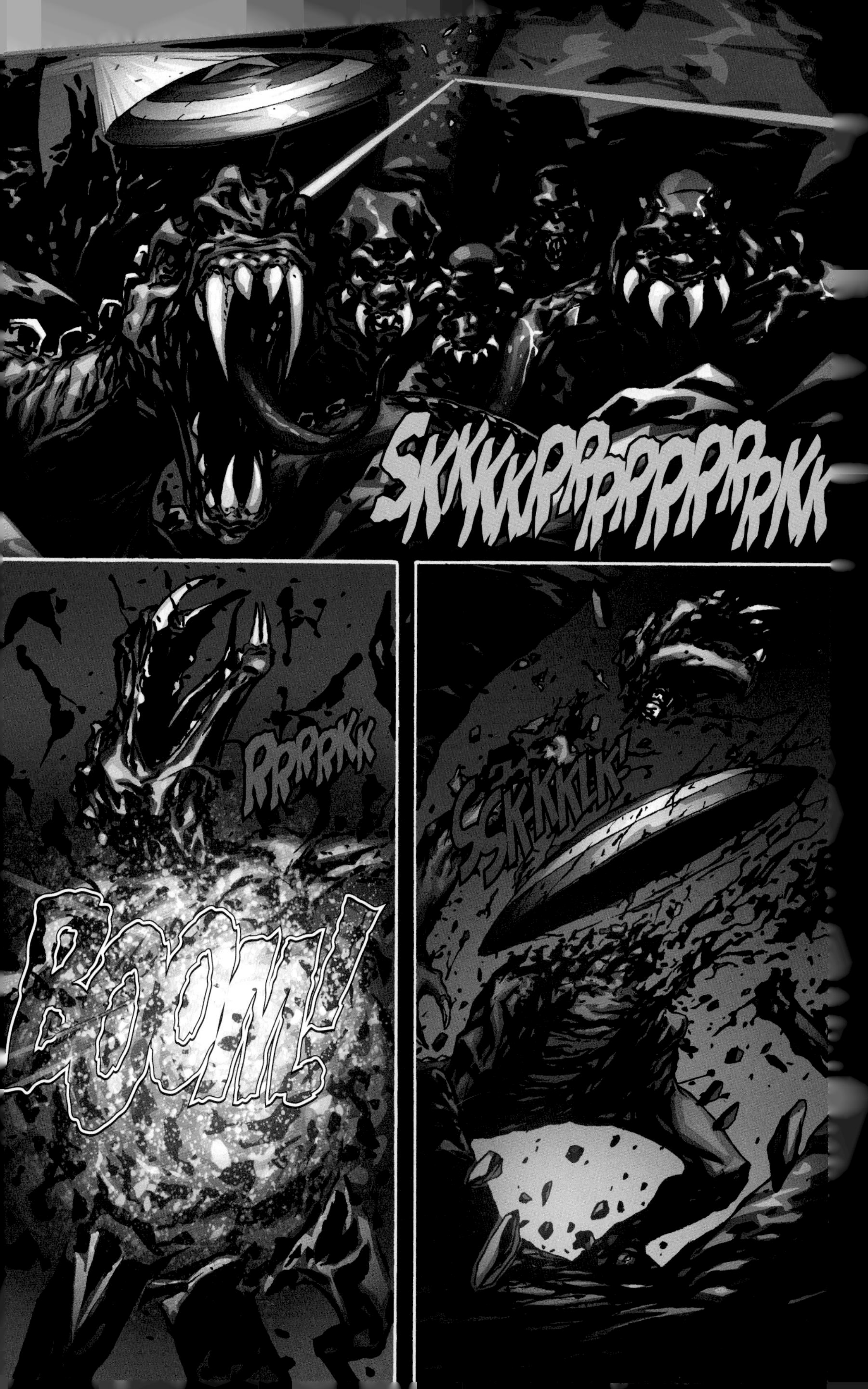
SKKKKRRRRRRRRRKK
RRRRKK
BOOM!
SSKKKLK!

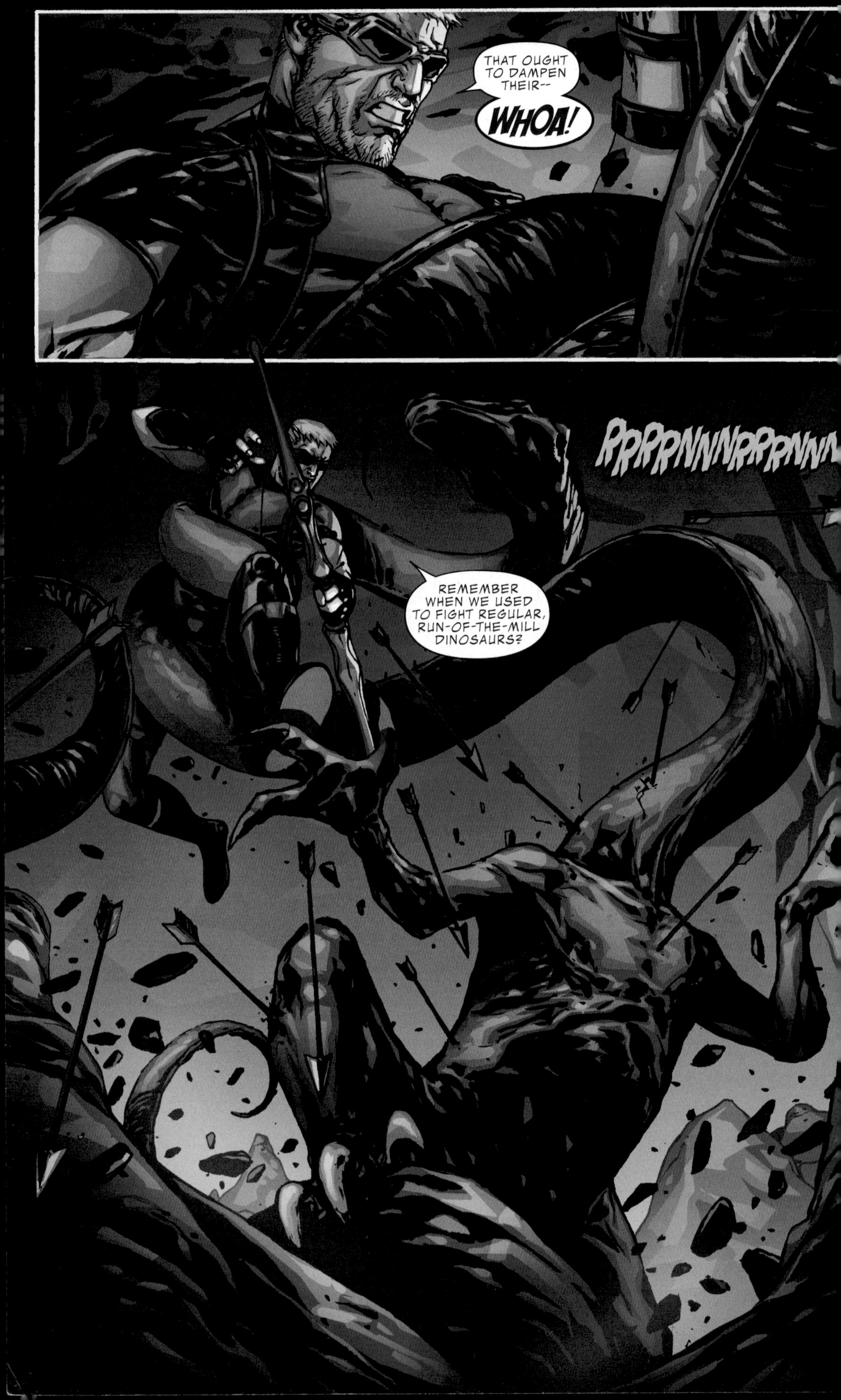

THAT OUGHT TO DAMPEN THEIR--
WHOA!
RRRRNNNRRRNNN
REMEMBER WHEN WE USED TO FIGHT REGULAR, RUN-OF-THE-MILL DINOSAURS?

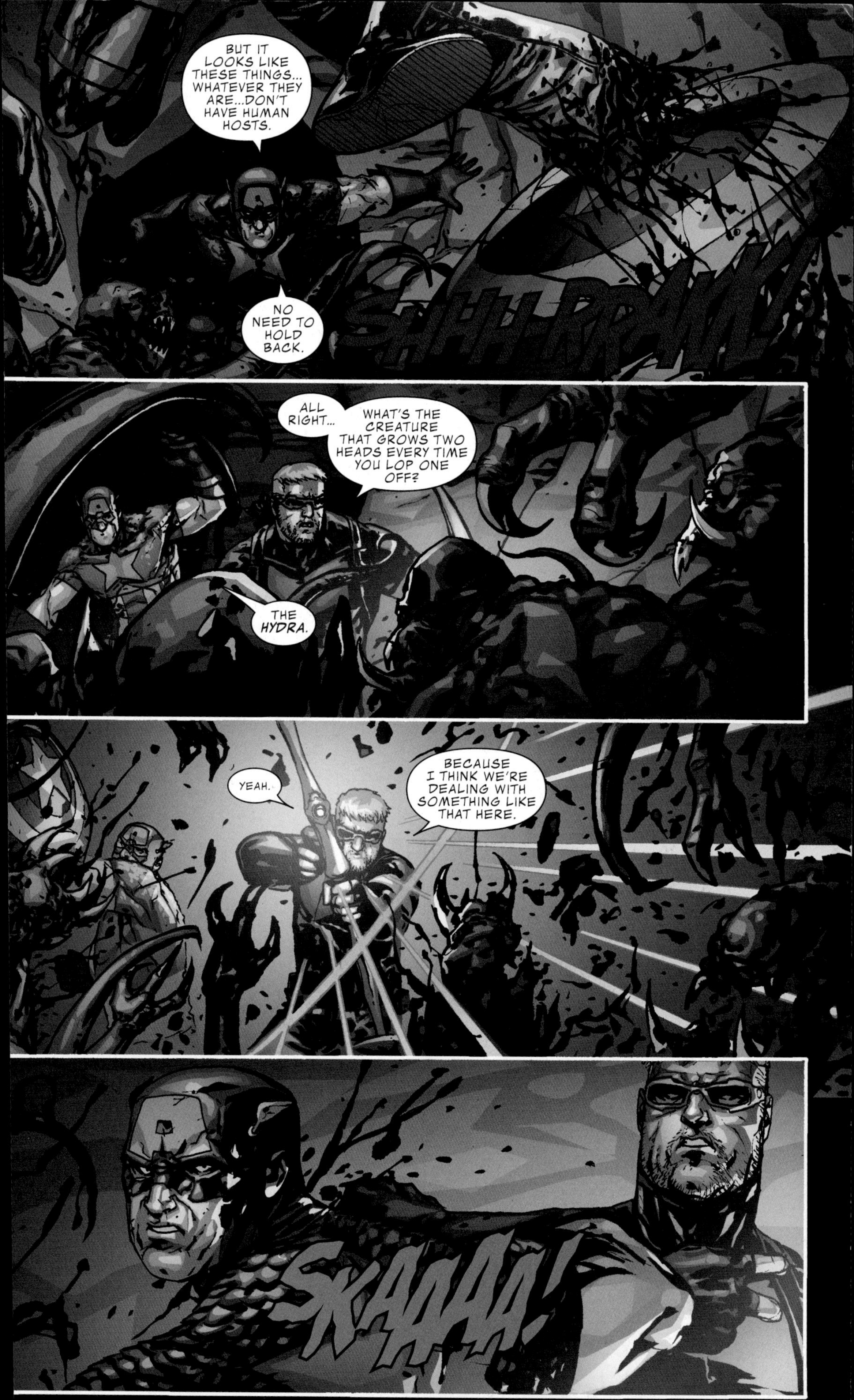

BUT IT LOOKS LIKE THESE THINGS... WHATEVER THEY ARE...DON'T HAVE HUMAN HOSTS.
NO NEED TO HOLD BACK.
SHHH-BRAWW!
ALL RIGHT...
WHAT'S THE CREATURE THAT GROWS TWO HEADS EVERY TIME YOU LOP ONE OFF?
THE *HYDRA.*
YEAH.
BECAUSE I THINK WE'RE DEALING WITH SOMETHING LIKE THAT HERE.
SKAAAA!

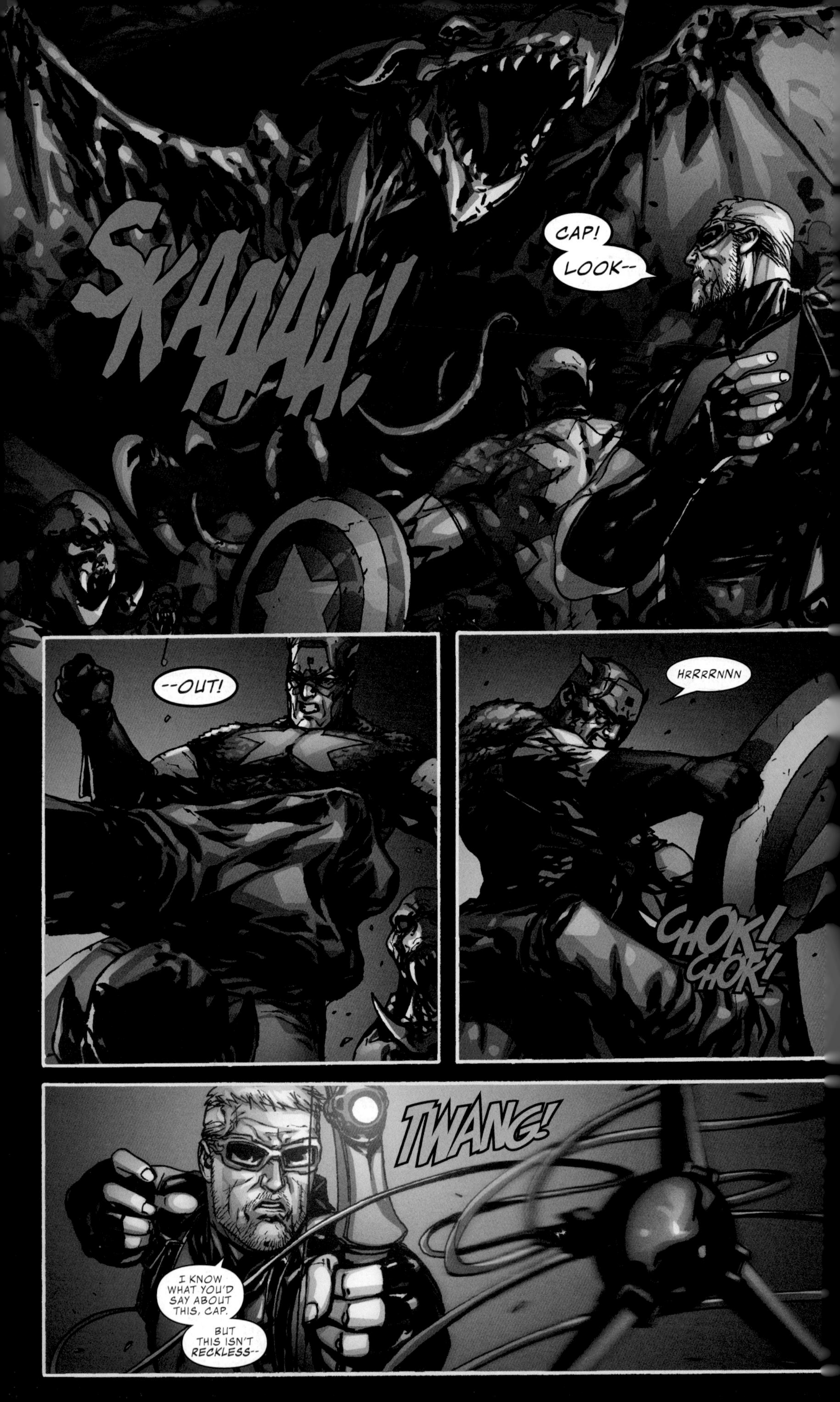
SKAAAA!
CAP!
LOOK--
--OUT!
HRRRRNNN
CHOK!
CHOK!
TWANG!
I KNOW WHAT YOU'D SAY ABOUT THIS, CAP.
BUT THIS ISN'T RECKLESS--

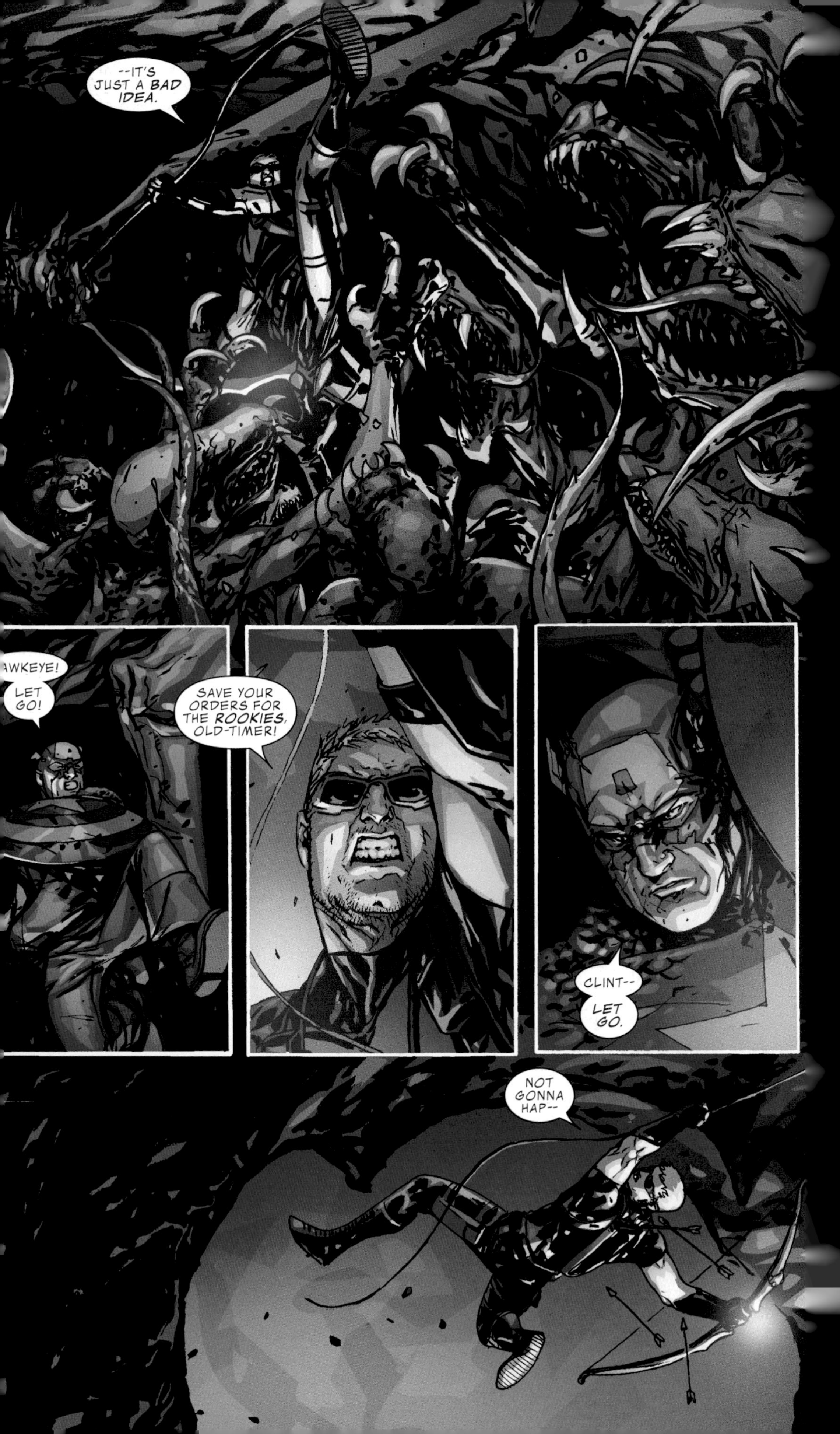
--IT'S JUST A BAD IDEA.
AWKEYE!
LET GO!
SAVE YOUR ORDERS FOR THE ROOKIES, OLD-TIMER!
CLINT--
LET GO.
NOT GONNA HAP--

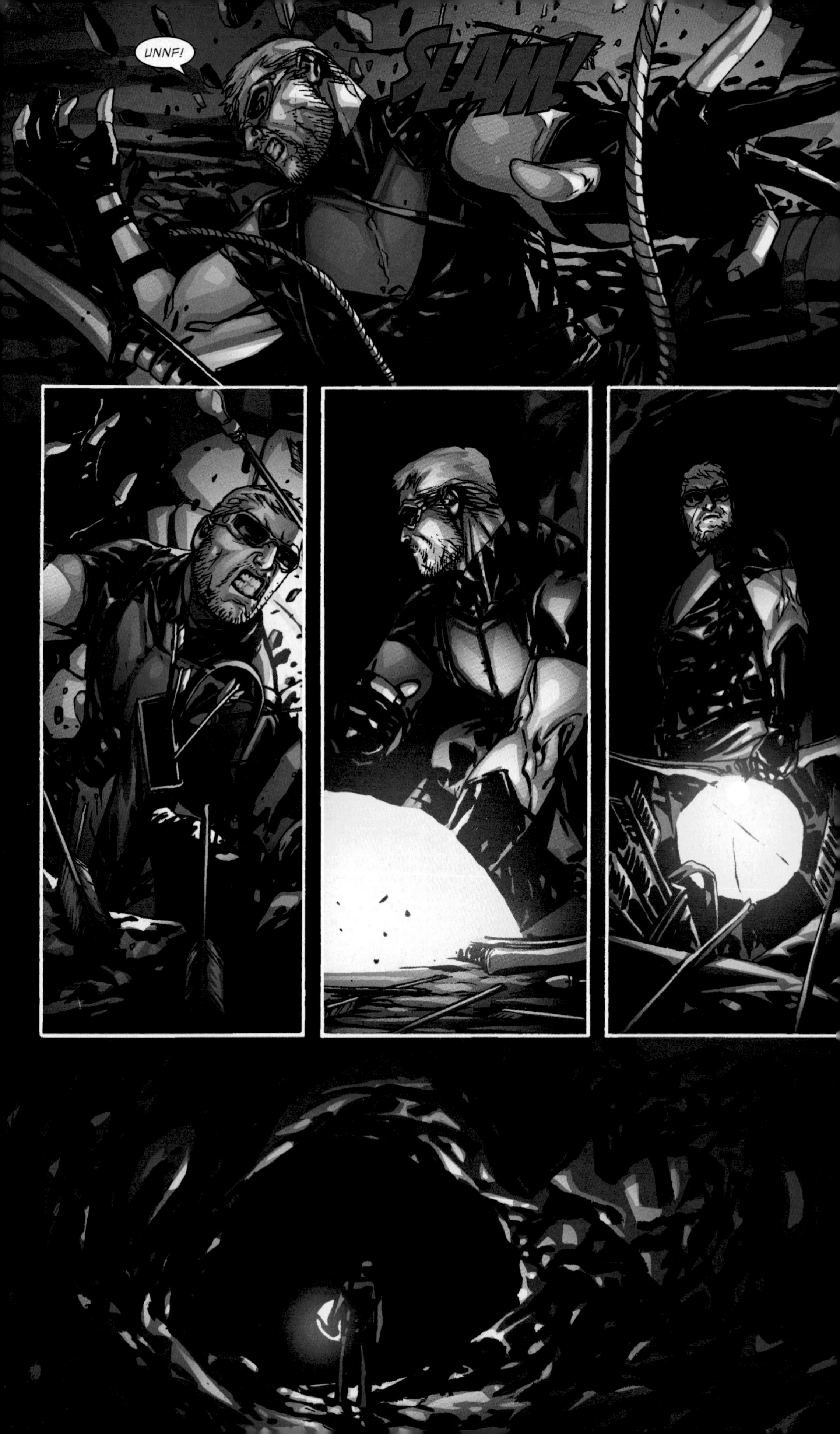
UNNF!
SLAM!

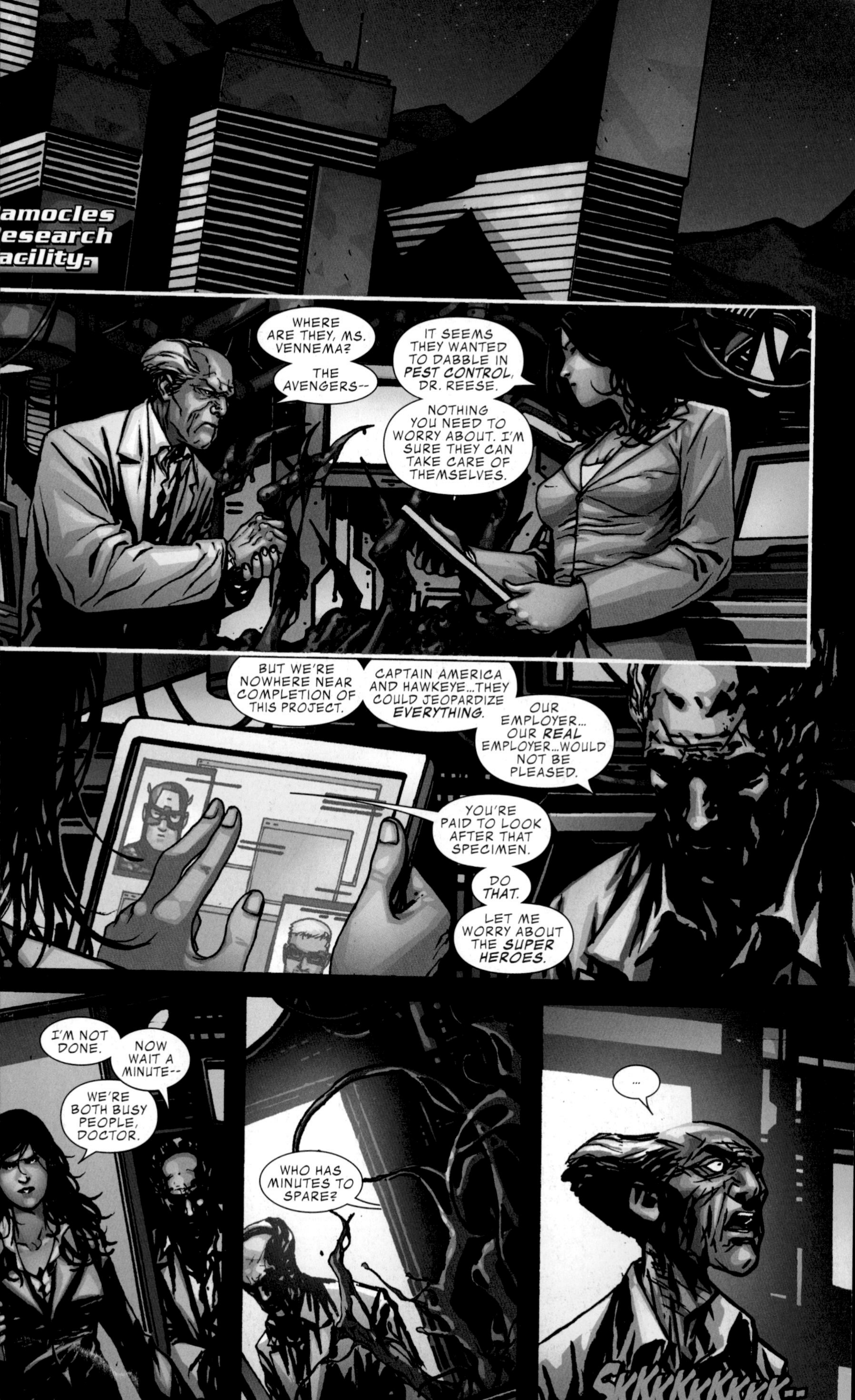

amocles
esearch
acility.
WHERE ARE THEY, MS. VENNEMA?
THE AVENGERS--
IT SEEMS THEY WANTED TO DABBLE IN PEST CONTROL, DR. REESE.
NOTHING YOU NEED TO WORRY ABOUT. I'M SURE THEY CAN TAKE CARE OF THEMSELVES.
BUT WE'RE NOWHERE NEAR COMPLETION OF THIS PROJECT.
CAPTAIN AMERICA AND HAWKEYE...THEY COULD JEOPARDIZE EVERYTHING.
OUR EMPLOYER... OUR REAL EMPLOYER...WOULD NOT BE PLEASED.
YOU'RE PAID TO LOOK AFTER THAT SPECIMEN.
DO THAT.
LET ME WORRY ABOUT THE SUPER HEROES.
I'M NOT DONE.
NOW WAIT A MINUTE--
WE'RE BOTH BUSY PEOPLE, DOCTOR.
WHO HAS MINUTES TO SPARE?
...

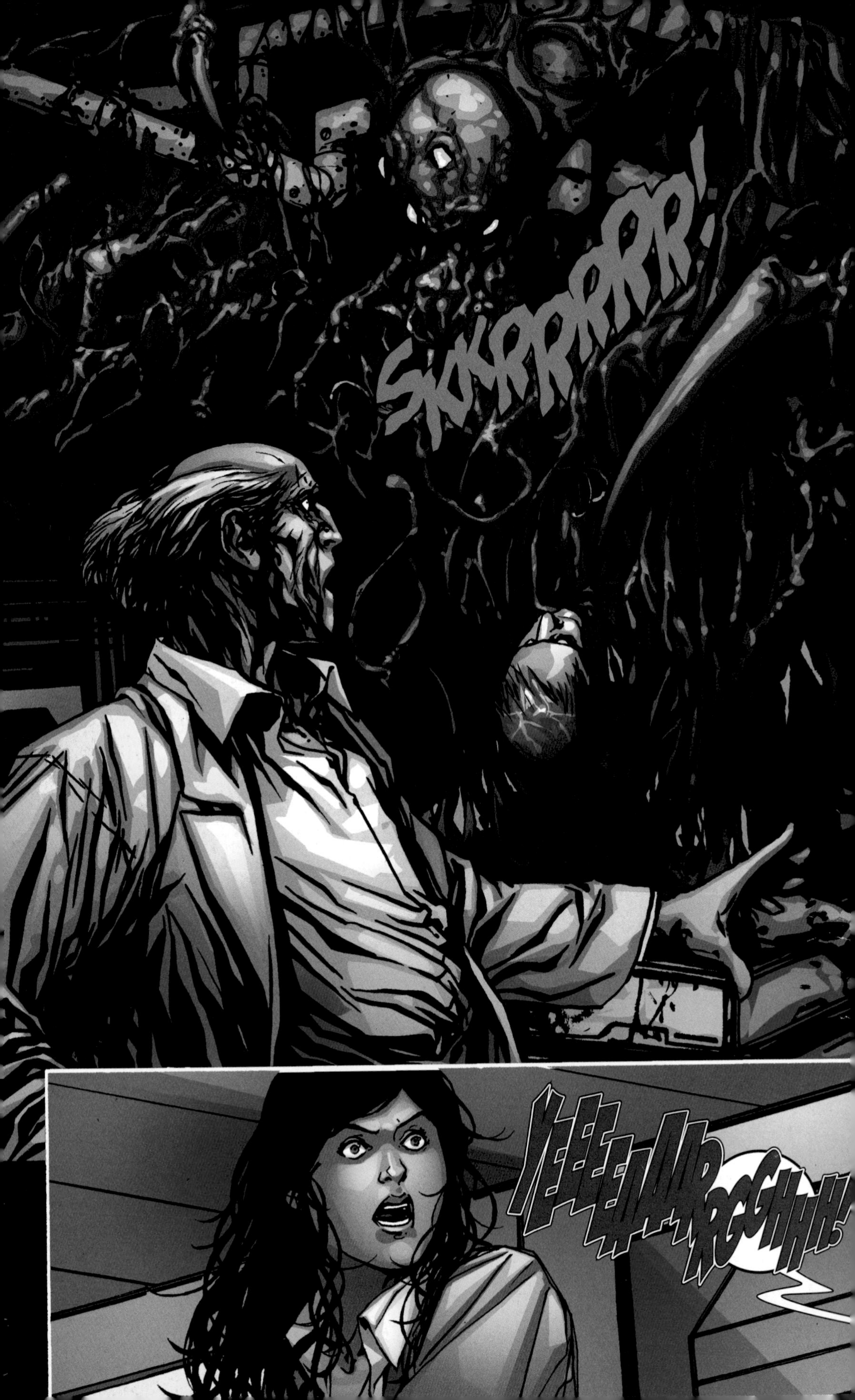
SKRRRRRRR!
YEEEEAARRGGHHH!

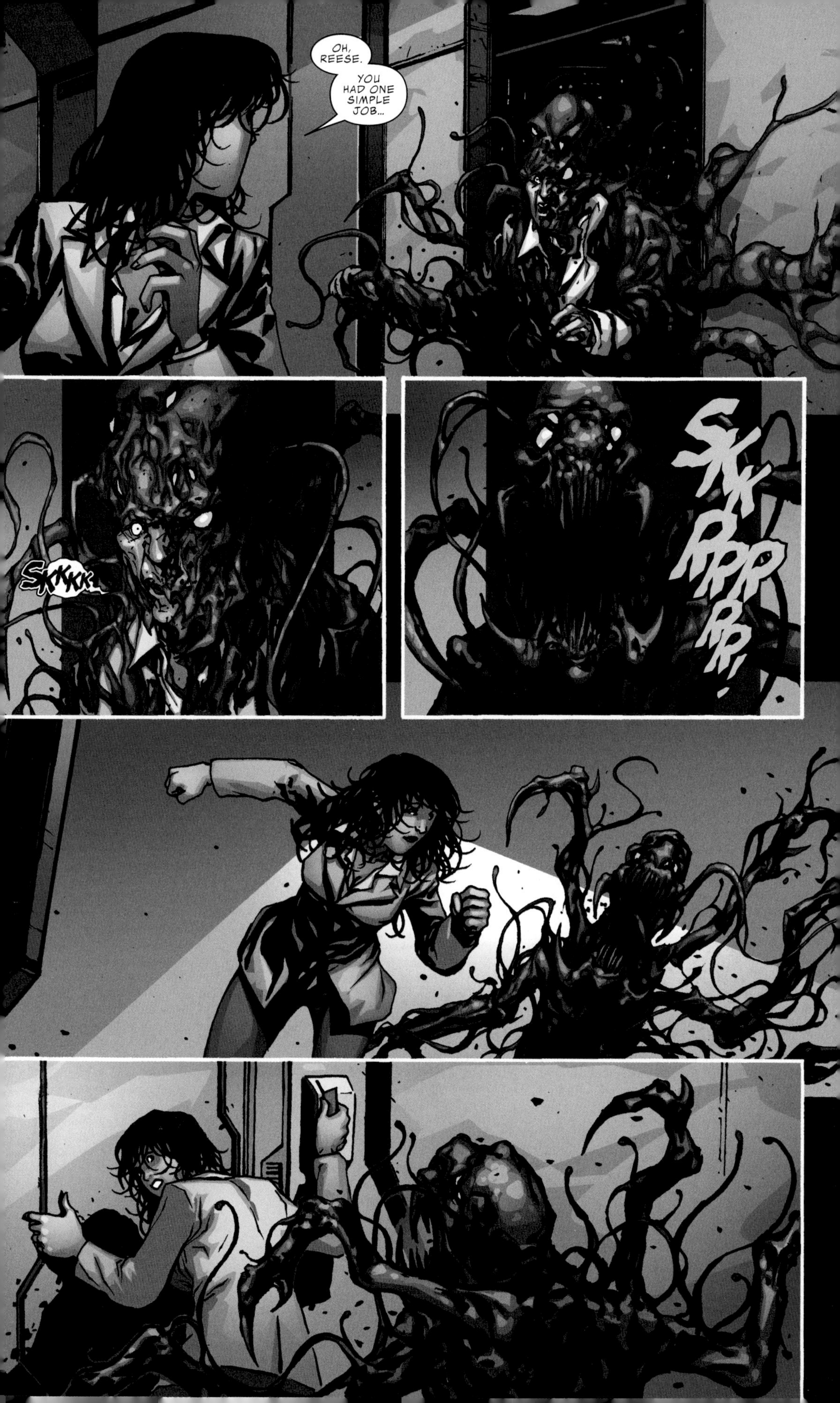
OH, REESE.
YOU HAD ONE SIMPLE JOB...
SKKKKK
SKKRRRRRR!

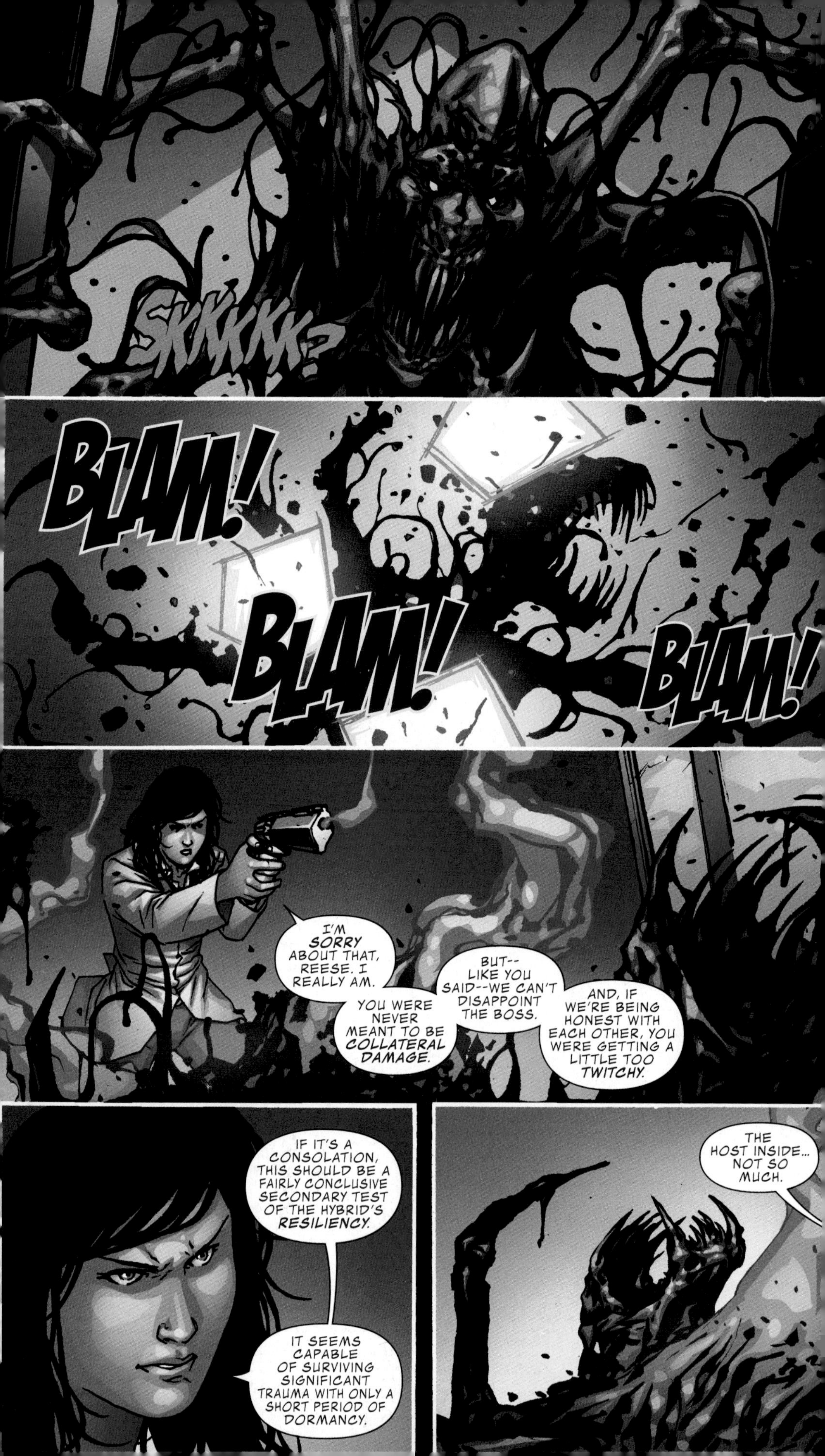

SKKKKK?
BLAM!
BLAM!
BLAM!
I'M SORRY ABOUT THAT, REESE. I REALLY AM.
YOU WERE NEVER MEANT TO BE COLLATERAL DAMAGE.
BUT-- LIKE YOU SAID--WE CAN'T DISAPPOINT THE BOSS.
AND, IF WE'RE BEING HONEST WITH EACH OTHER, YOU WERE GETTING A LITTLE TOO TWITCHY.
IF IT'S A CONSOLATION, THIS SHOULD BE A FAIRLY CONCLUSIVE SECONDARY TEST OF THE HYBRID'S RESILIENCY.
IT SEEMS CAPABLE OF SURVIVING SIGNIFICANT TRAUMA WITH ONLY A SHORT PERIOD OF DORMANCY.
THE HOST INSIDE... NOT SO MUCH.

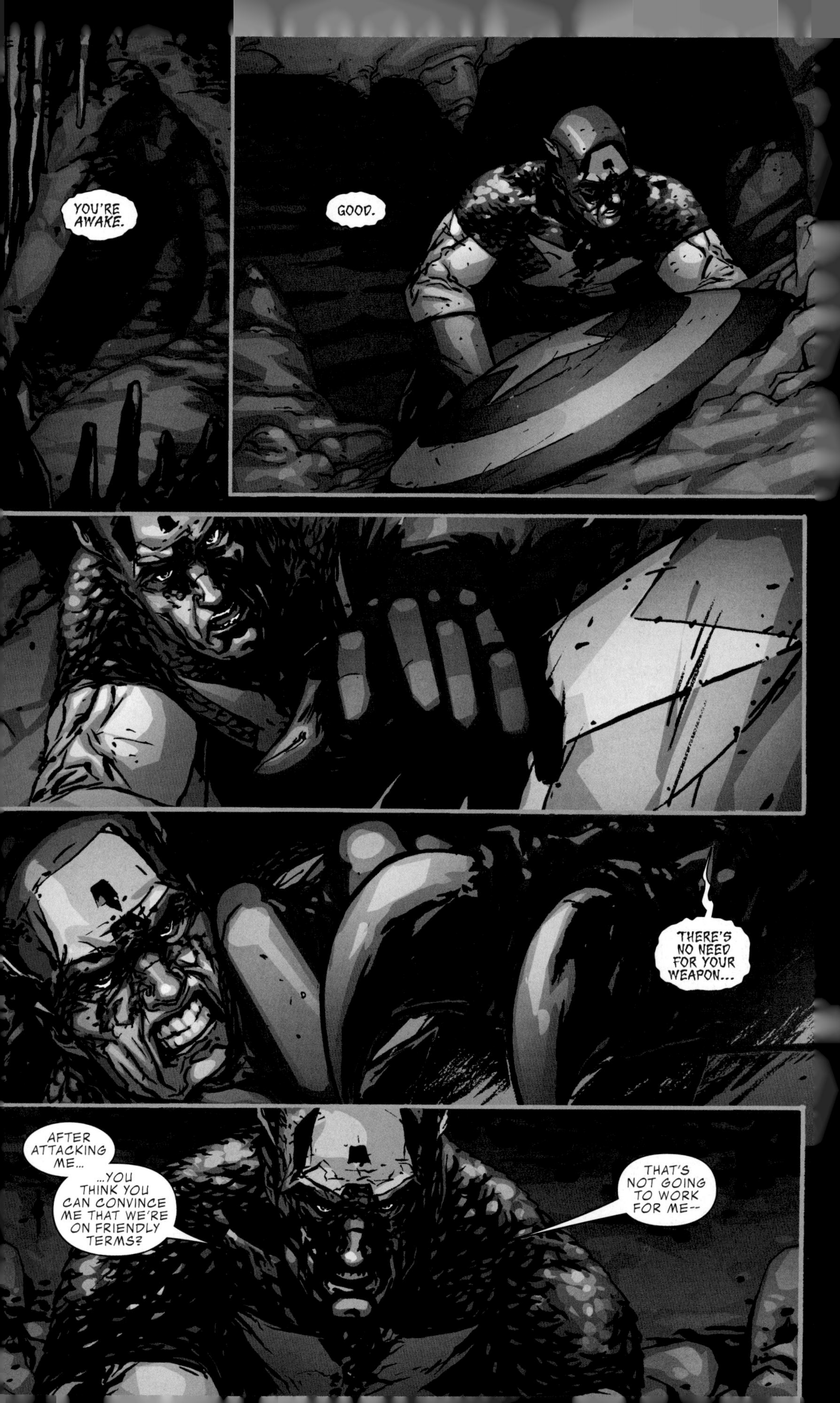
YOU'RE AWAKE.
GOOD.
THERE'S NO NEED FOR YOUR WEAPON...
AFTER ATTACKING ME...
...YOU THINK YOU CAN CONVINCE ME THAT WE'RE ON FRIENDLY TERMS?
THAT'S NOT GOING TO WORK FOR ME--

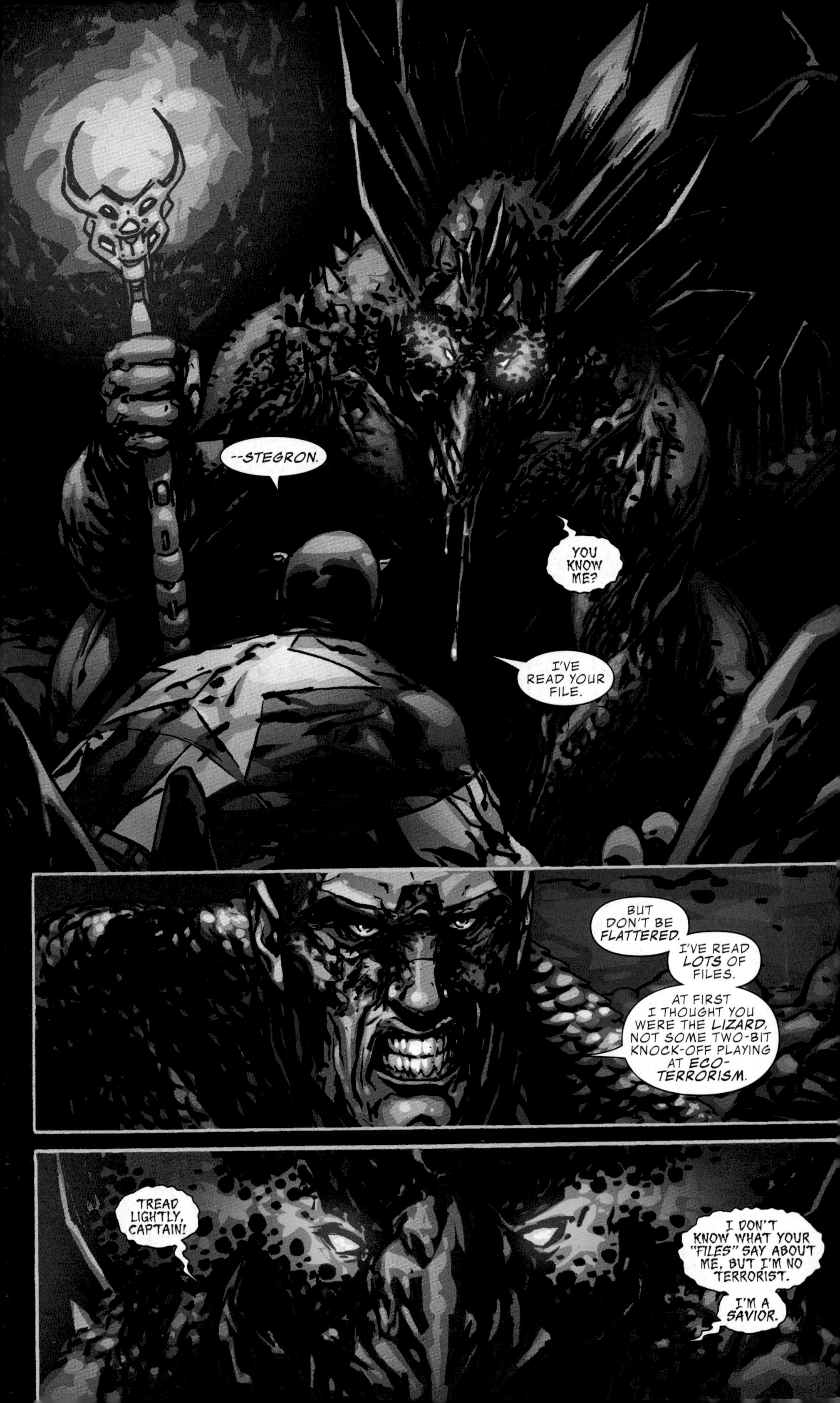
--STEGRON.
YOU KNOW ME?
I'VE READ YOUR FILE.
BUT DON'T BE FLATTERED.
I'VE READ LOTS OF FILES.
AT FIRST I THOUGHT YOU WERE THE LIZARD, NOT SOME TWO-BIT KNOCK-OFF PLAYING AT ECO-TERRORISM.
TREAD LIGHTLY, CAPTAIN!
I DON'T KNOW WHAT YOUR "FILES" SAY ABOUT ME, BUT I'M NO TERRORIST.
I'M A SAVIOR.

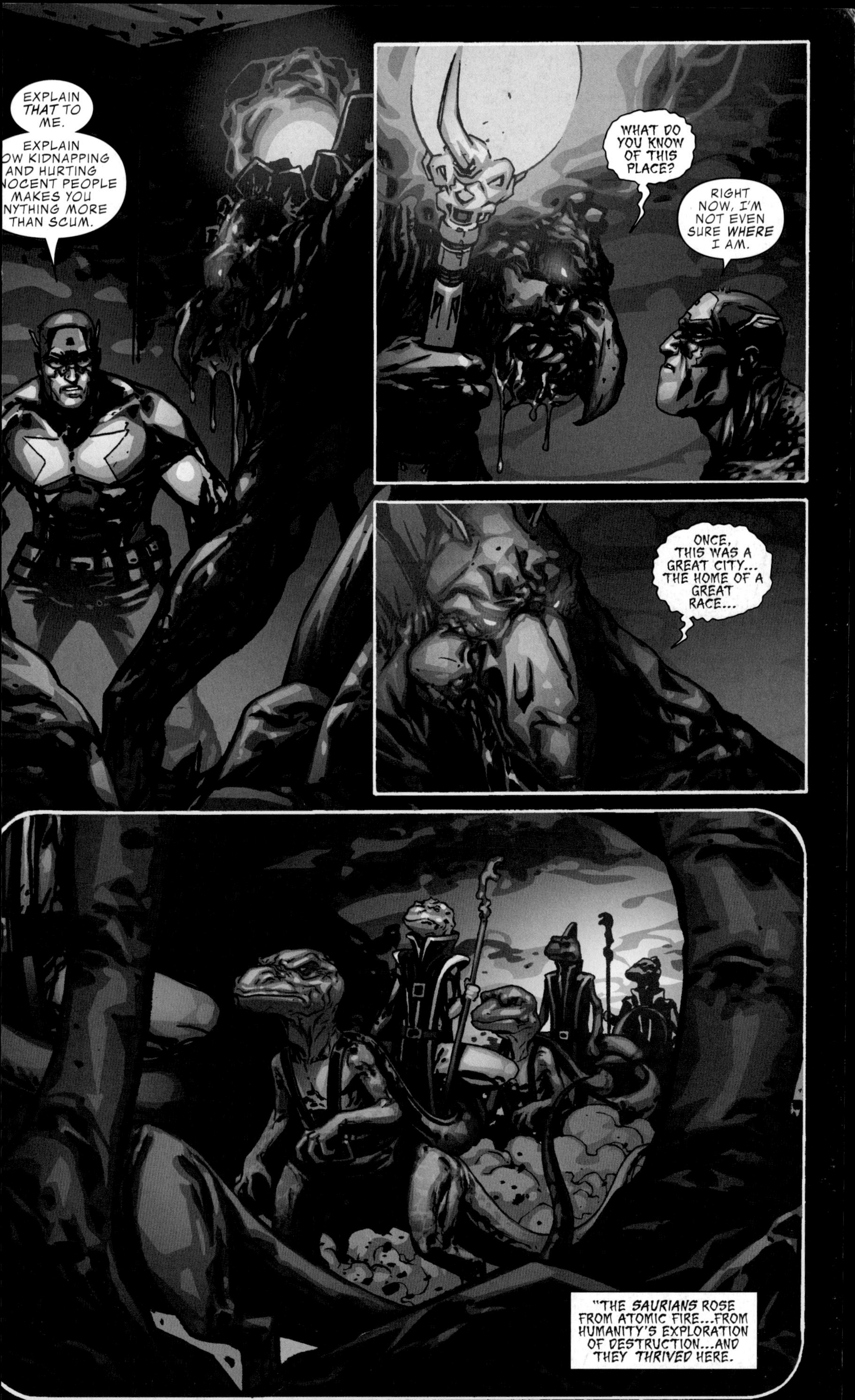
EXPLAIN THAT TO ME.
EXPLAIN OW KIDNAPPING AND HURTING NOCENT PEOPLE MAKES YOU NYTHING MORE THAN SCUM.
WHAT DO YOU KNOW OF THIS PLACE?
RIGHT NOW, I'M NOT EVEN SURE WHERE I AM.
ONCE, THIS WAS A GREAT CITY... THE HOME OF A GREAT RACE...
"THE SAURIANS ROSE FROM ATOMIC FIRE...FROM HUMANITY'S EXPLORATION OF DESTRUCTION...AND THEY THRIVED HERE.

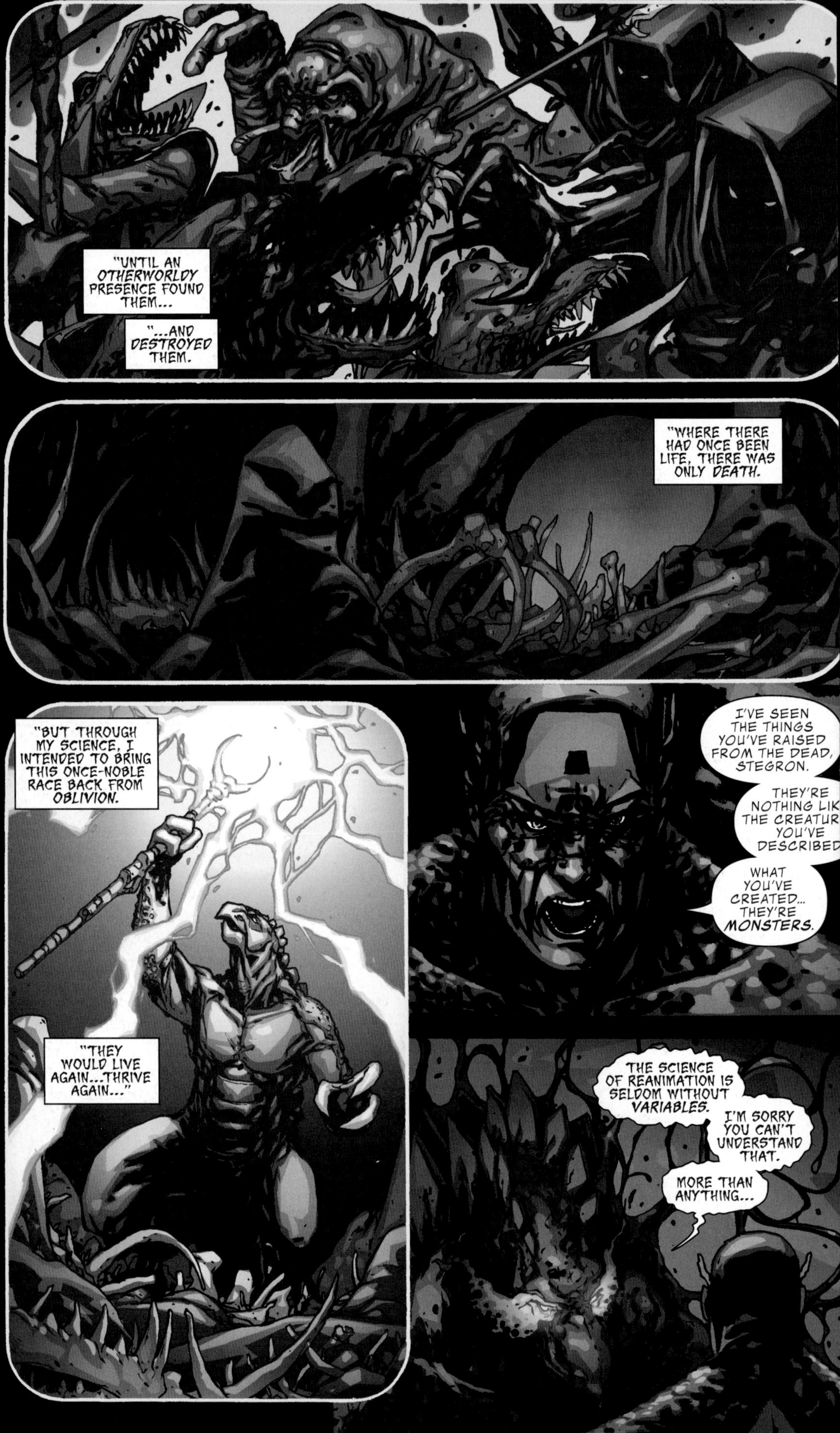
"UNTIL AN OTHERWORLDY PRESENCE FOUND THEM...
"...AND DESTROYED THEM.
"WHERE THERE HAD ONCE BEEN LIFE, THERE WAS ONLY DEATH.
"BUT THROUGH MY SCIENCE, I INTENDED TO BRING THIS ONCE-NOBLE RACE BACK FROM OBLIVION.
"THEY WOULD LIVE AGAIN...THRIVE AGAIN..."
I'VE SEEN THE THINGS YOU'VE RAISED FROM THE DEAD, STEGRON.
WHAT YOU'VE CREATED... THEY'RE MONSTERS.
THE SCIENCE OF REANIMATION IS SELDOM WITHOUT VARIABLES.
I'M SORRY YOU CAN'T UNDERSTAND THAT.
MORE THAN ANYTHING...

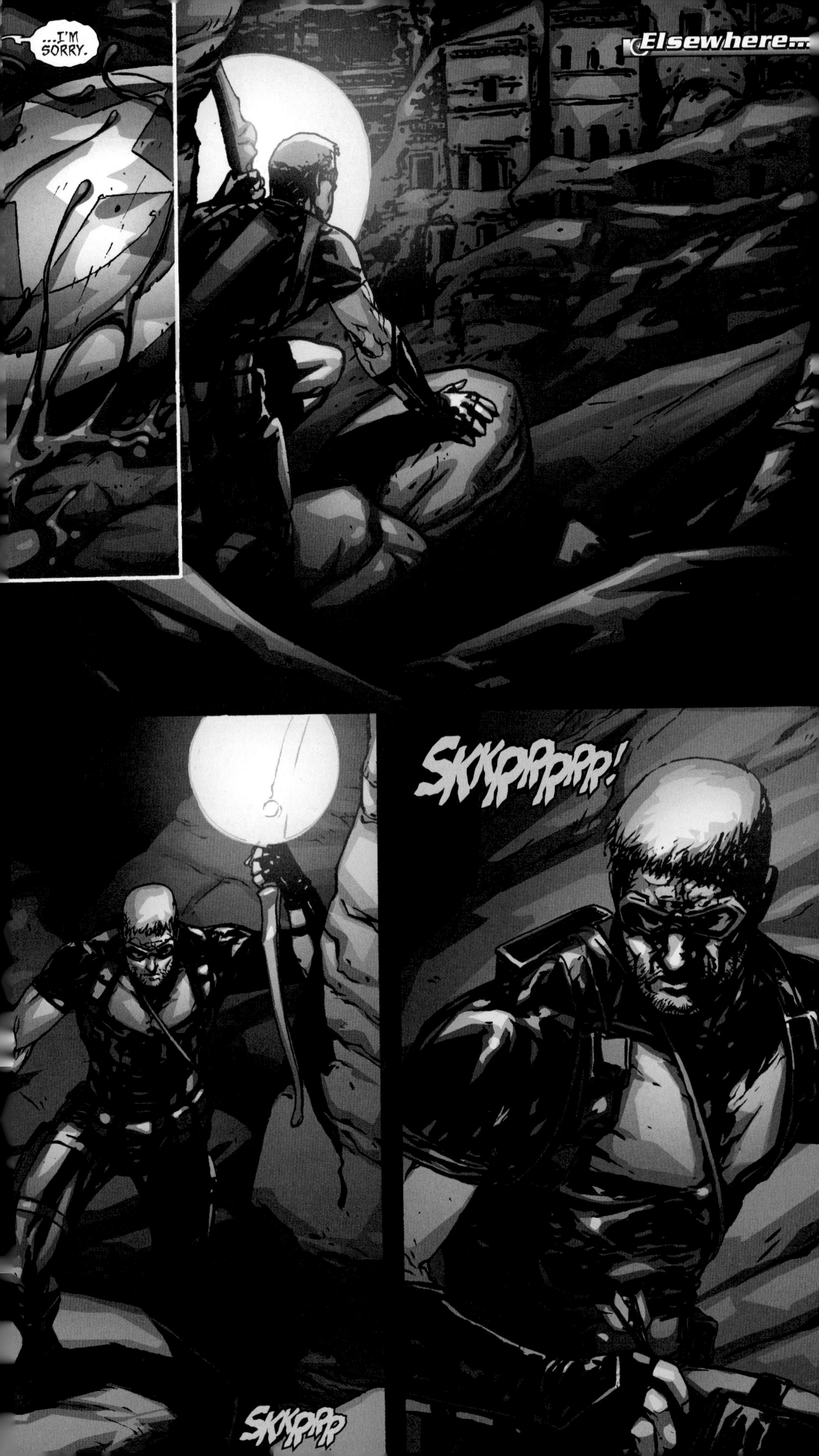
...I'M SORRY.
Elsewhere...
SKKRRRRR!
SKKRRR

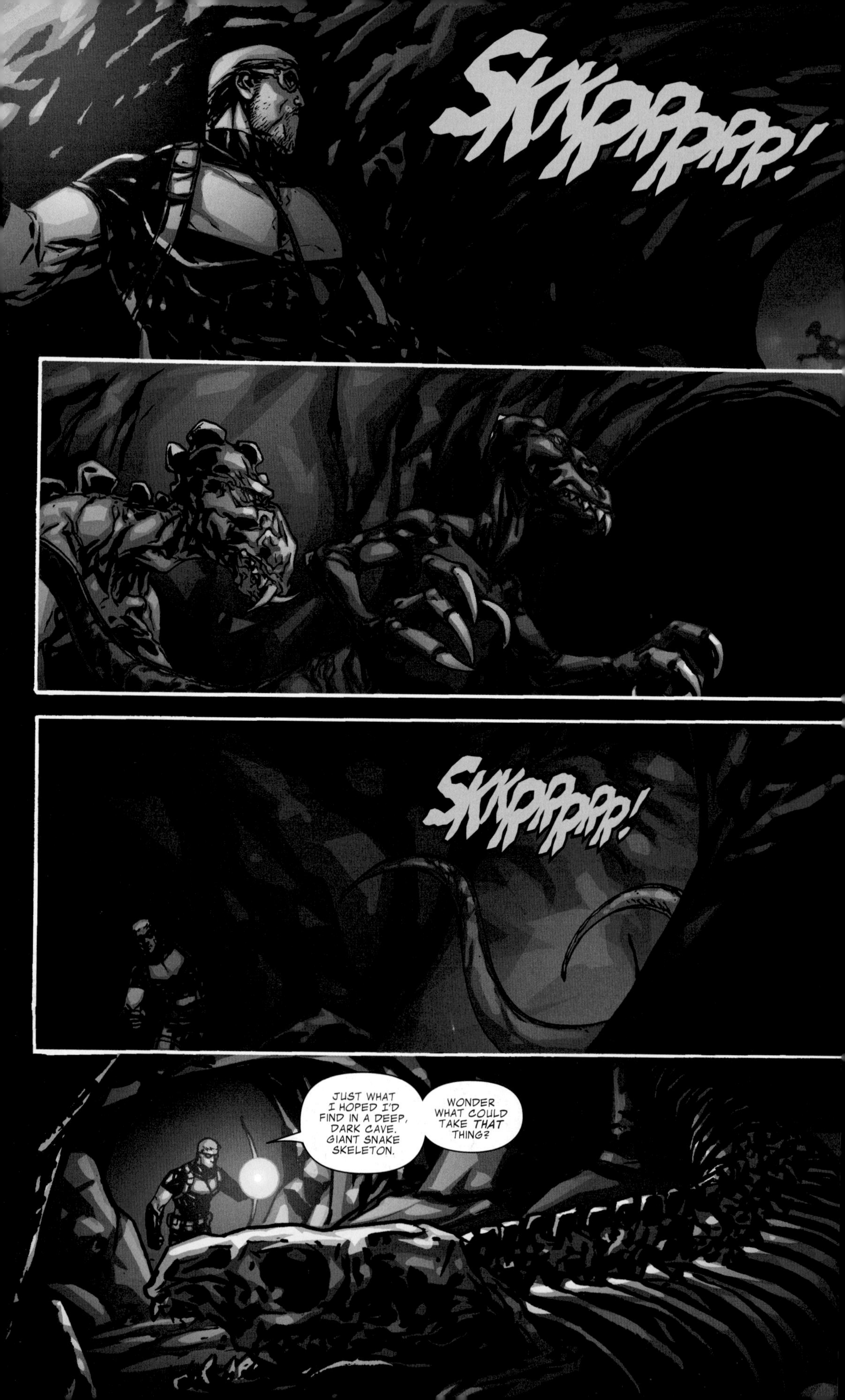
SKKRRRRR!
SKKRRRR!
JUST WHAT I HOPED I'D FIND IN A DEEP, DARK CAVE. GIANT SNAKE SKELETON.
WONDER WHAT COULD TAKE THAT THING?

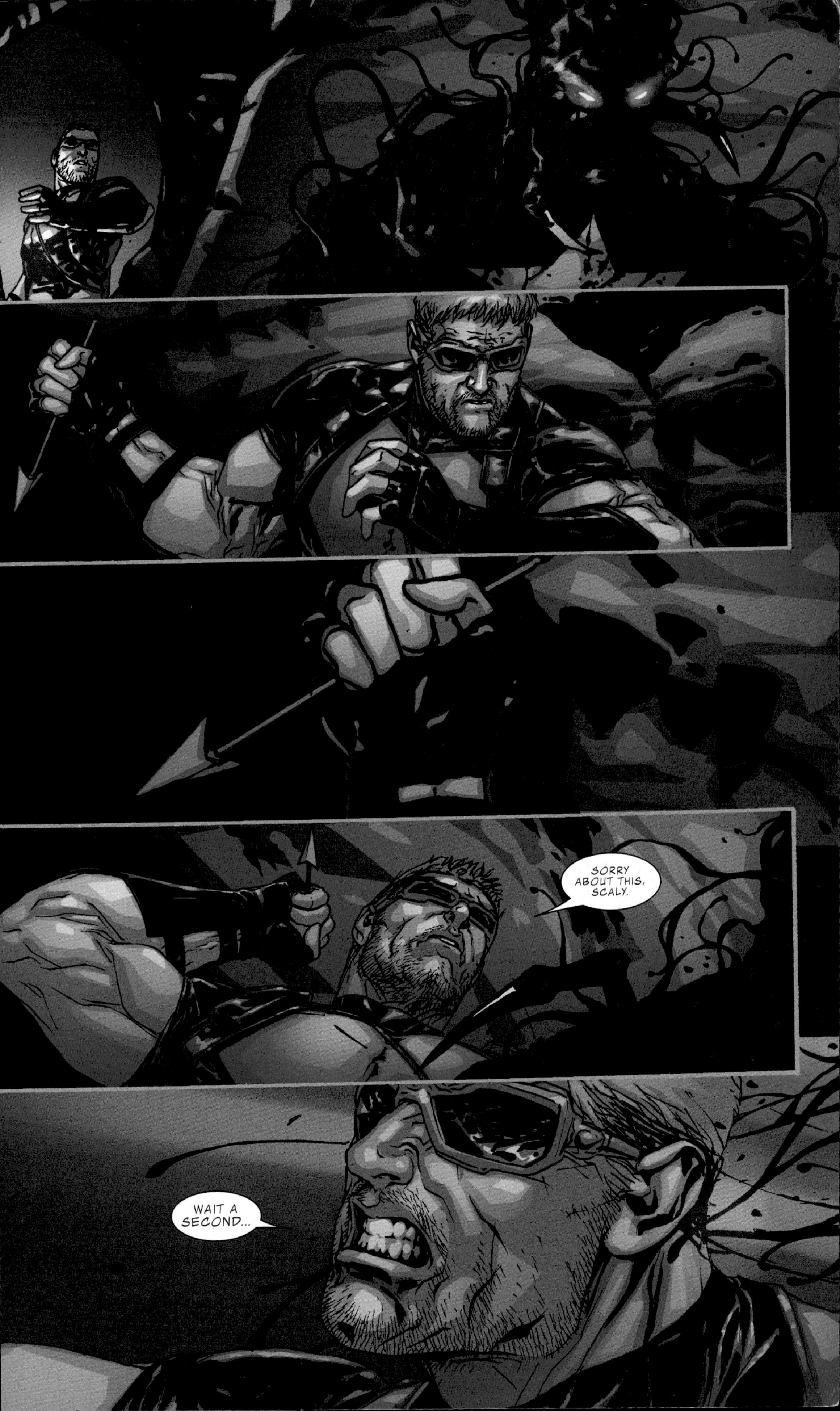
SORRY ABOUT THIS, SCALY.
WAIT A SECOND...

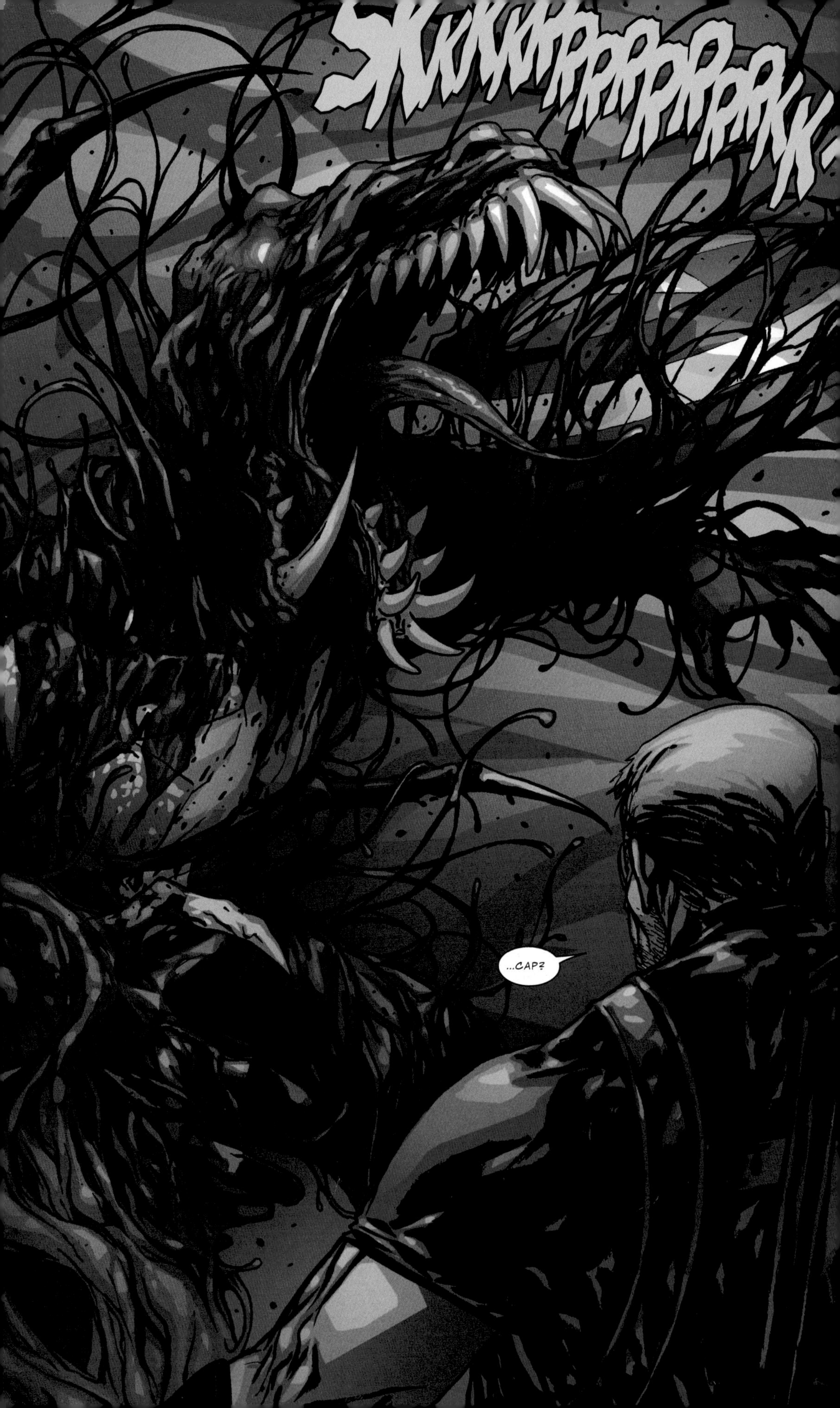
SKKKKRRRRRRRRRKK
...CAP?

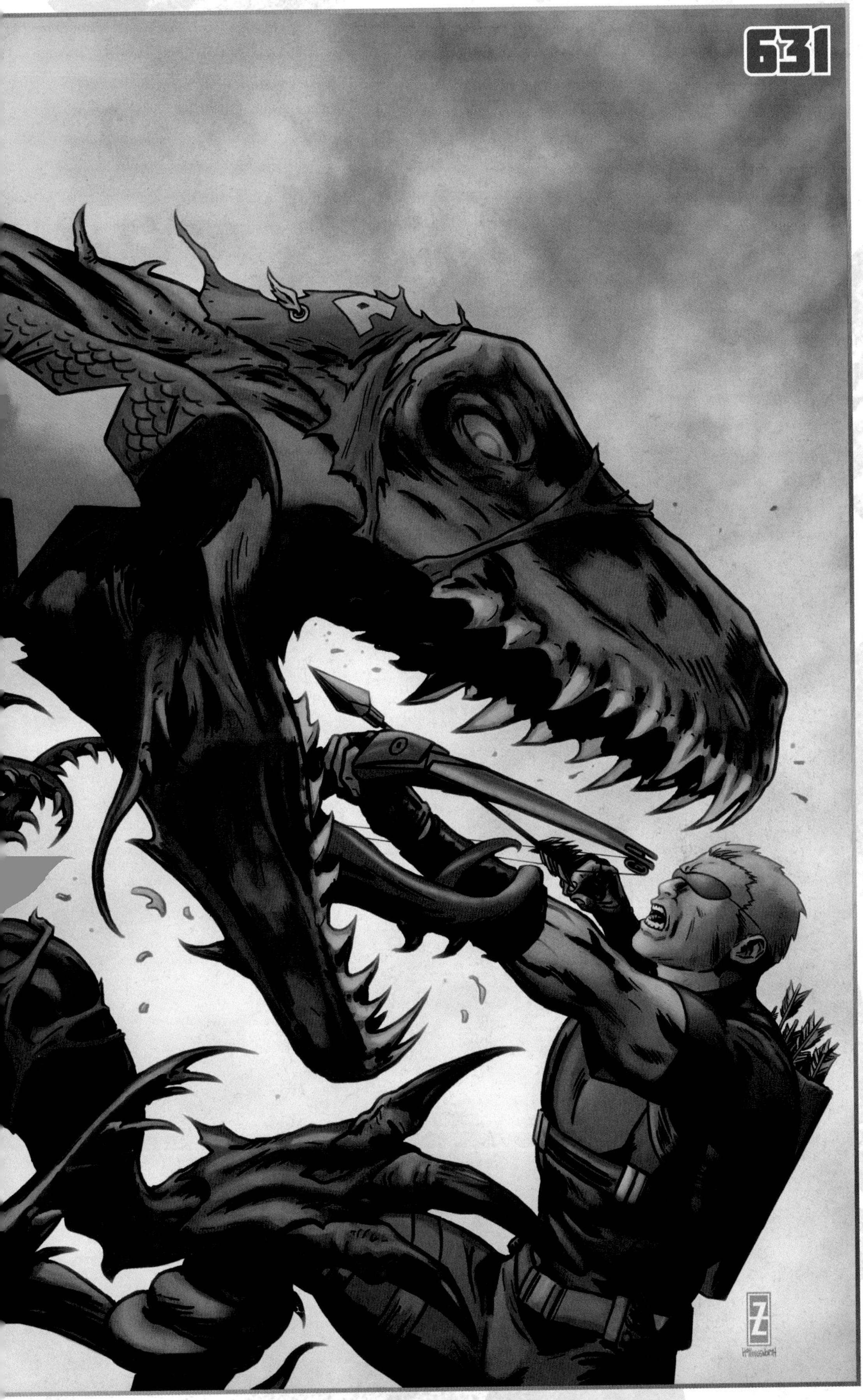
631

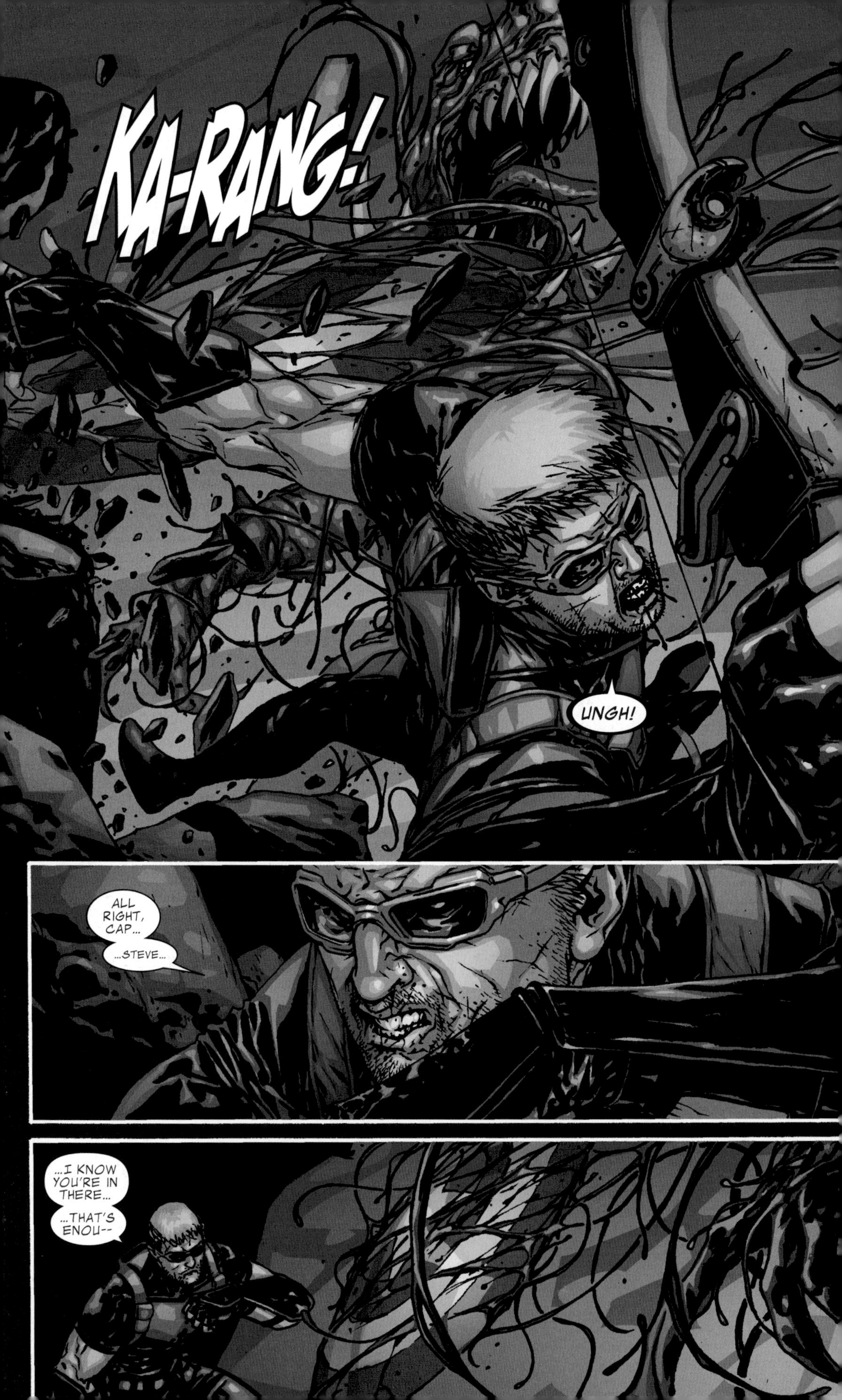
KA-RANG!
UNGH!
ALL RIGHT, CAP...
...STEVE...
...I KNOW YOU'RE IN THERE...
...THAT'S ENOU--

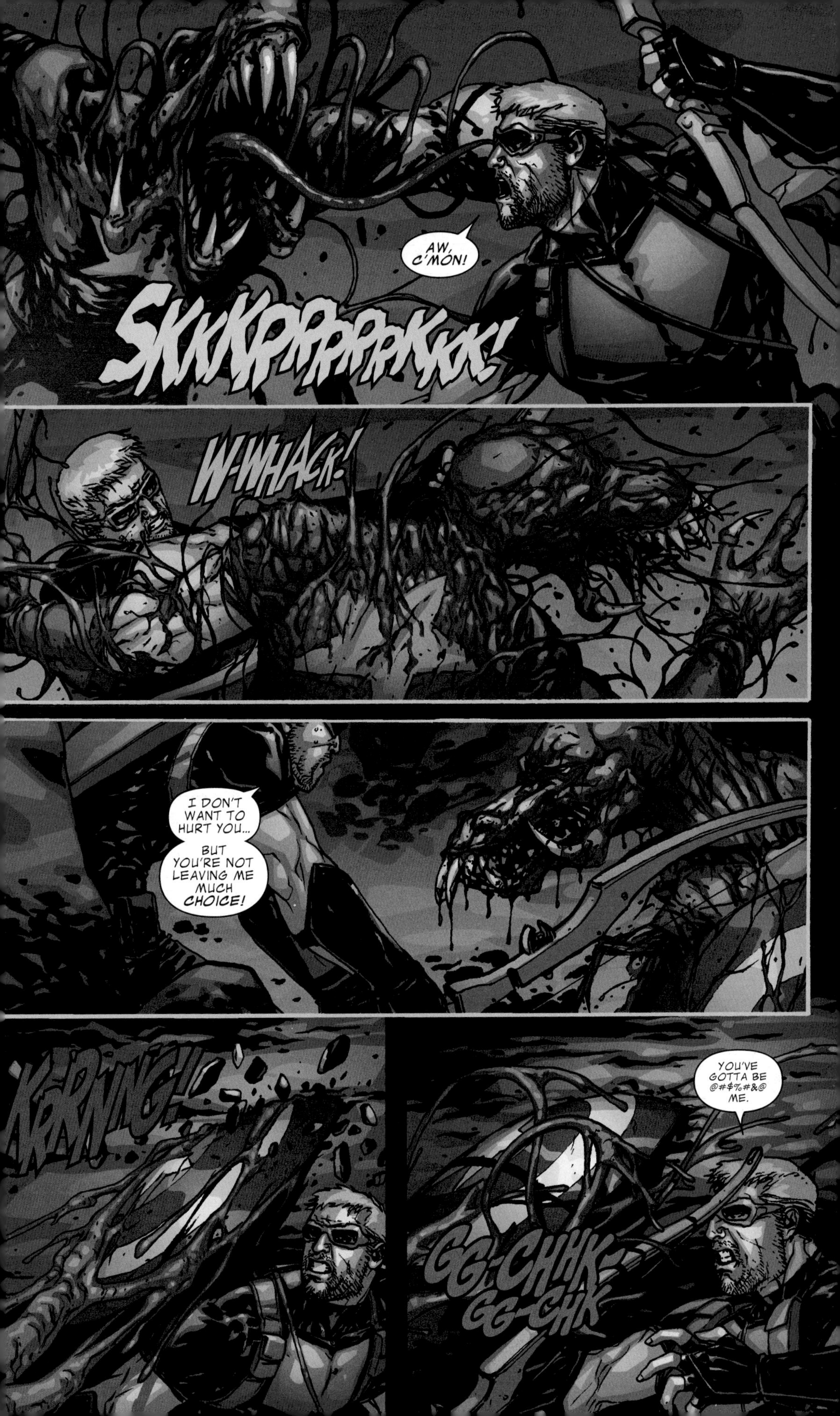
AW, C'MON!
SKKKRRRRRKKKK!
W-WHACK!
I DON'T WANT TO HURT YOU...
BUT YOU'RE NOT LEAVING ME MUCH CHOICE!
KRRANNG!!
YOU'VE GOTTA BE @#$%#&@ ME.
GG-CHHK
GG-CHK

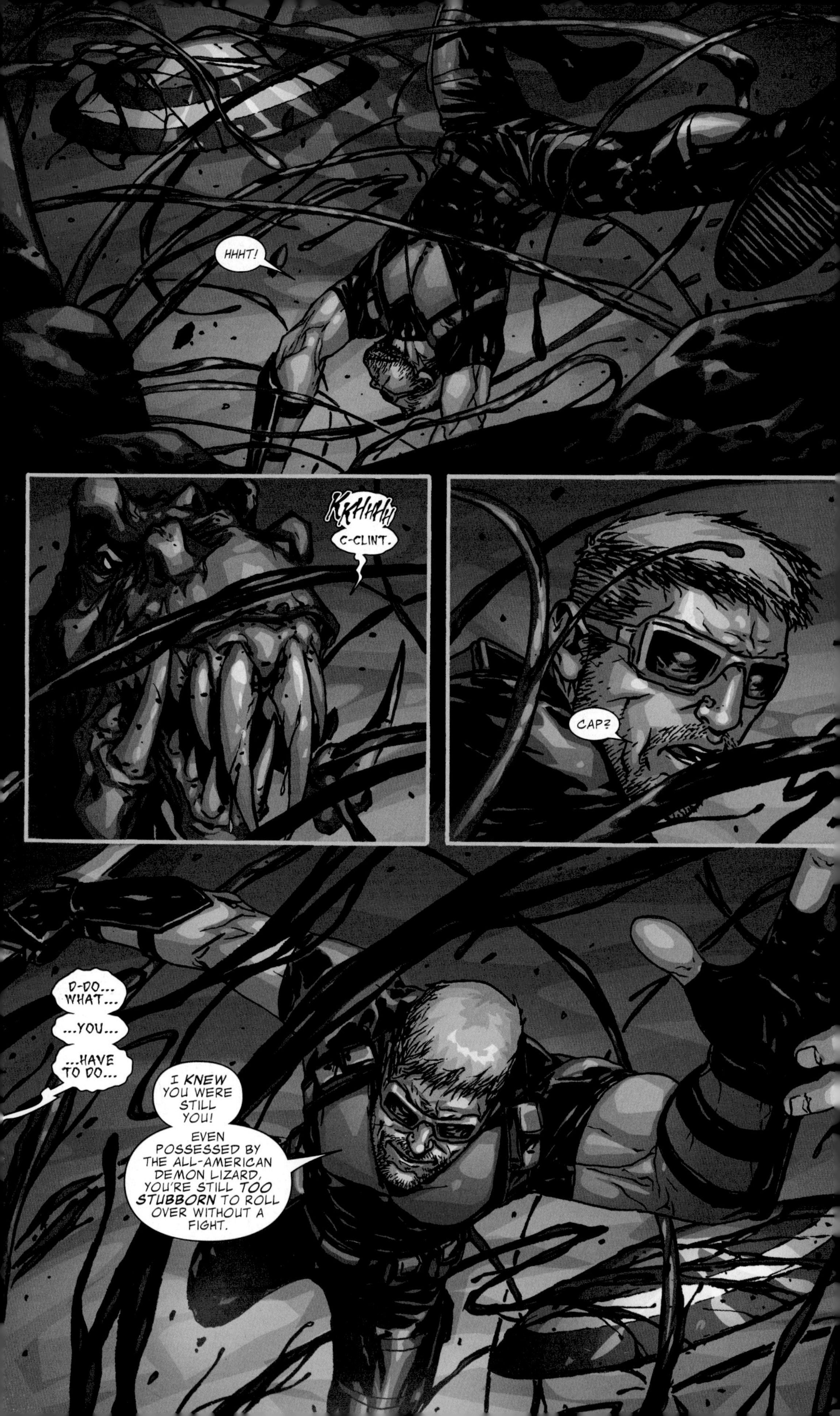
HHHT!
KKHHHH
C-CLINT.
CAP?
D-DO... WHAT...
...YOU...
...HAVE TO DO...
I KNEW YOU WERE STILL YOU!
EVEN POSSESSED BY THE ALL-AMERICAN DEMON LIZARD, YOU'RE STILL TOO STUBBORN TO ROLL OVER WITHOUT A FIGHT.

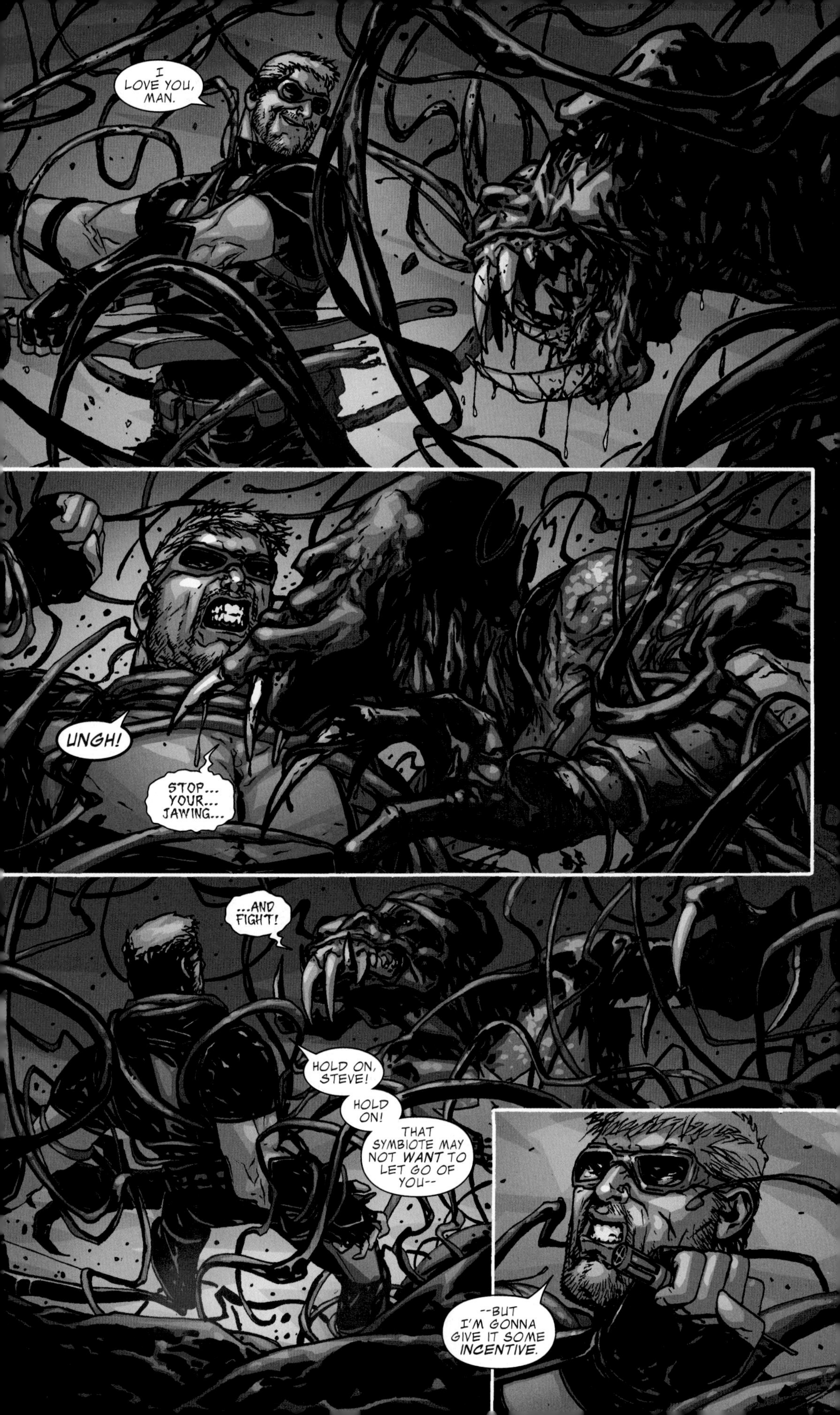
I LOVE YOU, MAN.
UNGH!
STOP... YOUR... JAWING...
...AND FIGHT!
HOLD ON, STEVE!
HOLD ON!
THAT SYMBIOTE MAY NOT *WANT* TO LET GO OF YOU--
--BUT I'M GONNA GIVE IT SOME *INCENTIVE*.

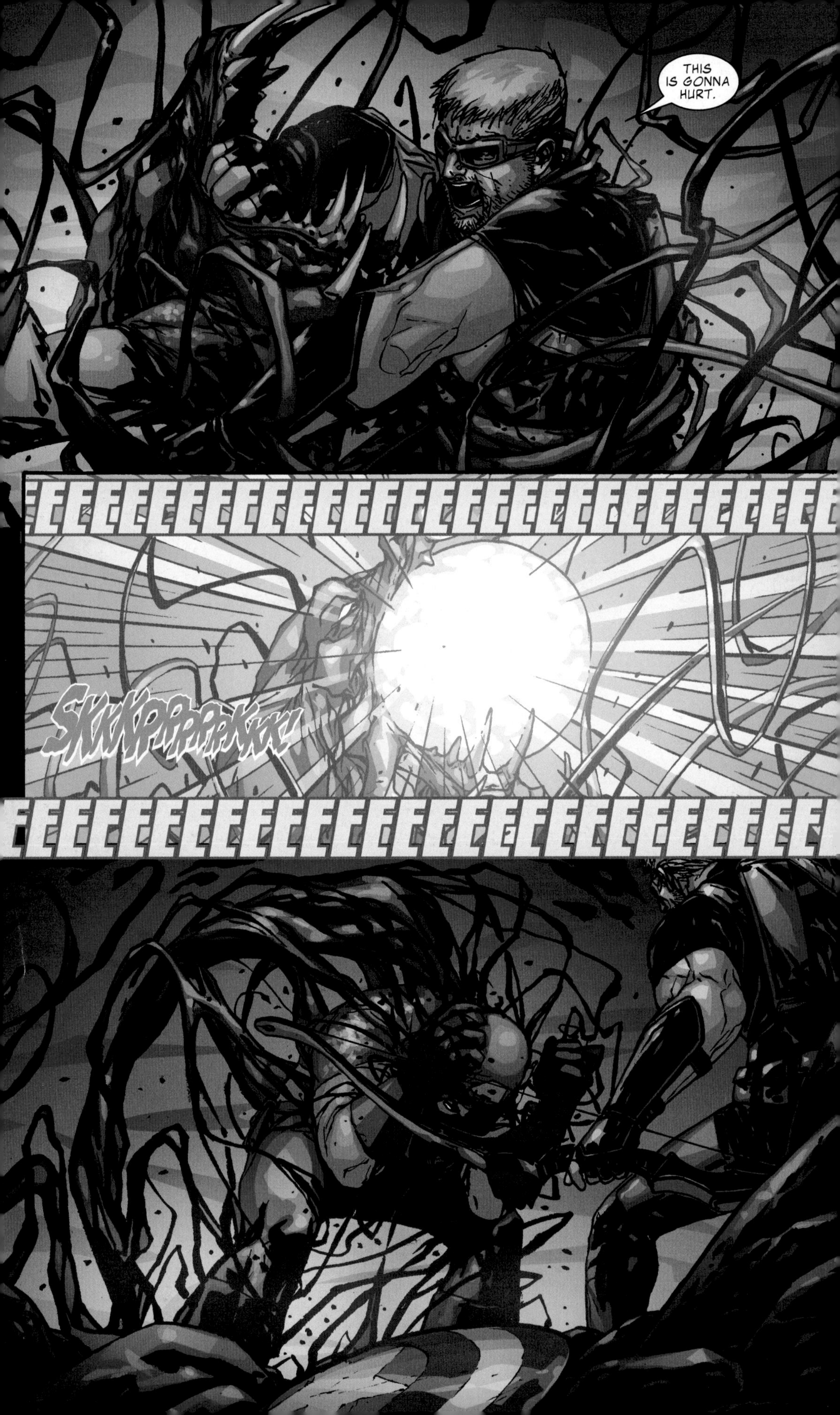
THIS IS GONNA HURT.

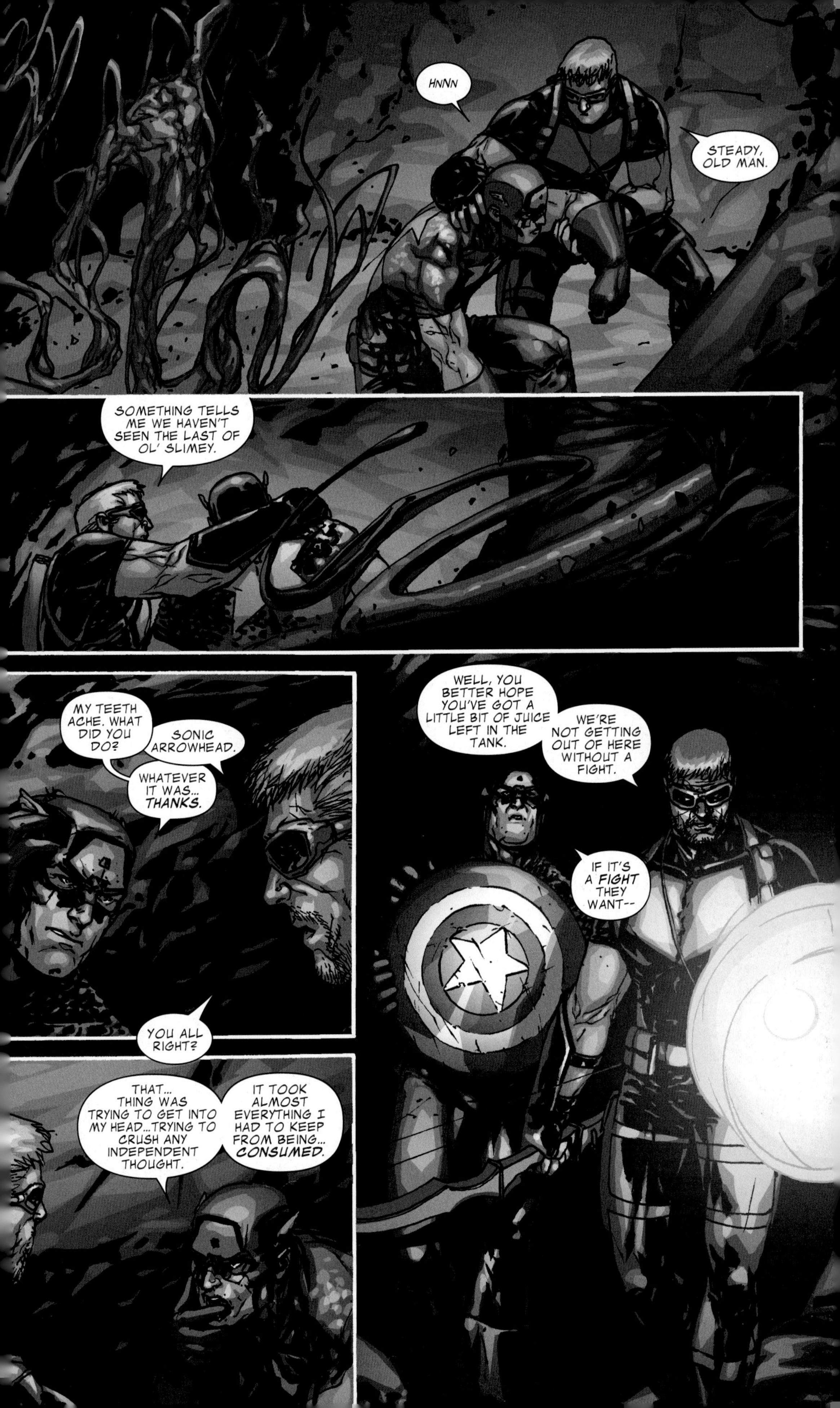
HNNN
STEADY, OLD MAN.
SOMETHING TELLS ME WE HAVEN'T SEEN THE LAST OF OL' SLIMEY.
MY TEETH ACHE. WHAT DID YOU DO?
SONIC ARROWHEAD.
WHATEVER IT WAS... THANKS.
YOU ALL RIGHT?
THAT... THING WAS TRYING TO GET INTO MY HEAD...TRYING TO CRUSH ANY INDEPENDENT THOUGHT.
IT TOOK ALMOST EVERYTHING I HAD TO KEEP FROM BEING... CONSUMED.
WELL, YOU BETTER HOPE YOU'VE GOT A LITTLE BIT OF JUICE LEFT IN THE TANK.
WE'RE NOT GETTING OUT OF HERE WITHOUT A FIGHT.
IF IT'S A FIGHT THEY WANT--

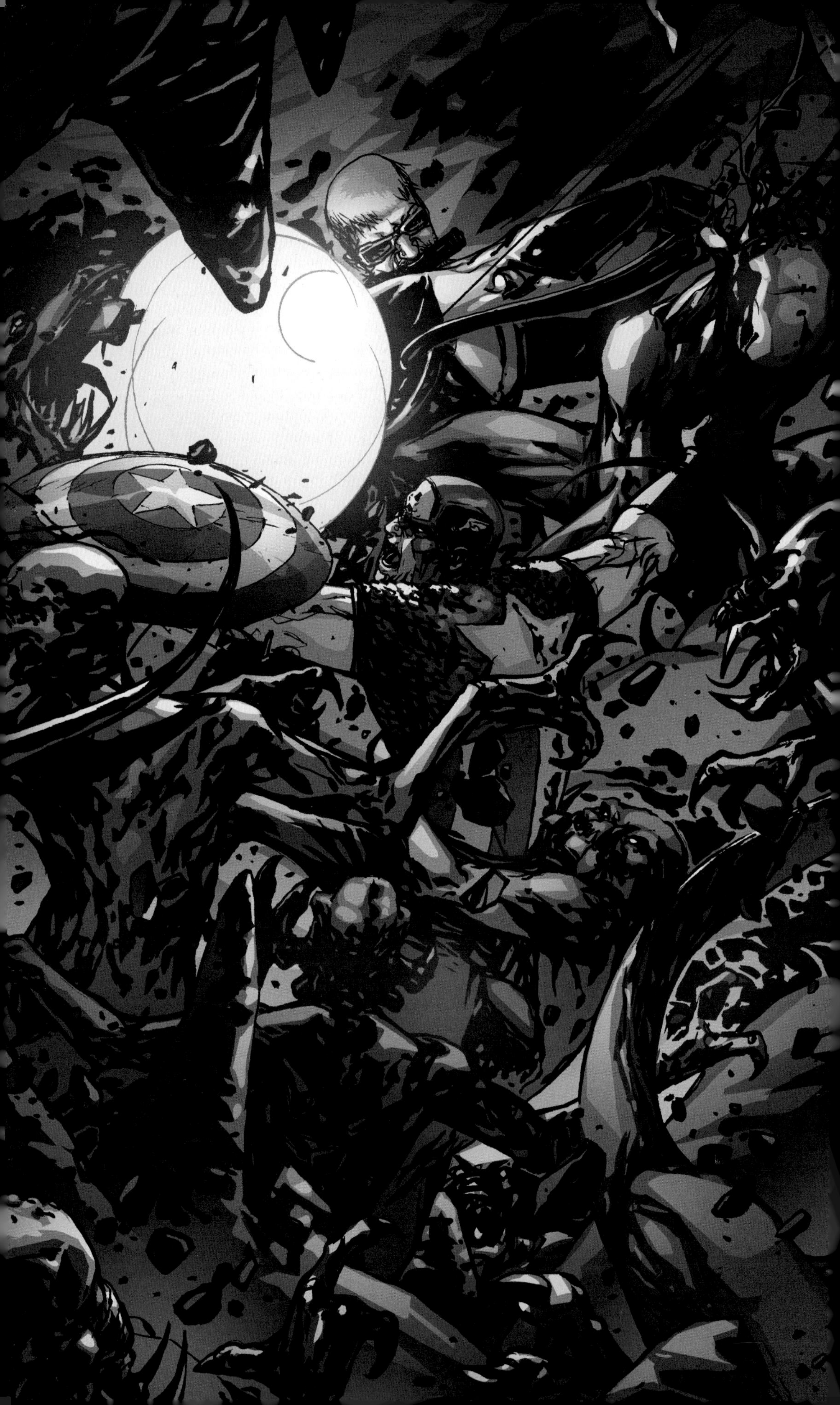

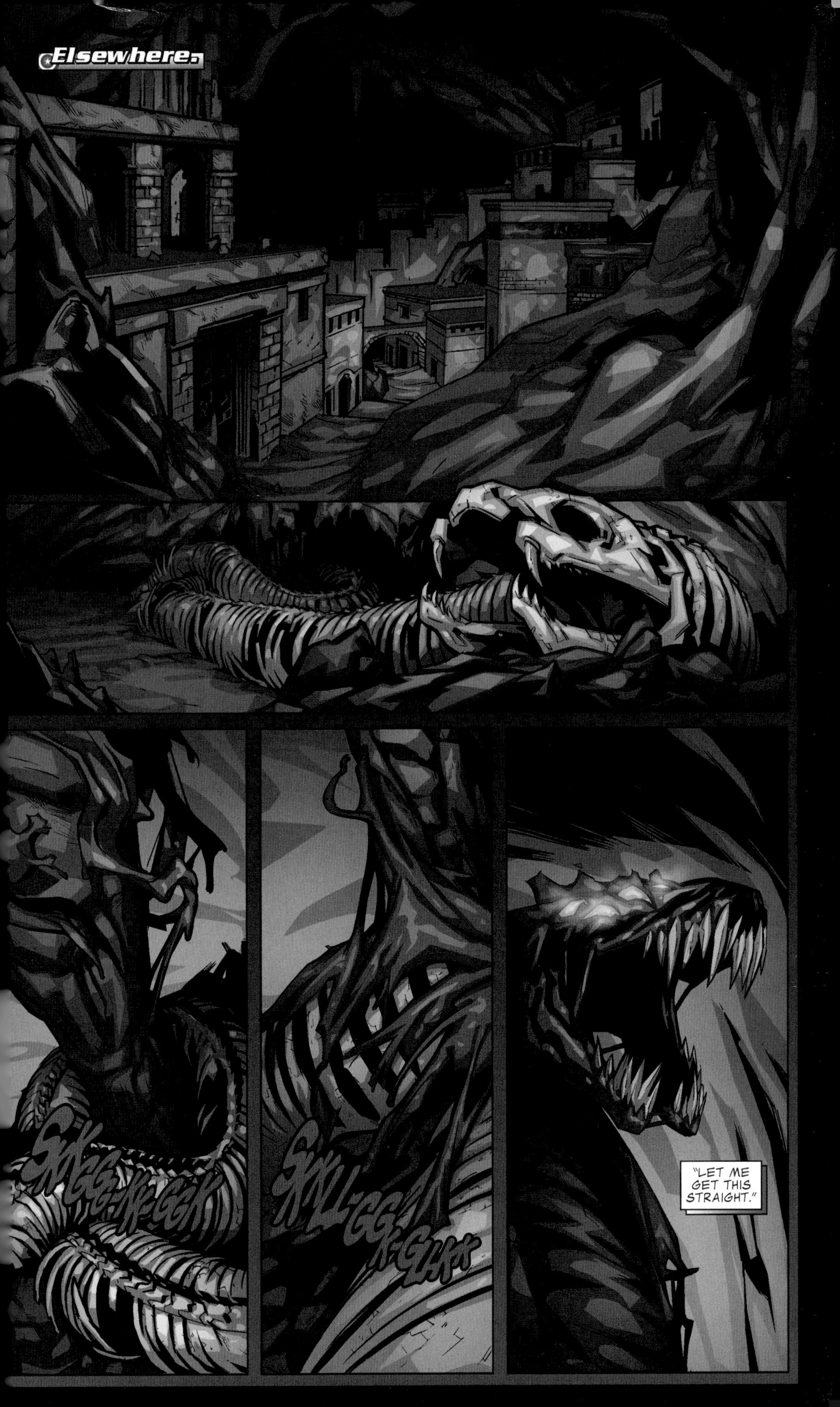
Elsewhere.
SKGG-KK-GGK
SKLL-GGK-GLK
"LET ME GET THIS STRAIGHT."

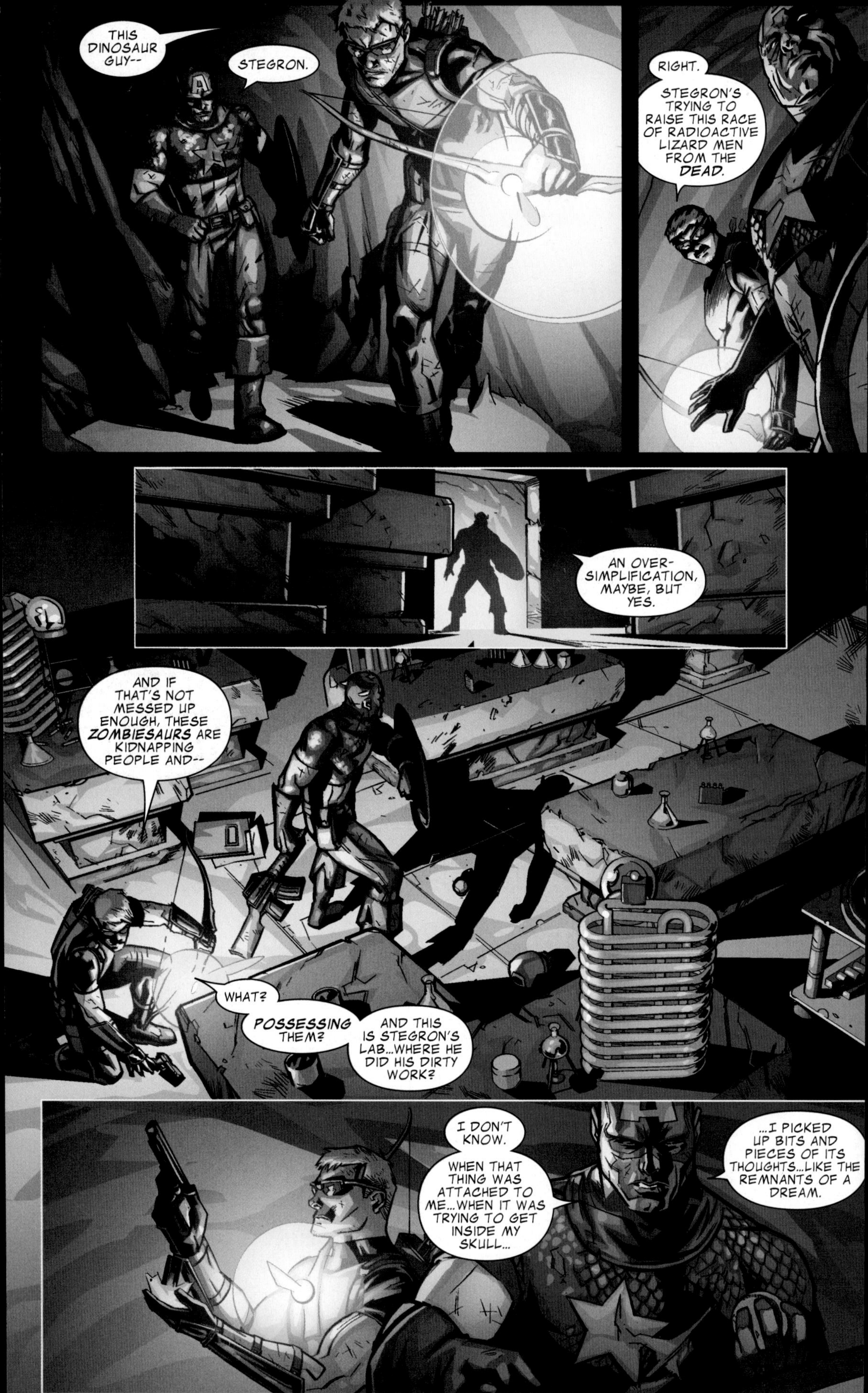
THIS DINOSAUR GUY--
STEGRON.
RIGHT.
STEGRON'S TRYING TO RAISE THIS RACE OF RADIOACTIVE LIZARD MEN FROM THE *DEAD*.
AN OVER-SIMPLIFICATION, MAYBE, BUT YES.
AND IF THAT'S NOT MESSED UP ENOUGH, THESE *ZOMBIESAURS* ARE KIDNAPPING PEOPLE AND--
WHAT?
POSSESSING THEM?
AND THIS IS STEGRON'S LAB...WHERE HE DID HIS DIRTY WORK?
I DON'T KNOW.
WHEN THAT THING WAS ATTACHED TO ME...WHEN IT WAS TRYING TO GET INSIDE MY SKULL...
...I PICKED UP BITS AND PIECES OF ITS THOUGHTS...LIKE THE REMNANTS OF A DREAM.

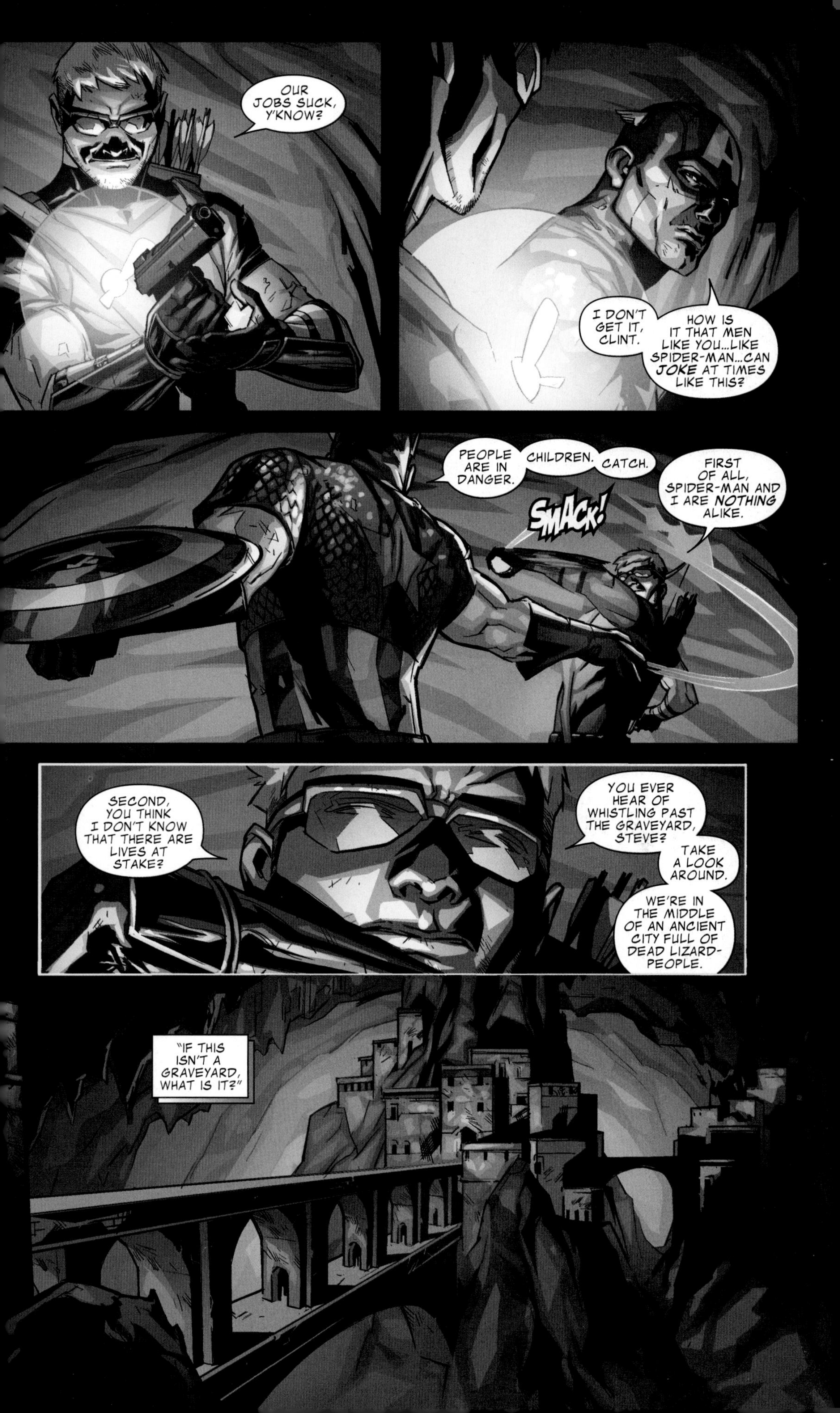
OUR JOBS SUCK, Y'KNOW?
I DON'T GET IT, CLINT.
HOW IS IT THAT MEN LIKE YOU...LIKE SPIDER-MAN...CAN JOKE AT TIMES LIKE THIS?
PEOPLE ARE IN DANGER.
CHILDREN.
CATCH.
SMACK!
FIRST OF ALL, SPIDER-MAN AND I ARE NOTHING ALIKE.
SECOND, YOU THINK I DON'T KNOW THAT THERE ARE LIVES AT STAKE?
YOU EVER HEAR OF WHISTLING PAST THE GRAVEYARD, STEVE?
TAKE A LOOK AROUND.
WE'RE IN THE MIDDLE OF AN ANCIENT CITY FULL OF DEAD LIZARD-PEOPLE.
"IF THIS ISN'T A GRAVEYARD, WHAT IS IT?"

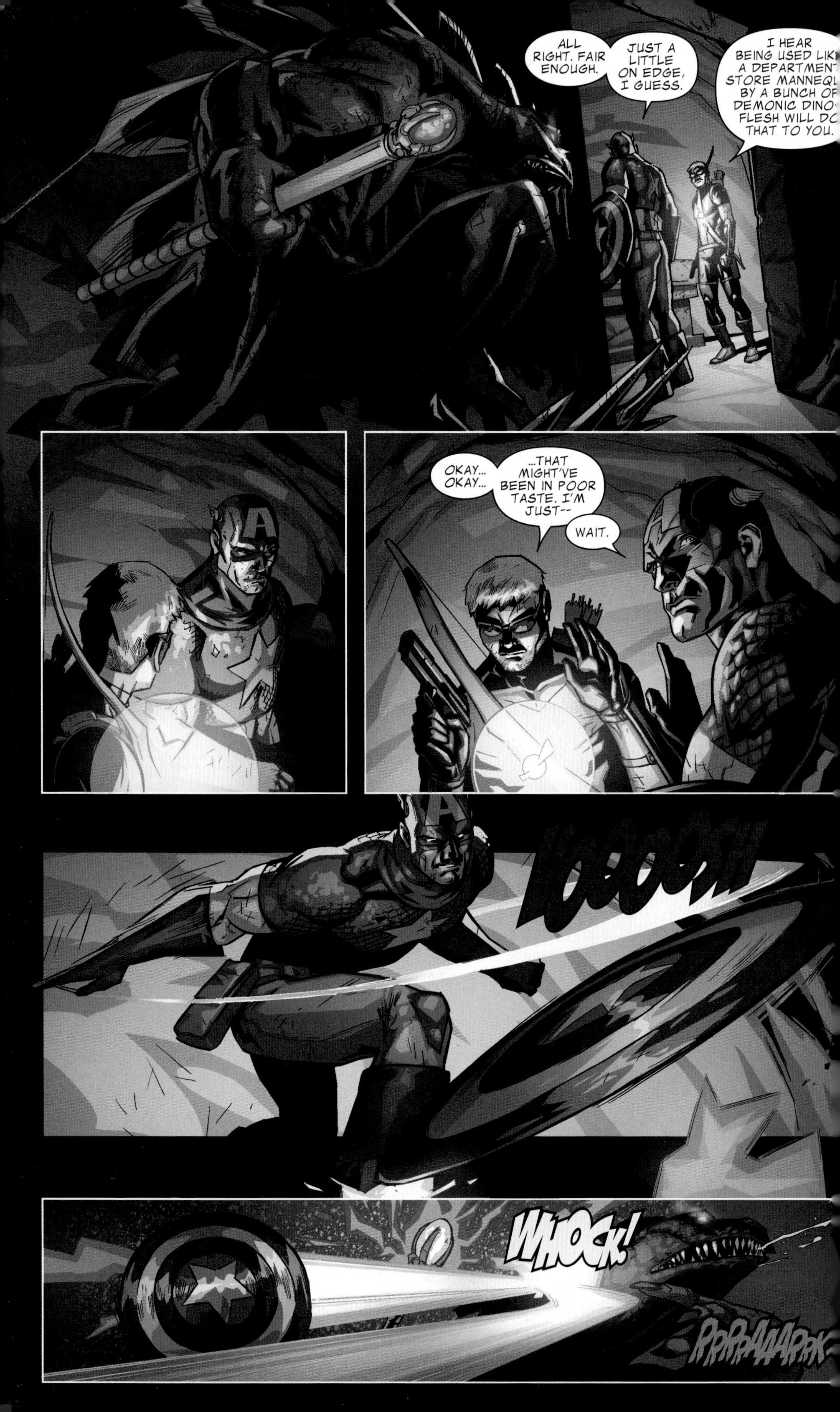
ALL RIGHT. FAIR ENOUGH.
JUST A LITTLE ON EDGE, I GUESS.
I HEAR BEING USED LIK A DEPARTMENT STORE MANNEQ BY A BUNCH OF DEMONIC DINO- FLESH WILL DO THAT TO YOU.
OKAY... OKAY...
...THAT MIGHT'VE BEEN IN POOR TASTE. I'M JUST--
WAIT.
WHOCK!
RRRRAAAARRK

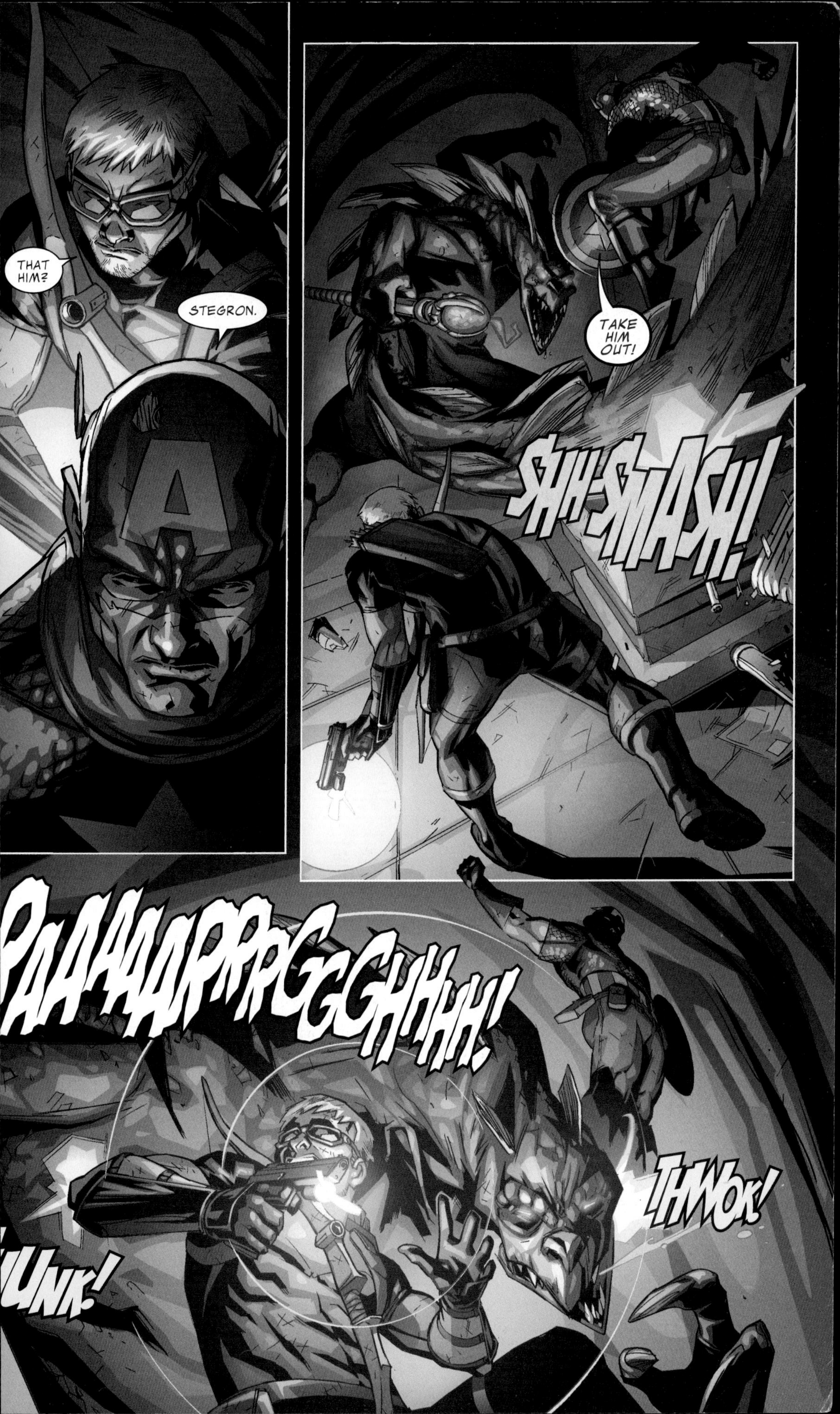
THAT HIM?
STEGRON.
TAKE HIM OUT!
SHH-SMASH!
PAAAAARRRGGHHHH!
THWOK!
UNK!

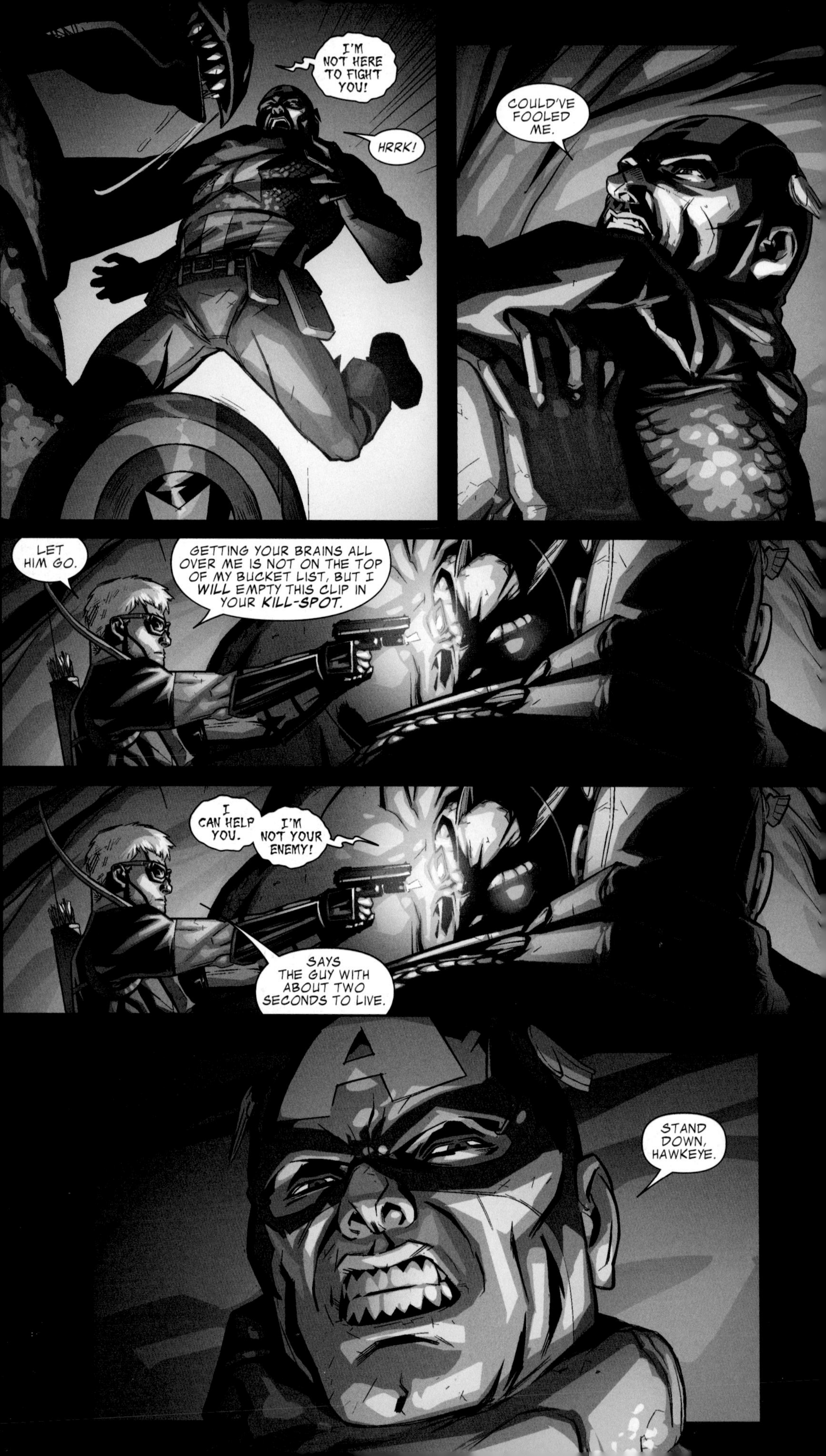
I'M NOT HERE TO FIGHT YOU!
HRRK!
COULD'VE FOOLED ME.
LET HIM GO.
GETTING YOUR BRAINS ALL OVER ME IS NOT ON THE TOP OF MY BUCKET LIST, BUT I WILL EMPTY THIS CLIP IN YOUR KILL-SPOT.
I CAN HELP YOU.
I'M NOT YOUR ENEMY!
SAYS THE GUY WITH ABOUT TWO SECONDS TO LIVE.
STAND DOWN, HAWKEYE.

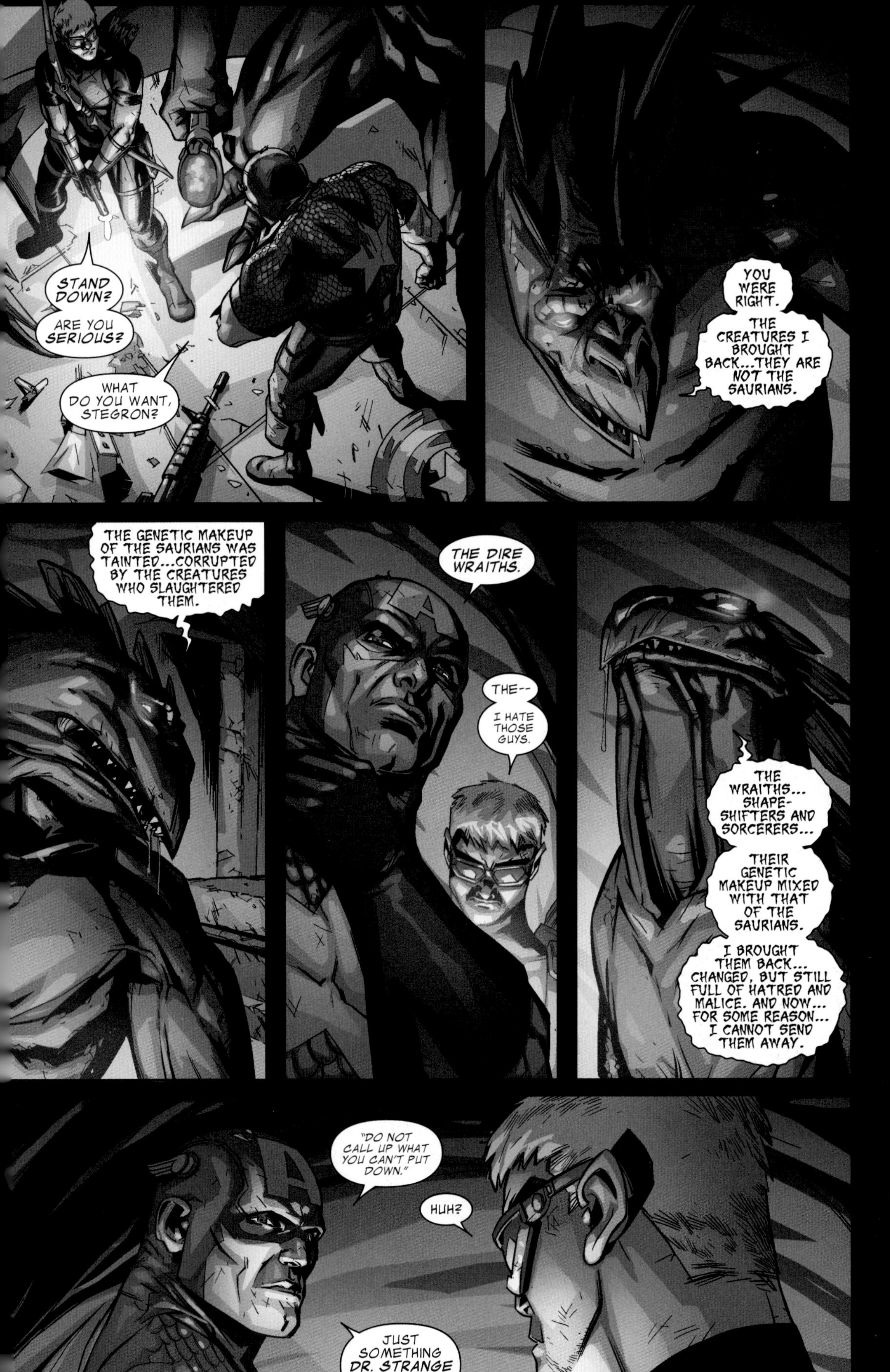
STAND DOWN?
ARE YOU SERIOUS?
WHAT DO YOU WANT, STEGRON?
YOU WERE RIGHT.
THE CREATURES I BROUGHT BACK...THEY ARE NOT THE SAURIANS.
THE GENETIC MAKEUP OF THE SAURIANS WAS TAINTED...CORRUPTED BY THE CREATURES WHO SLAUGHTERED THEM.
THE DIRE WRAITHS.
THE--
I HATE THOSE GUYS.
THE WRAITHS... SHAPE-SHIFTERS AND SORCERERS...
THEIR GENETIC MAKEUP MIXED WITH THAT OF THE SAURIANS.
I BROUGHT THEM BACK... CHANGED, BUT STILL FULL OF HATRED AND MALICE. AND NOW... FOR SOME REASON... I CANNOT SEND THEM AWAY.
"DO NOT CALL UP WHAT YOU CAN'T PUT DOWN."
HUH?
JUST SOMETHING DR. STRANGE USED TO SAY.

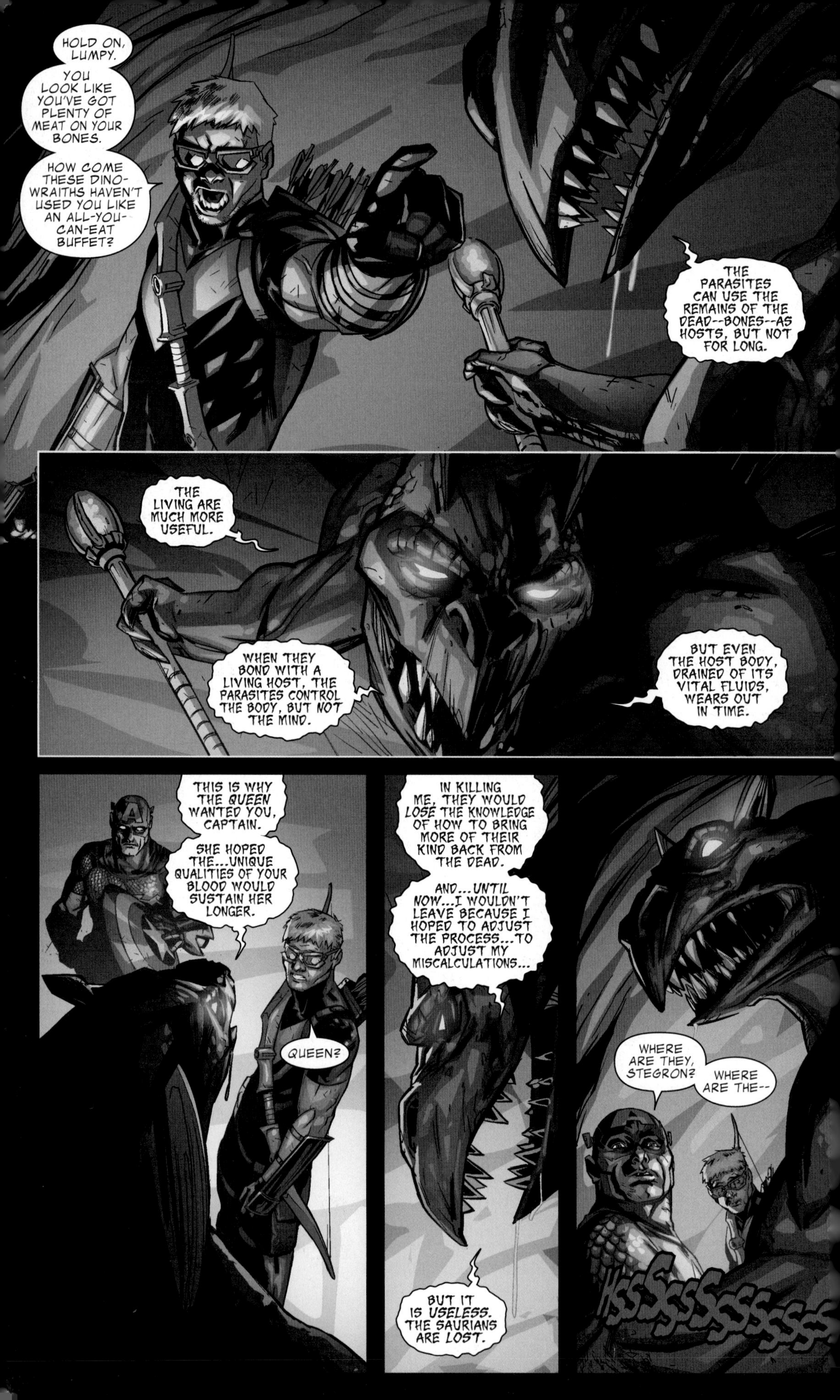

HOLD ON, LUMPY.
YOU LOOK LIKE YOU'VE GOT PLENTY OF MEAT ON YOUR BONES.
HOW COME THESE DINO-WRAITHS HAVEN'T USED YOU LIKE AN ALL-YOU-CAN-EAT BUFFET?
THE PARASITES CAN USE THE REMAINS OF THE DEAD--BONES--AS HOSTS, BUT NOT FOR LONG.
THE LIVING ARE MUCH MORE USEFUL.
WHEN THEY BOND WITH A LIVING HOST, THE PARASITES CONTROL THE BODY, BUT NOT THE MIND.
BUT EVEN THE HOST BODY, DRAINED OF ITS VITAL FLUIDS, WEARS OUT IN TIME.
THIS IS WHY THE QUEEN WANTED YOU, CAPTAIN.
SHE HOPED THE...UNIQUE QUALITIES OF YOUR BLOOD WOULD SUSTAIN HER LONGER.
QUEEN?
IN KILLING ME, THEY WOULD LOSE THE KNOWLEDGE OF HOW TO BRING MORE OF THEIR KIND BACK FROM THE DEAD.
AND...UNTIL NOW...I WOULDN'T LEAVE BECAUSE I HOPED TO ADJUST THE PROCESS...TO ADJUST MY MISCALCULATIONS...
BUT IT IS USELESS. THE SAURIANS ARE LOST.
WHERE ARE THEY, STEGRON?
WHERE ARE THE--
HSSSSSSSSSSSSS

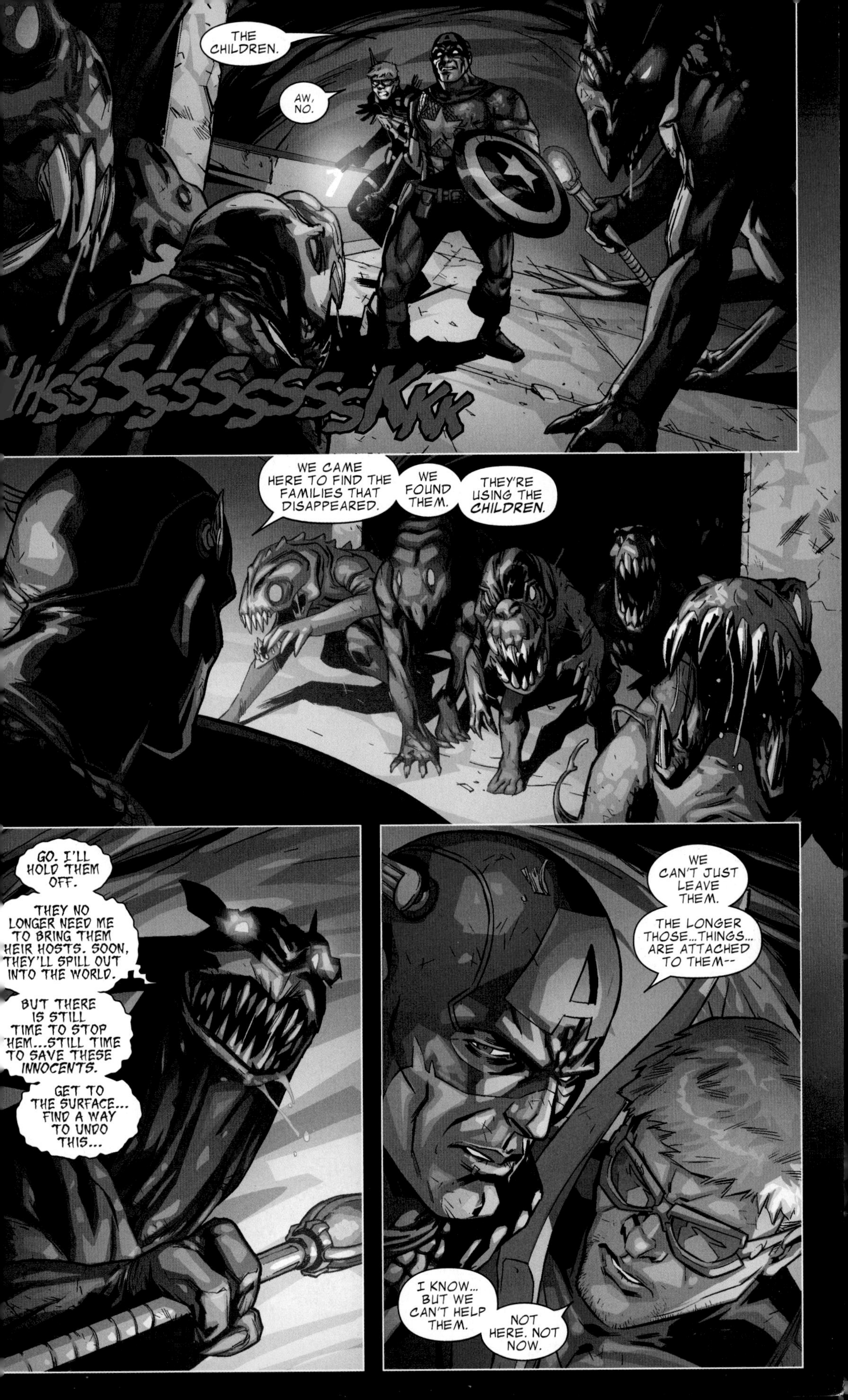

THE CHILDREN.
AW, NO.
WE CAME HERE TO FIND THE FAMILIES THAT DISAPPEARED.
WE FOUND THEM.
THEY'RE USING THE CHILDREN.
GO. I'LL HOLD THEM OFF.
THEY NO LONGER NEED ME TO BRING THEM HEIR HOSTS. SOON, THEY'LL SPILL OUT INTO THE WORLD.
BUT THERE IS STILL TIME TO STOP HEM...STILL TIME TO SAVE THESE INNOCENTS.
GET TO THE SURFACE... FIND A WAY TO UNDO THIS...
WE CAN'T JUST LEAVE THEM.
THE LONGER THOSE...THINGS... ARE ATTACHED TO THEM--
I KNOW... BUT WE CAN'T HELP THEM.
NOT HERE. NOT NOW.

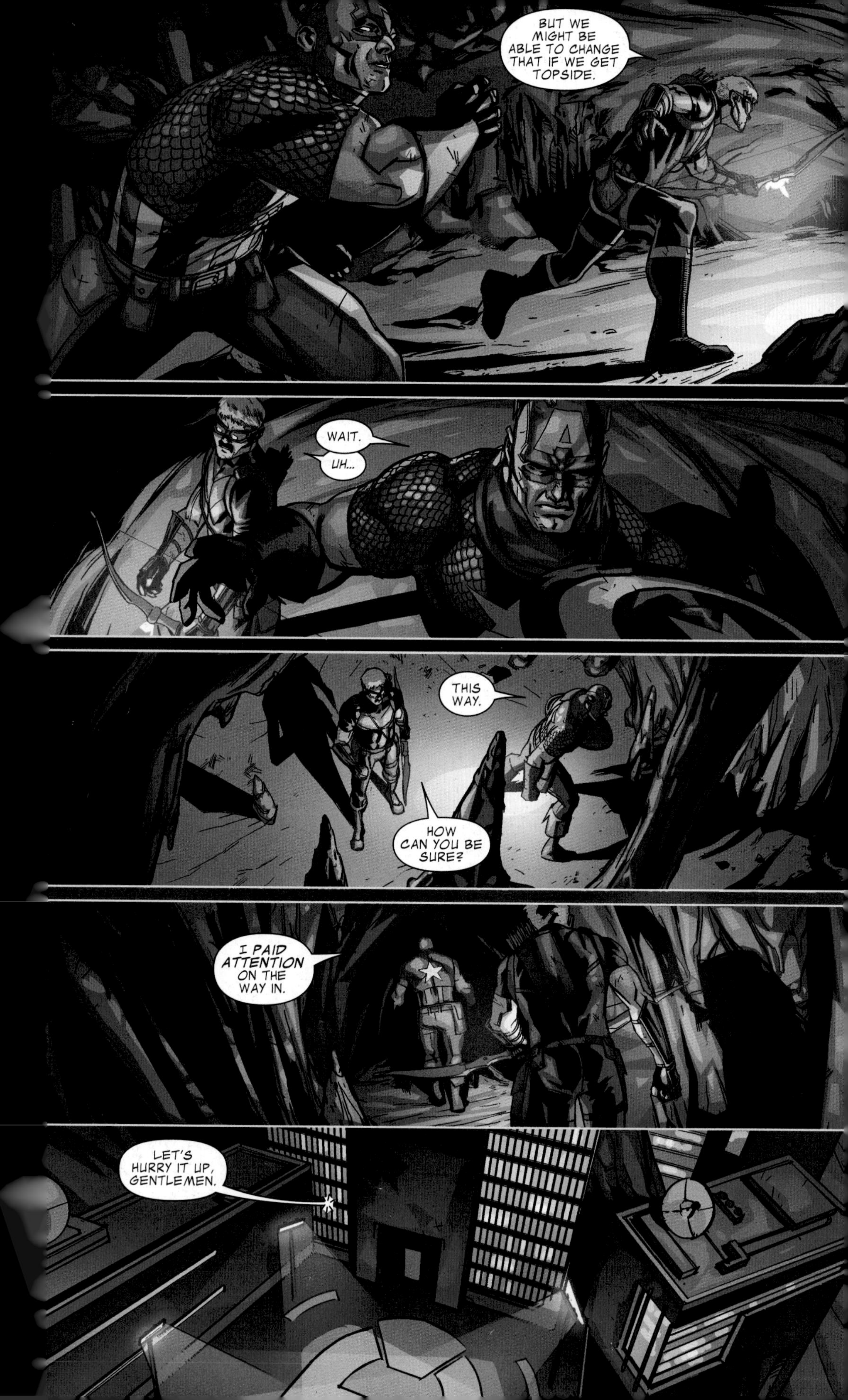
BUT WE MIGHT BE ABLE TO CHANGE THAT IF WE GET TOPSIDE.
WAIT.
UH...
THIS WAY.
HOW CAN YOU BE SURE?
I PAID ATTENTION ON THE WAY IN.
LET'S HURRY IT UP, GENTLEMEN.

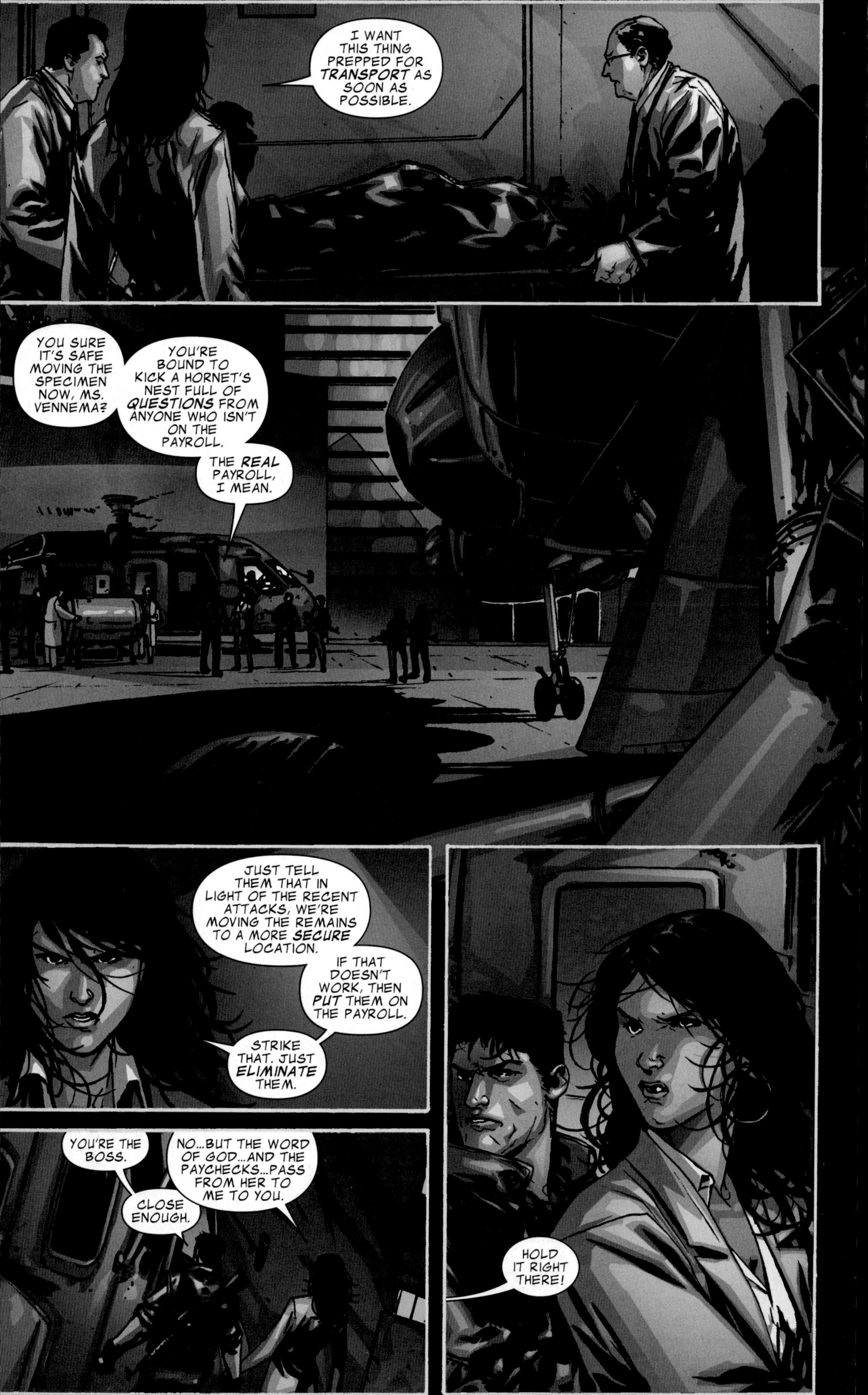

I WANT THIS THING PREPPED FOR TRANSPORT AS SOON AS POSSIBLE.
YOU SURE IT'S SAFE MOVING THE SPECIMEN NOW, MS. VENNEMA?
YOU'RE BOUND TO KICK A HORNET'S NEST FULL OF QUESTIONS FROM ANYONE WHO ISN'T ON THE PAYROLL.
THE REAL PAYROLL, I MEAN.
JUST TELL THEM THAT IN LIGHT OF THE RECENT ATTACKS, WE'RE MOVING THE REMAINS TO A MORE SECURE LOCATION.
IF THAT DOESN'T WORK, THEN PUT THEM ON THE PAYROLL.
STRIKE THAT. JUST ELIMINATE THEM.
YOU'RE THE BOSS.
NO...BUT THE WORD OF GOD...AND THE PAYCHECKS...PASS FROM HER TO ME TO YOU.
CLOSE ENOUGH.
HOLD IT RIGHT THERE!

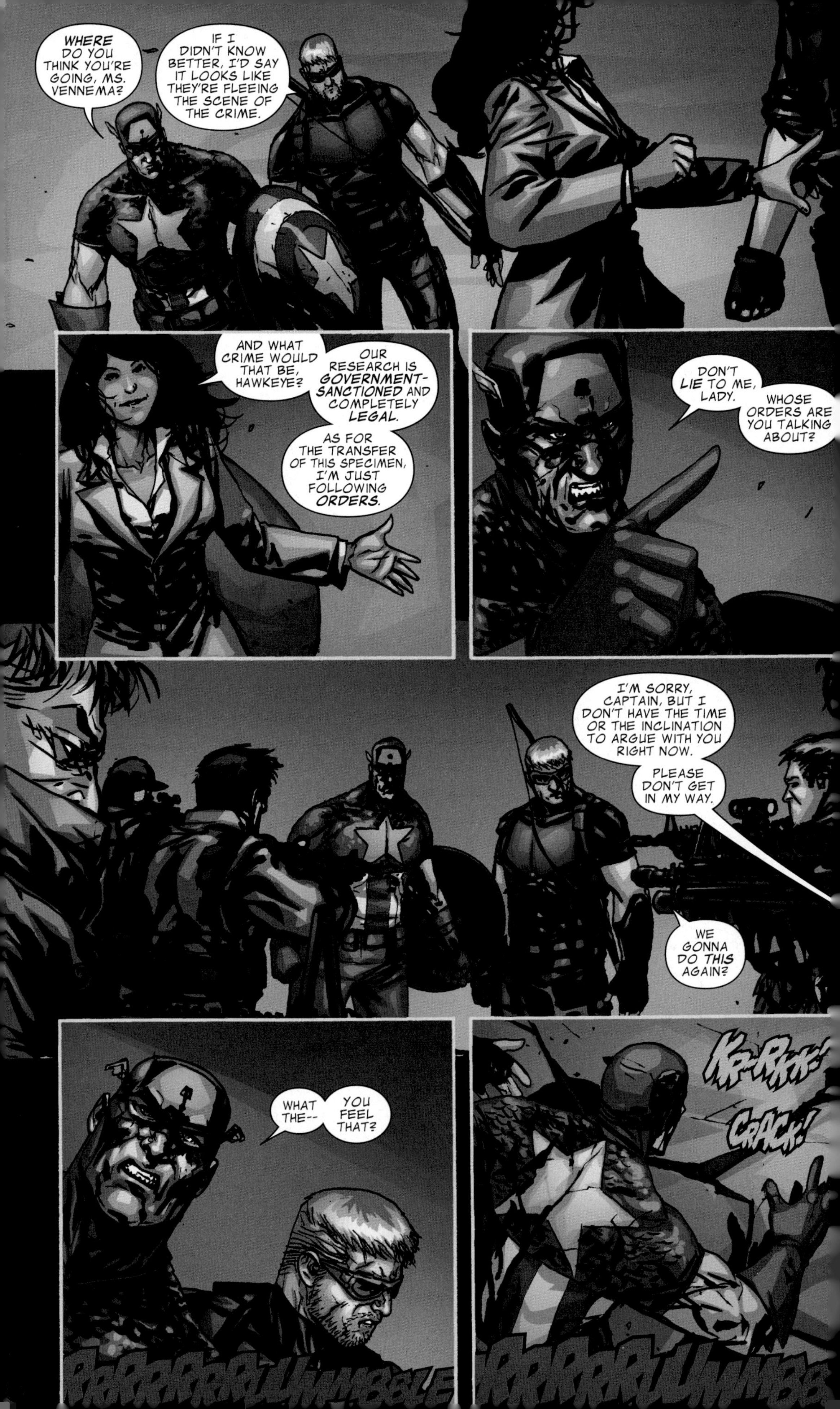
WHERE DO YOU THINK YOU'RE GOING, MS. VENNEMA?
IF I DIDN'T KNOW BETTER, I'D SAY IT LOOKS LIKE THEY'RE FLEEING THE SCENE OF THE CRIME.
AND WHAT CRIME WOULD THAT BE, HAWKEYE?
OUR RESEARCH IS GOVERNMENT-SANCTIONED AND COMPLETELY LEGAL.
AS FOR THE TRANSFER OF THIS SPECIMEN, I'M JUST FOLLOWING ORDERS.
DON'T LIE TO ME, LADY.
WHOSE ORDERS ARE YOU TALKING ABOUT?
I'M SORRY, CAPTAIN, BUT I DON'T HAVE THE TIME OR THE INCLINATION TO ARGUE WITH YOU RIGHT NOW.
PLEASE DON'T GET IN MY WAY.
WE GONNA DO THIS AGAIN?
WHAT THE--
YOU FEEL THAT?
RRRRRRRUMMMBBLE
KR-RKK!
CRACK!
RRRRRRRUMMBB

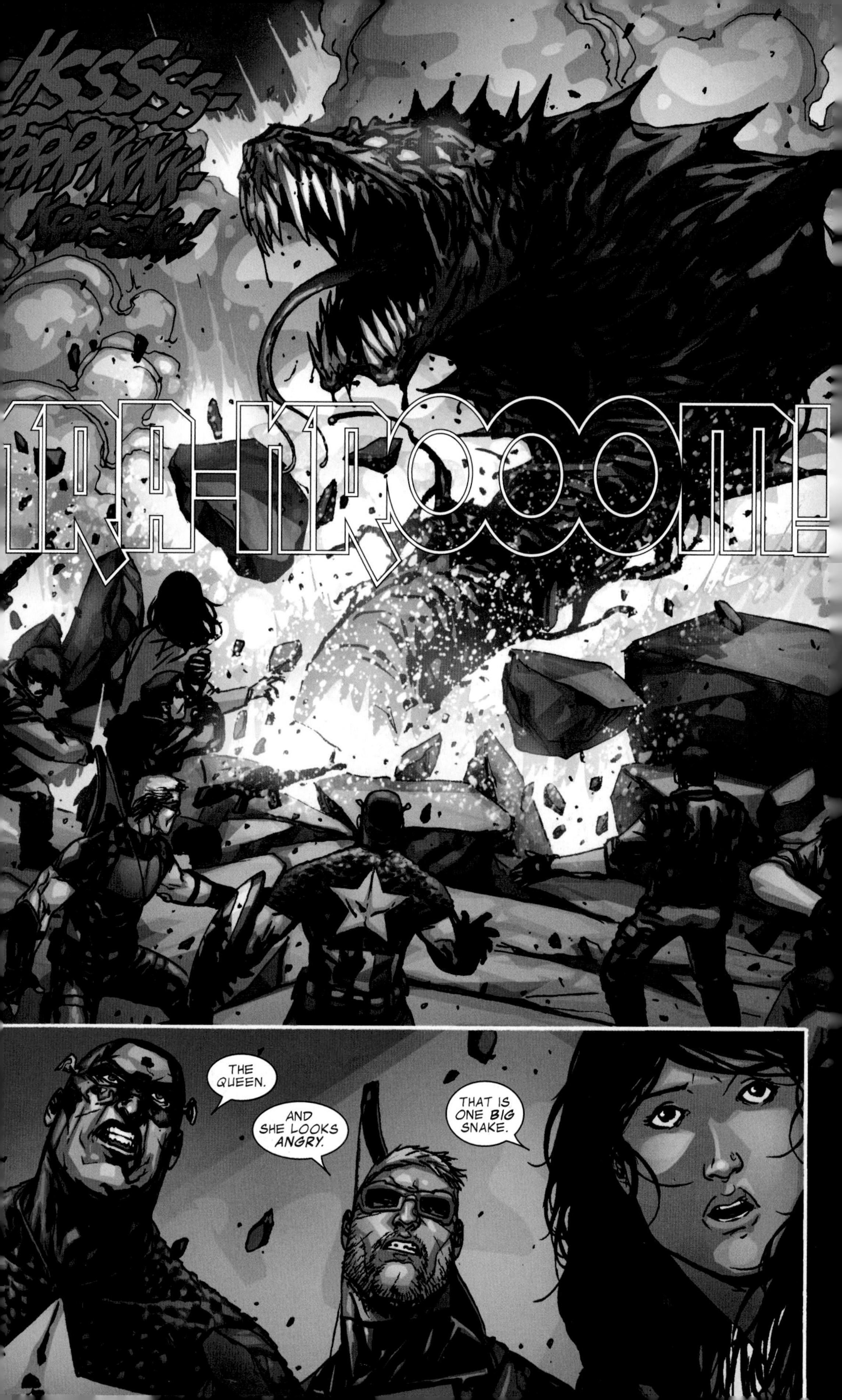
DRA-KROOOM!
THE QUEEN.
AND SHE LOOKS ANGRY.
THAT IS ONE BIG SNAKE.

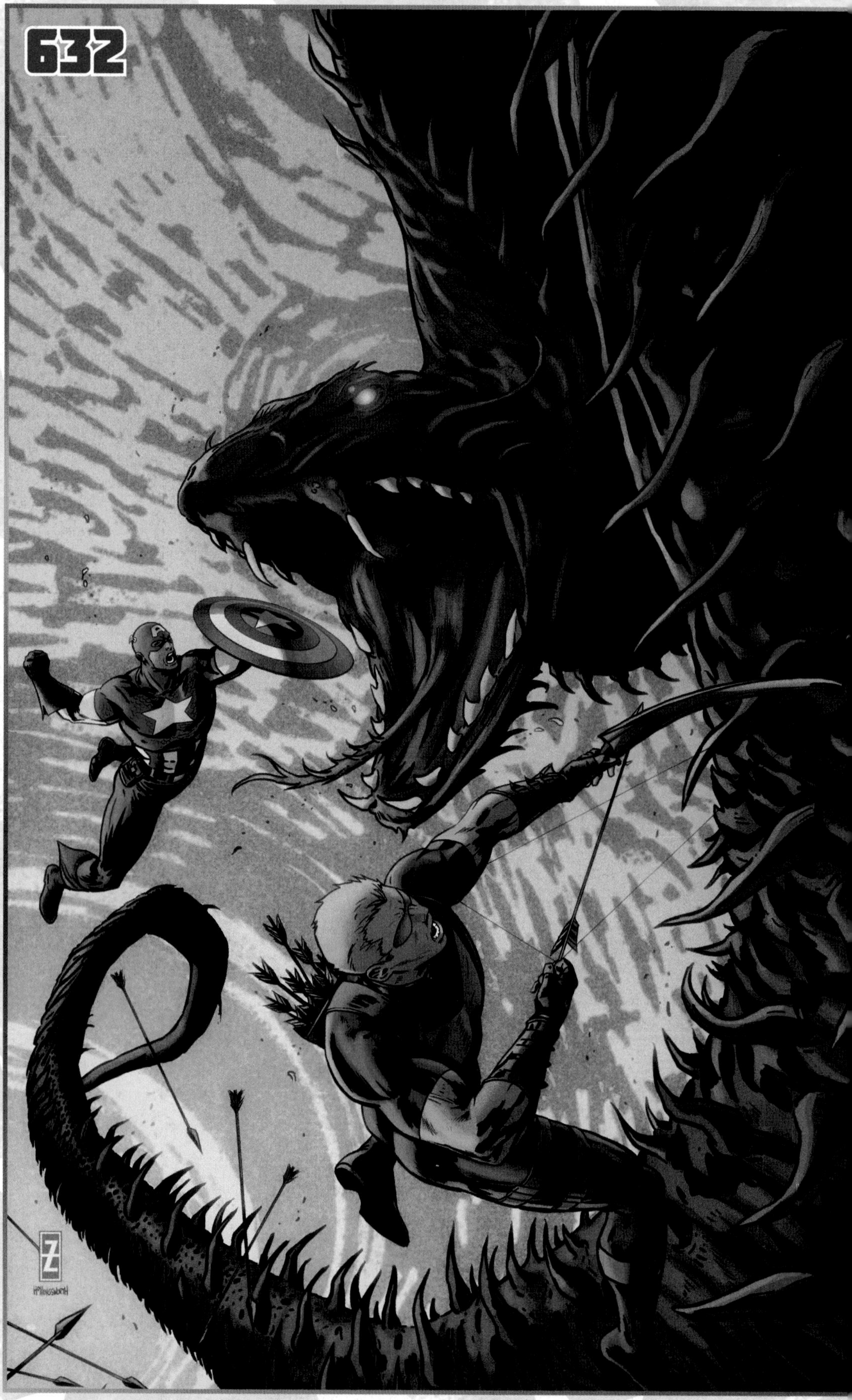
632

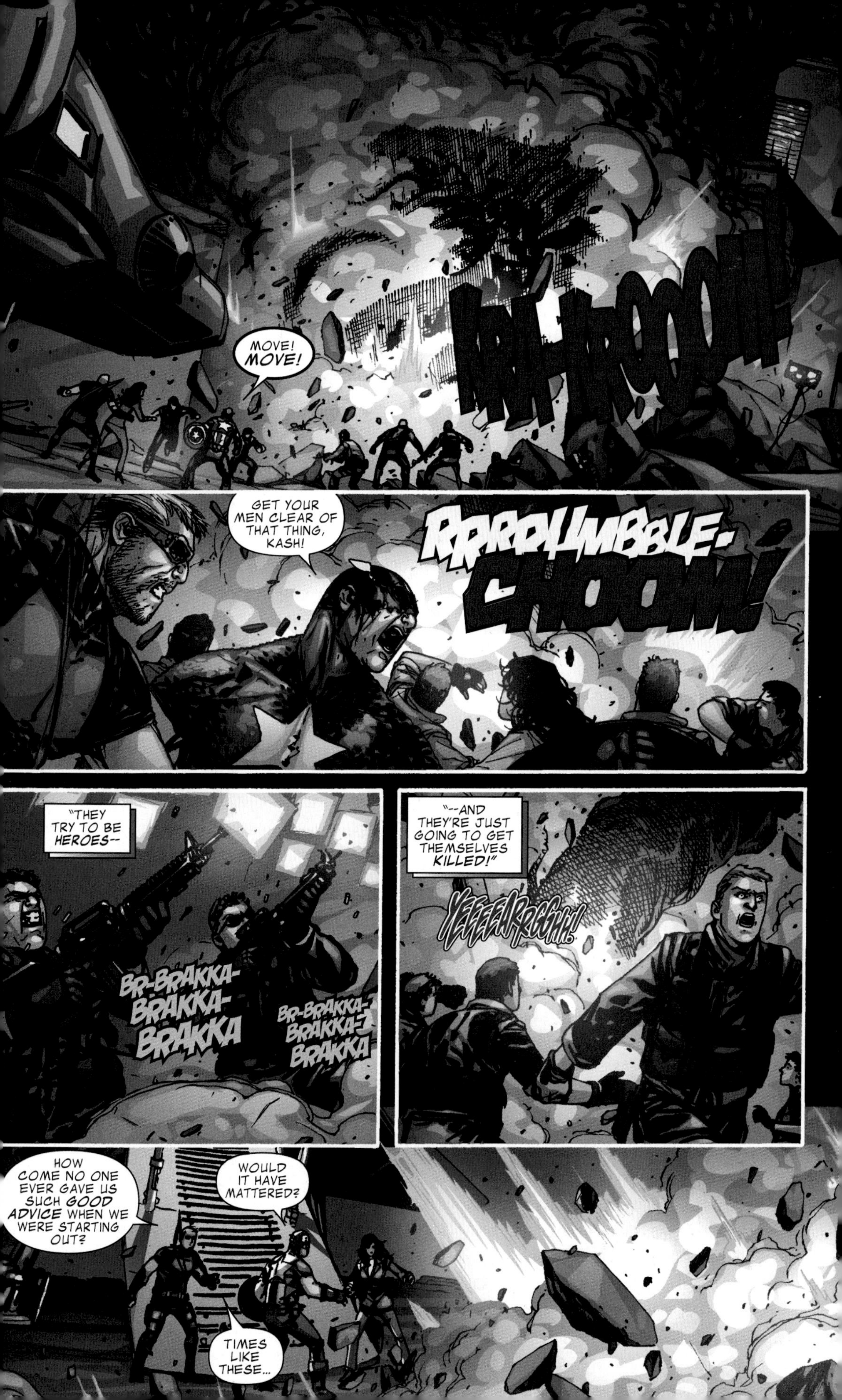

MOVE! MOVE!
KRHHROOOM!!
GET YOUR MEN CLEAR OF THAT THING, KASH!
RRRUMBBLE-CHOOM!
"THEY TRY TO BE HEROES--
BR-BRAKKA-BRAKKA-BRAKKA
BR-BRAKKA-BRAKKA-BRAKKA
"--AND THEY'RE JUST GOING TO GET THEMSELVES KILLED!"
YEEEEARRGGHH!
HOW COME NO ONE EVER GAVE US SUCH GOOD ADVICE WHEN WE WERE STARTING OUT?
WOULD IT HAVE MATTERED?
TIMES LIKE THESE...

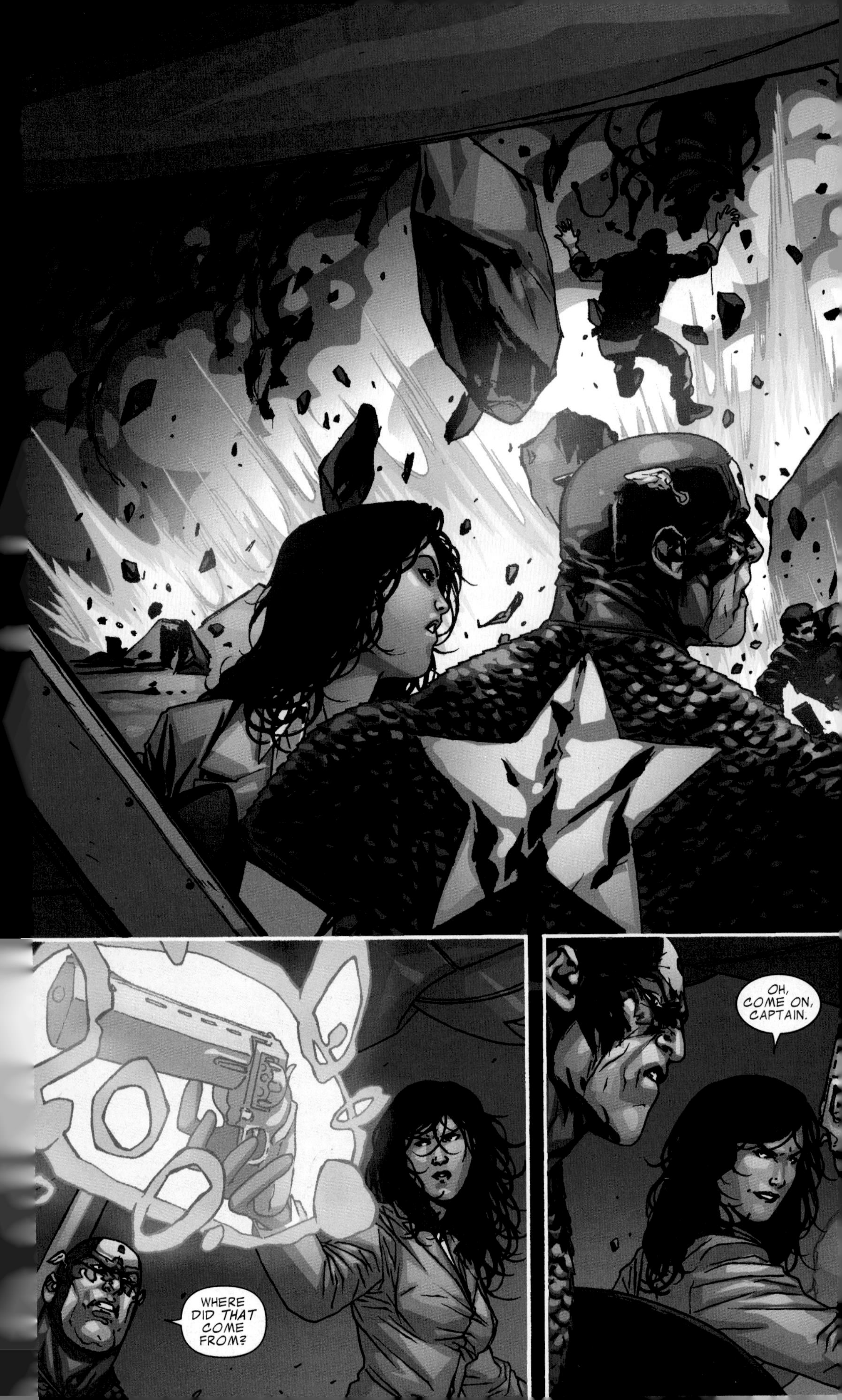
WHERE DID THAT COME FROM?
OH, COME ON, CAPTAIN.

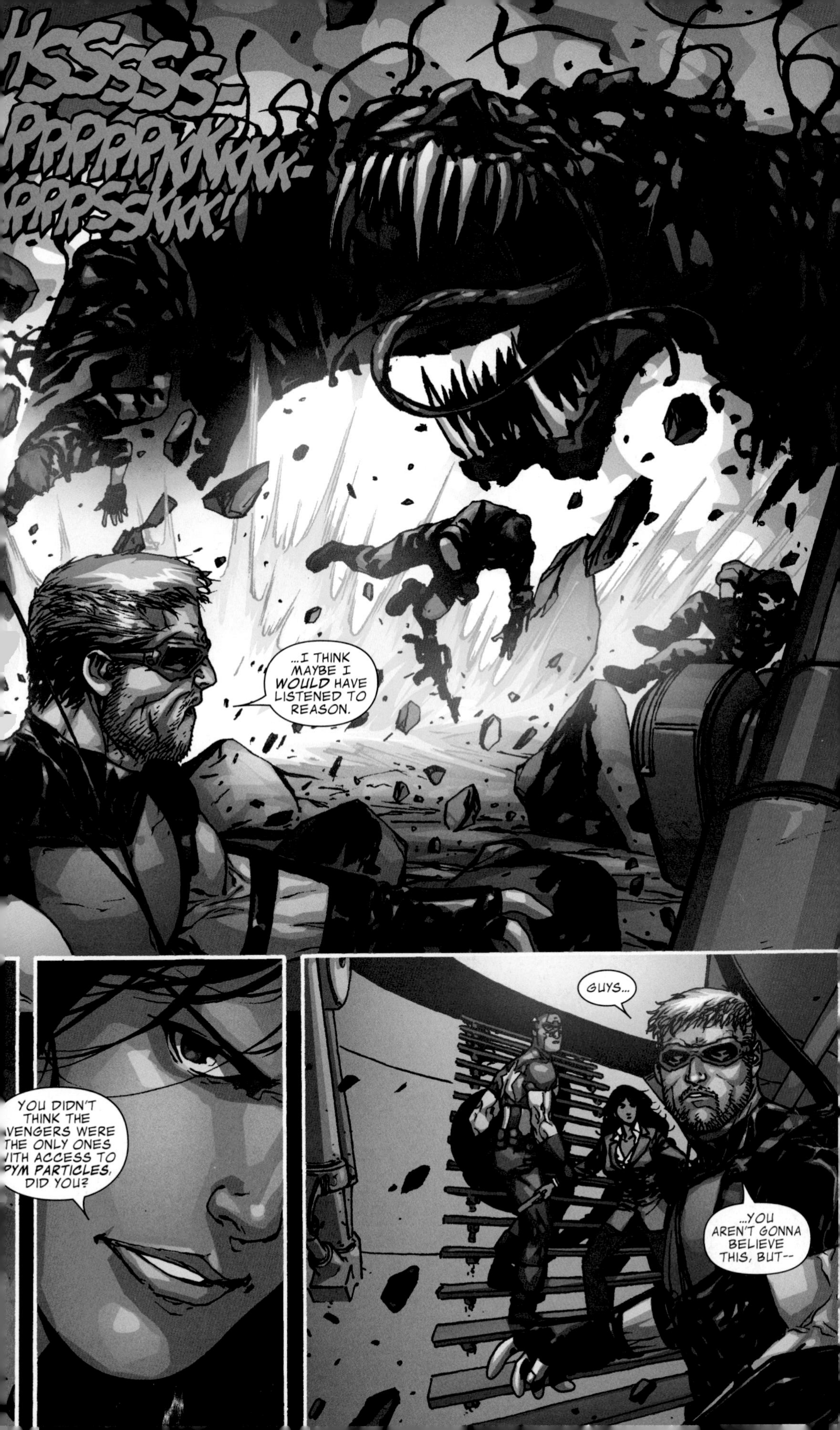

HSSSSS-PPPPPKKKKK-PPPSSKKK!
...I THINK MAYBE I *WOULD* HAVE LISTENED TO REASON.
YOU DIDN'T THINK THE VENGERS WERE THE ONLY ONES WITH ACCESS TO *PYM PARTICLES*, DID YOU?
GUYS...
...YOU AREN'T GONNA BELIEVE THIS, BUT--

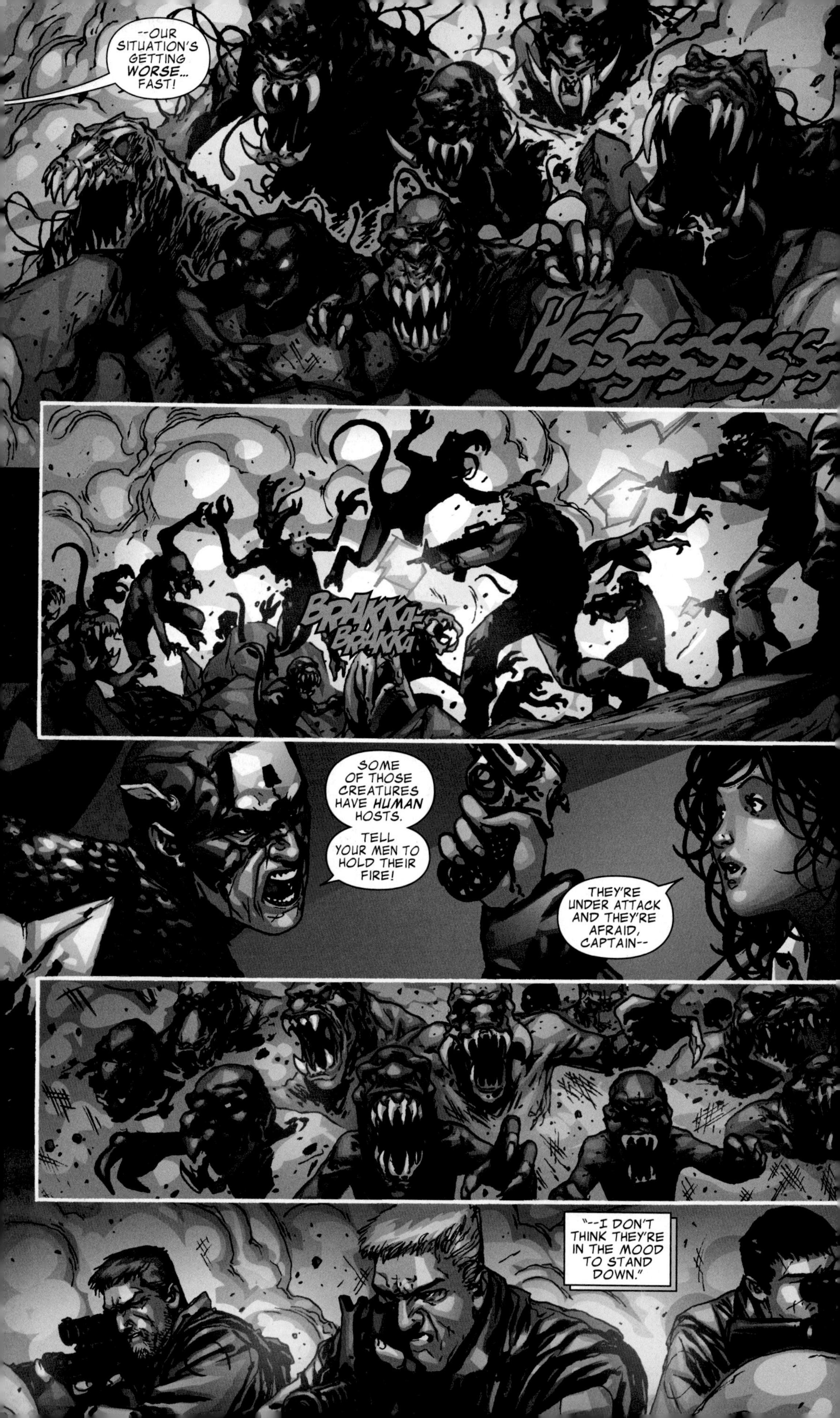
--OUR SITUATION'S GETTING WORSE... FAST!
HSSSSSSSS
BRAKKA-BRAKKA
SOME OF THOSE CREATURES HAVE HUMAN HOSTS.
TELL YOUR MEN TO HOLD THEIR FIRE!
THEY'RE UNDER ATTACK AND THEY'RE AFRAID, CAPTAIN--
"--I DON'T THINK THEY'RE IN THE MOOD TO STAND DOWN."

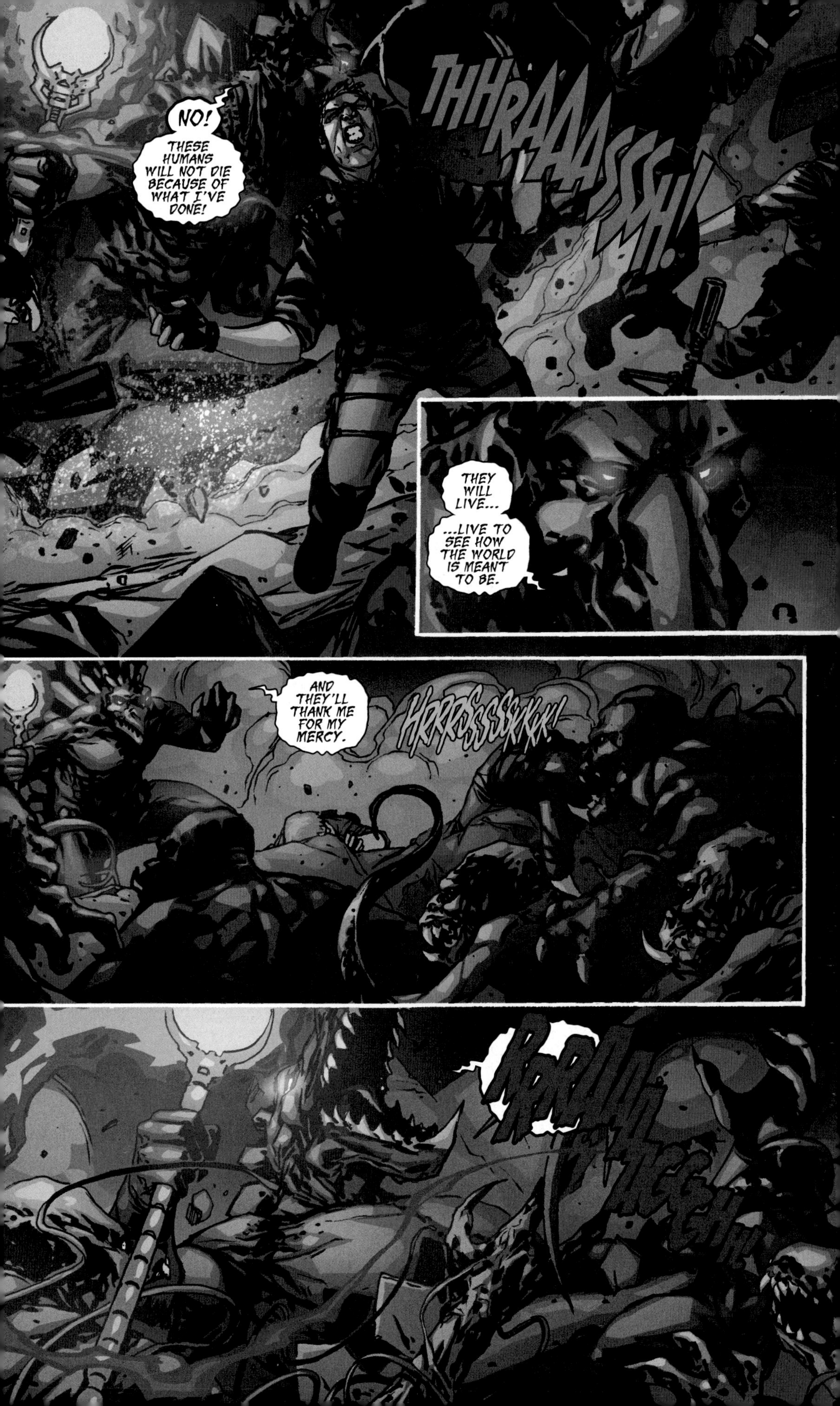
NO!
THESE HUMANS WILL NOT DIE BECAUSE OF WHAT I'VE DONE!
THHRAAASSSH!
THEY WILL LIVE...
...LIVE TO SEE HOW THE WORLD IS MEANT TO BE.
AND THEY'LL THANK ME FOR MY MERCY.

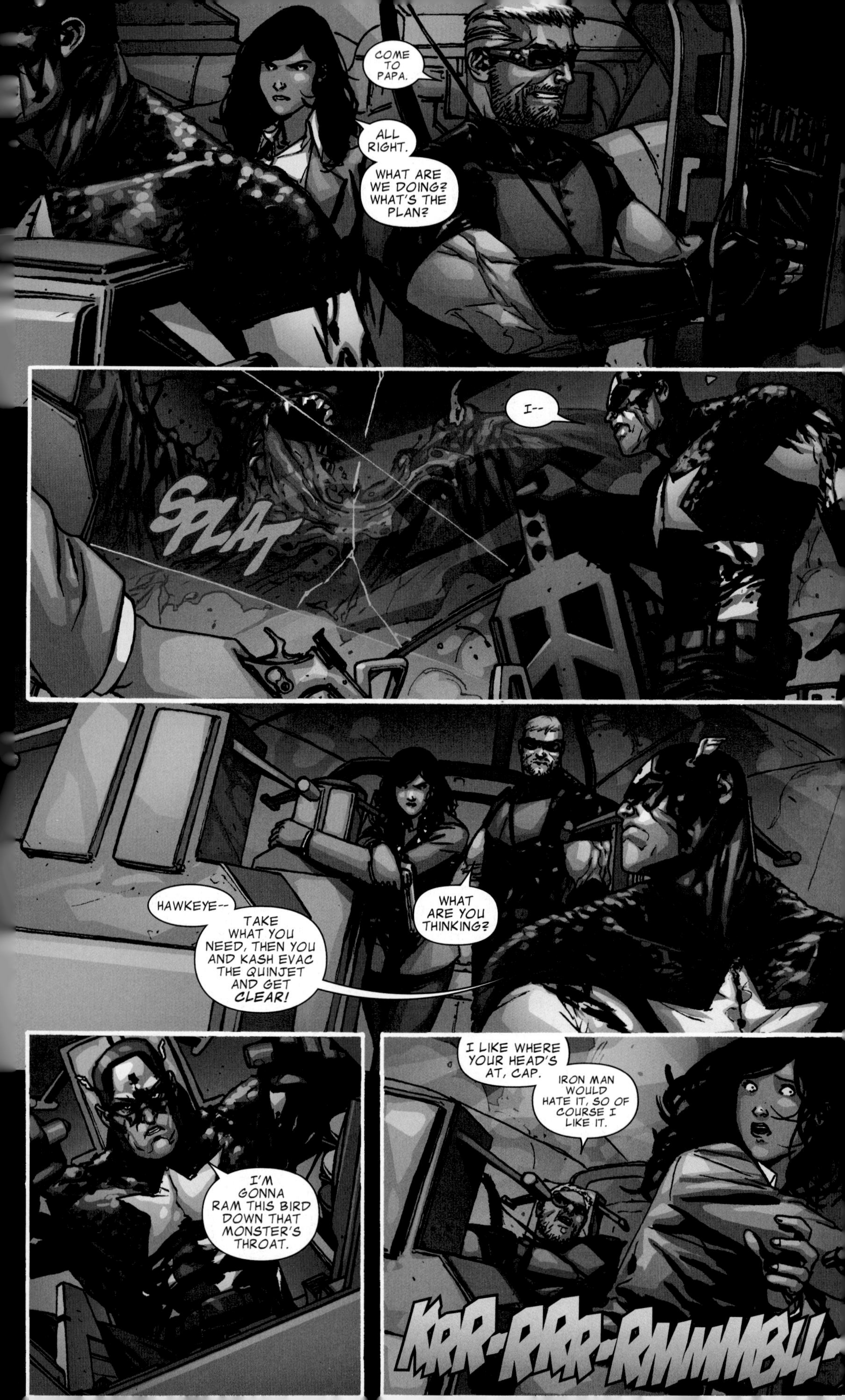
COME TO PAPA.
ALL RIGHT.
WHAT ARE WE DOING? WHAT'S THE PLAN?
SPLAT
I--
HAWKEYE--
TAKE WHAT YOU NEED, THEN YOU AND KASH EVAC THE QUINJET AND GET CLEAR!
WHAT ARE YOU THINKING?
I'M GONNA RAM THIS BIRD DOWN THAT MONSTER'S THROAT.
I LIKE WHERE YOUR HEAD'S AT, CAP.
IRON MAN WOULD HATE IT, SO OF COURSE I LIKE IT.
KRR-RRR-RMMMBLL-

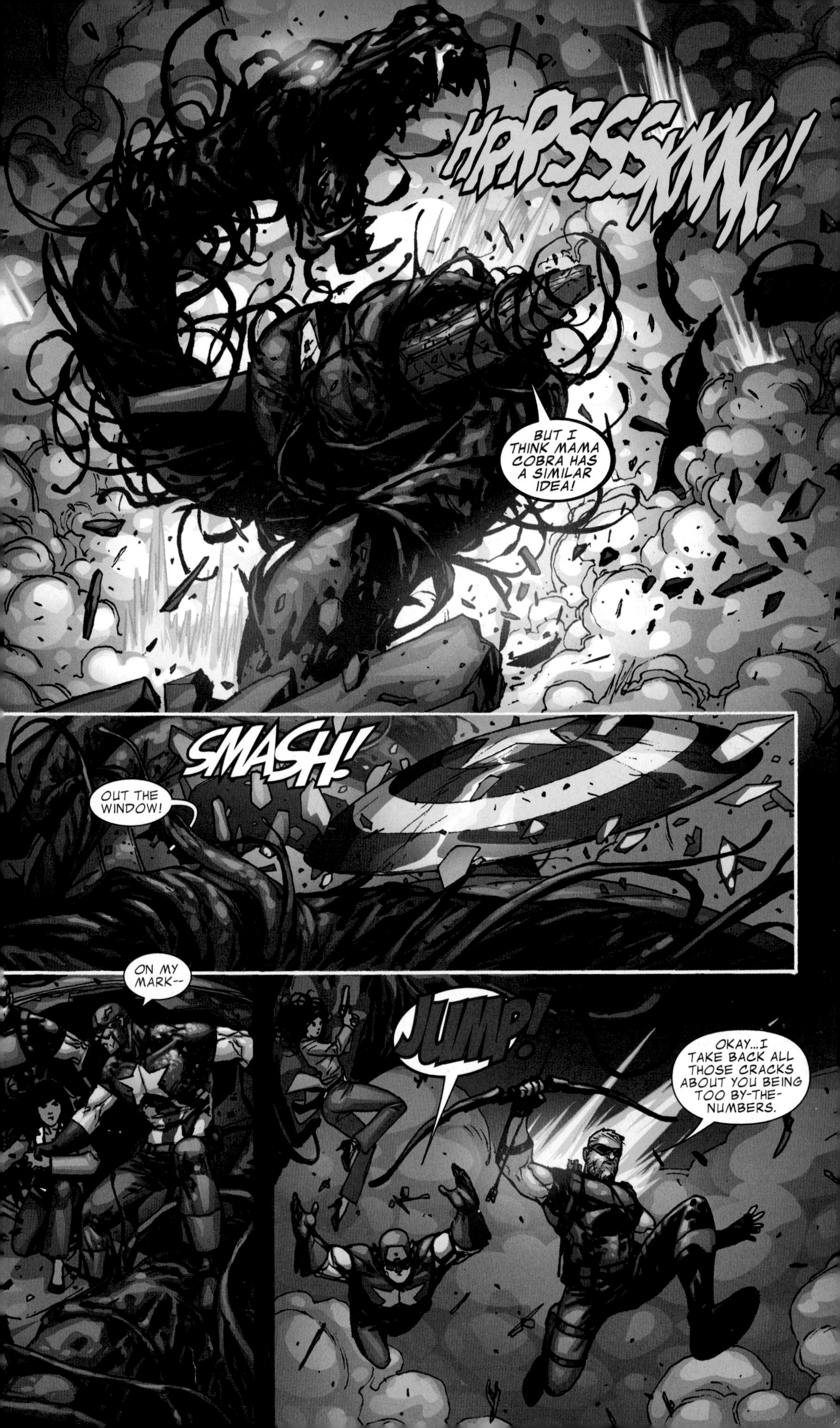
HRRSSSKKKK!
BUT I THINK MAMA COBRA HAS A SIMILAR IDEA!
SMASH!
OUT THE WINDOW!
ON MY MARK--
JUMP!
OKAY...I TAKE BACK ALL THOSE CRACKS ABOUT YOU BEING TOO BY-THE-NUMBERS.

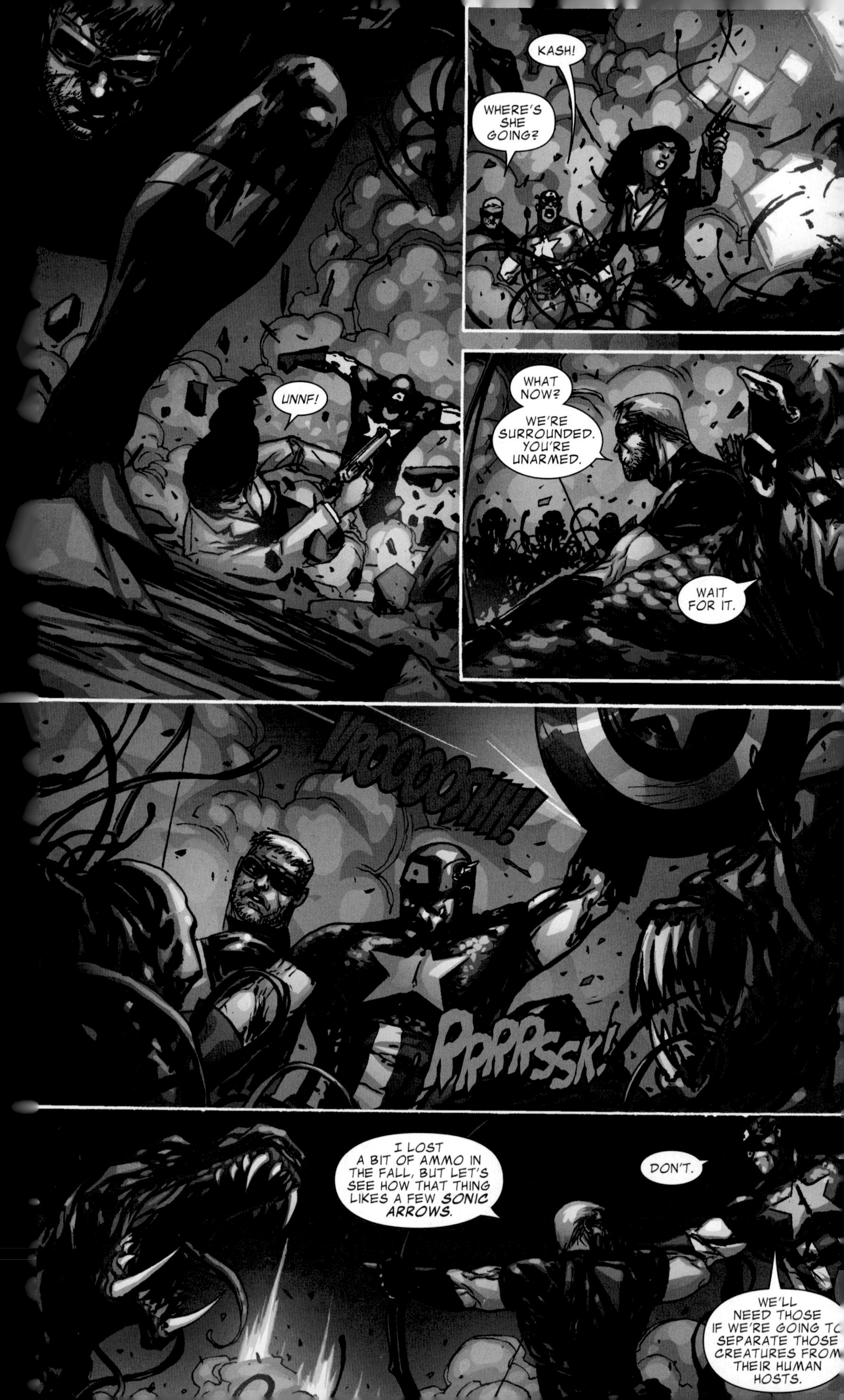
UNNF!
KASH!
WHERE'S SHE GOING?
WHAT NOW?
WE'RE SURROUNDED. YOU'RE UNARMED.
WAIT FOR IT.
ROOOOOM!
RPPPSSK!
I LOST A BIT OF AMMO IN THE FALL, BUT LET'S SEE HOW THAT THING LIKES A FEW SONIC ARROWS.
DON'T.
WE'LL NEED THOSE IF WE'RE GOING TO SEPARATE THOSE CREATURES FROM THEIR HUMAN HOSTS.

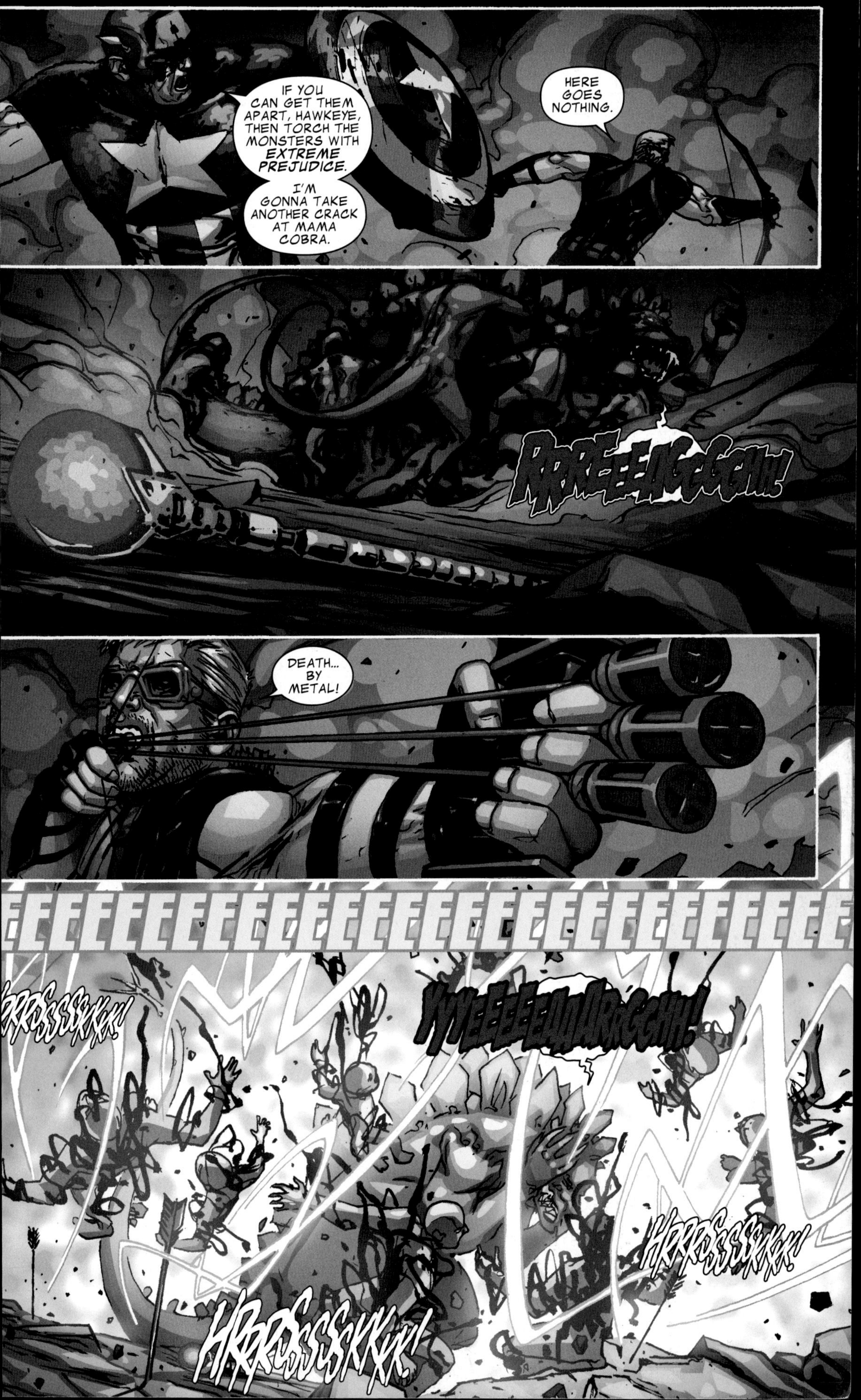

IF YOU CAN GET THEM APART, HAWKEYE, THEN TORCH THE MONSTERS WITH EXTREME PREJUDICE.
I'M GONNA TAKE ANOTHER CRACK AT MAMA COBRA.
HERE GOES NOTHING.
RRREEEAGGGHH!
DEATH... BY METAL!
EEEEEEEEEEEEEEEEEEEEEEEEEEE
YYYEEEEEAAARRGGHH!
HRRRSSSSKKKK!
HRRRSSSSKKKK!
HRRRSSSSKKKK!

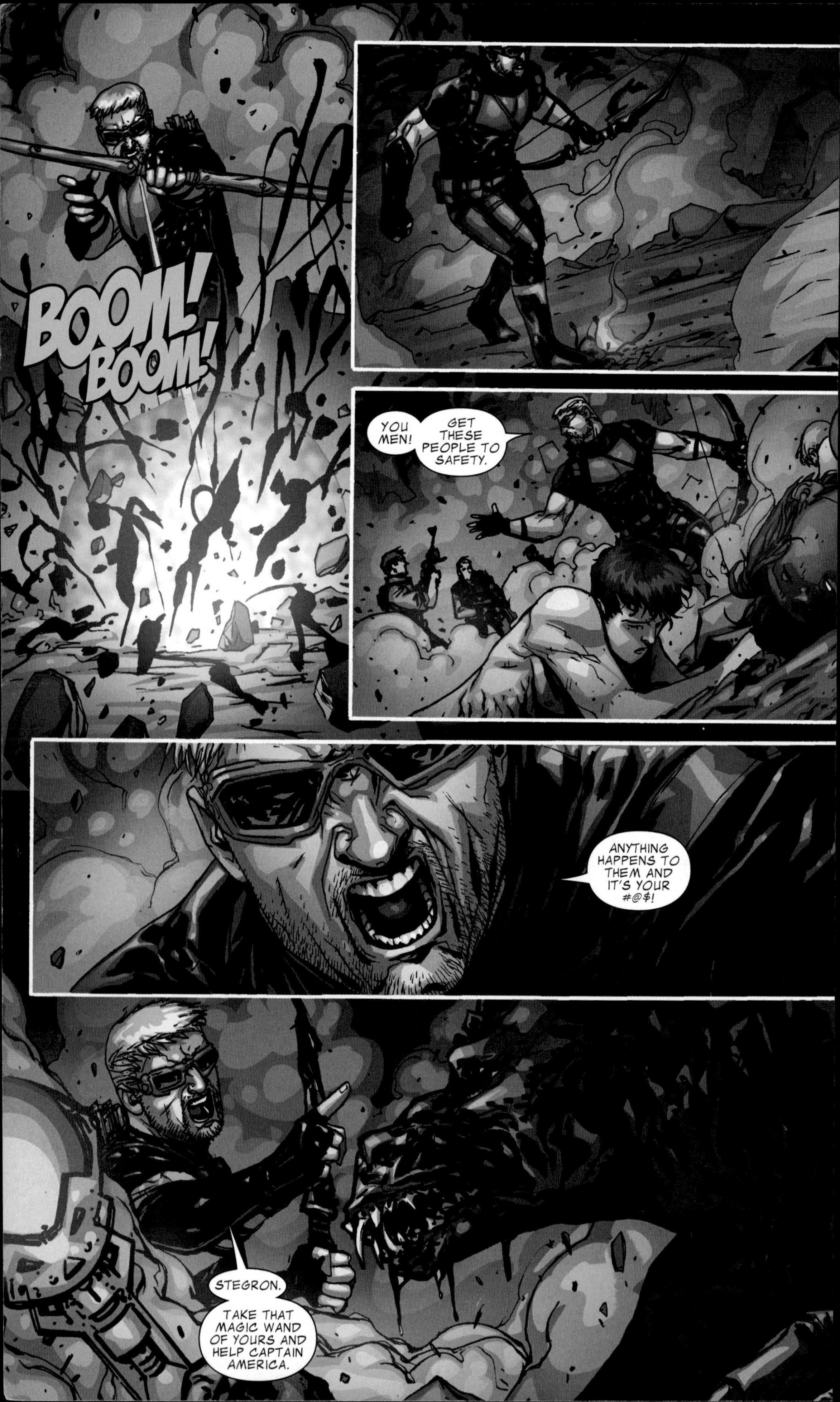
BOOM! BOOM!
YOU MEN!
GET THESE PEOPLE TO SAFETY.
ANYTHING HAPPENS TO THEM AND IT'S YOUR #@$!
STEGRON.
TAKE THAT MAGIC WAND OF YOURS AND HELP CAPTAIN AMERICA.

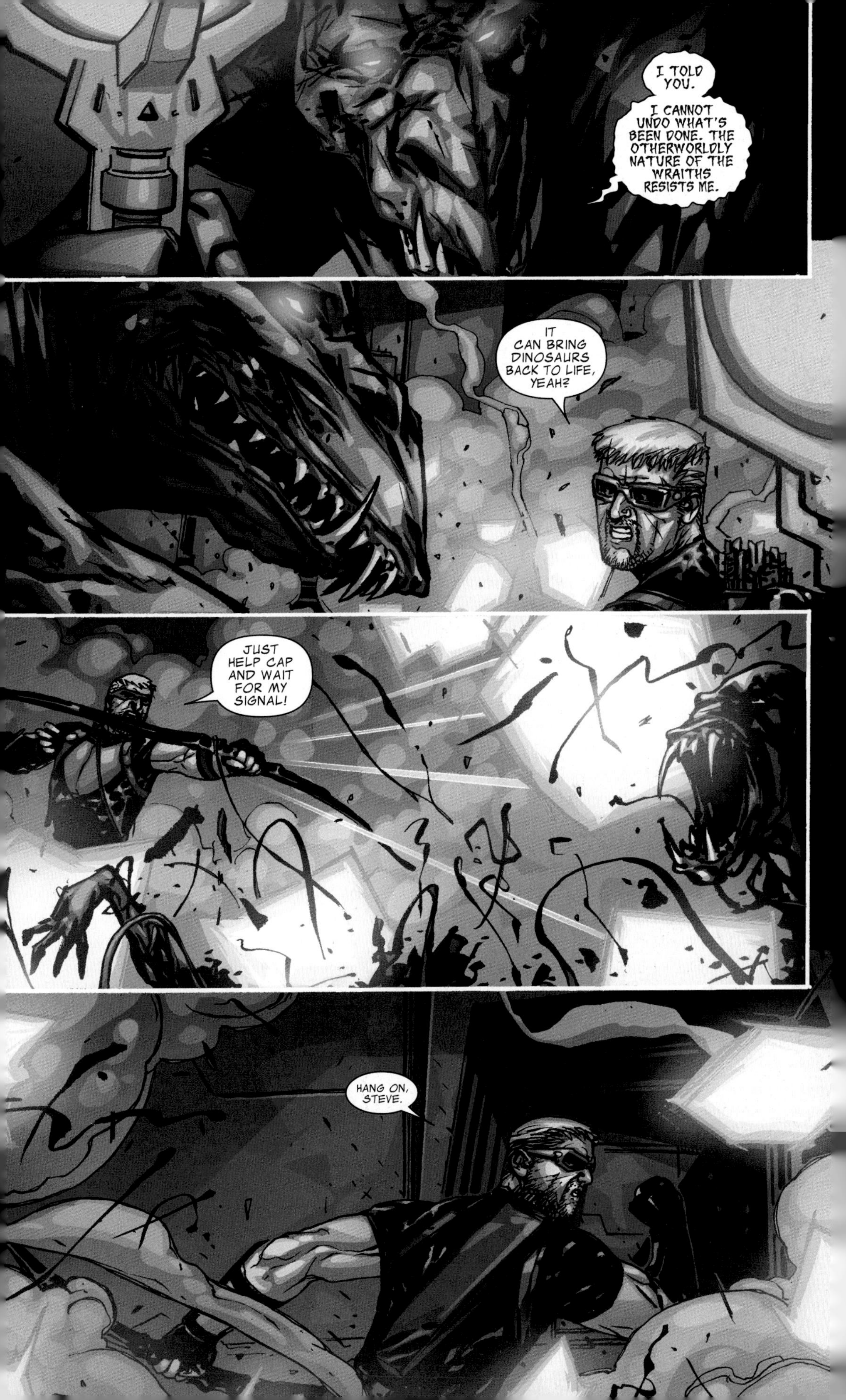
I TOLD YOU.
I CANNOT UNDO WHAT'S BEEN DONE. THE OTHERWORLDLY NATURE OF THE WRAITHS RESISTS ME.
IT CAN BRING DINOSAURS BACK TO LIFE, YEAH?
JUST HELP CAP AND WAIT FOR MY SIGNAL!
HANG ON, STEVE.

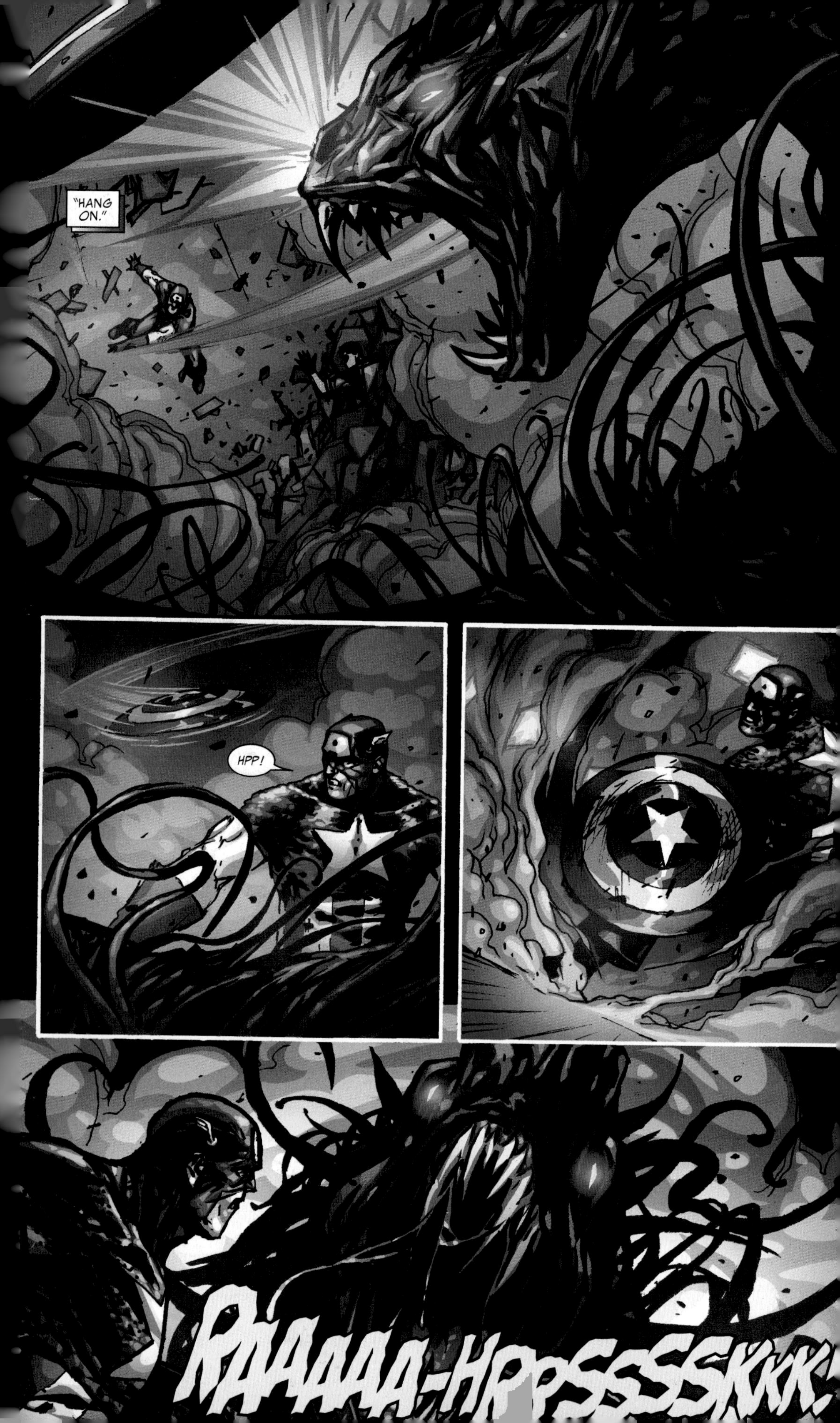
"HANG ON."
HPP!
RAAAAA-HRPSSSSSKKK!

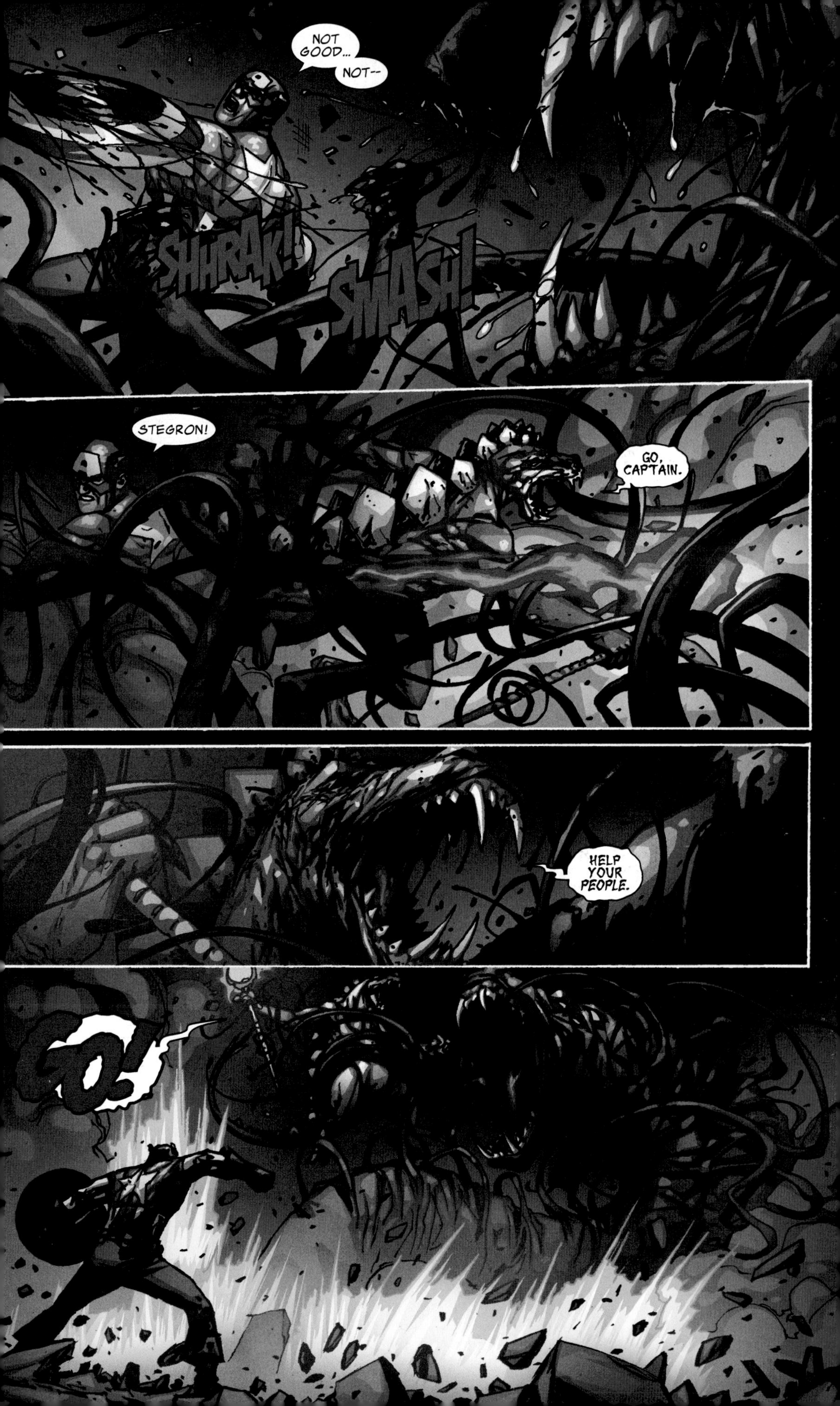
NOT GOOD...
NOT--
SHHRAK!
SMASH!
STEGRON!
GO, CAPTAIN.
HELP YOUR PEOPLE.
GO!

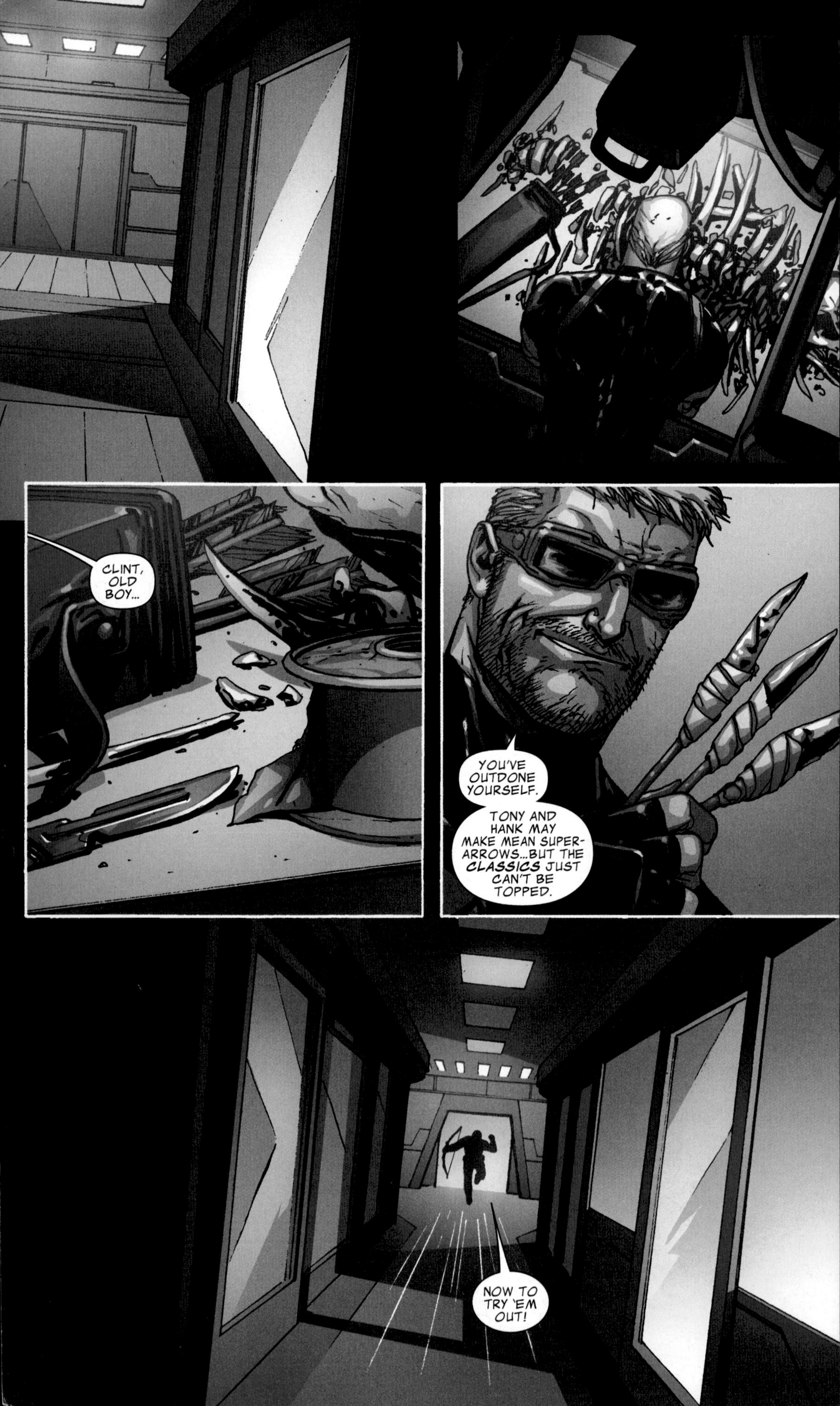
CLINT, OLD BOY...
YOU'VE OUTDONE YOURSELF.
TONY AND HANK MAY MAKE MEAN SUPER-ARROWS...BUT THE CLASSICS JUST CAN'T BE TOPPED.
NOW TO TRY 'EM OUT!

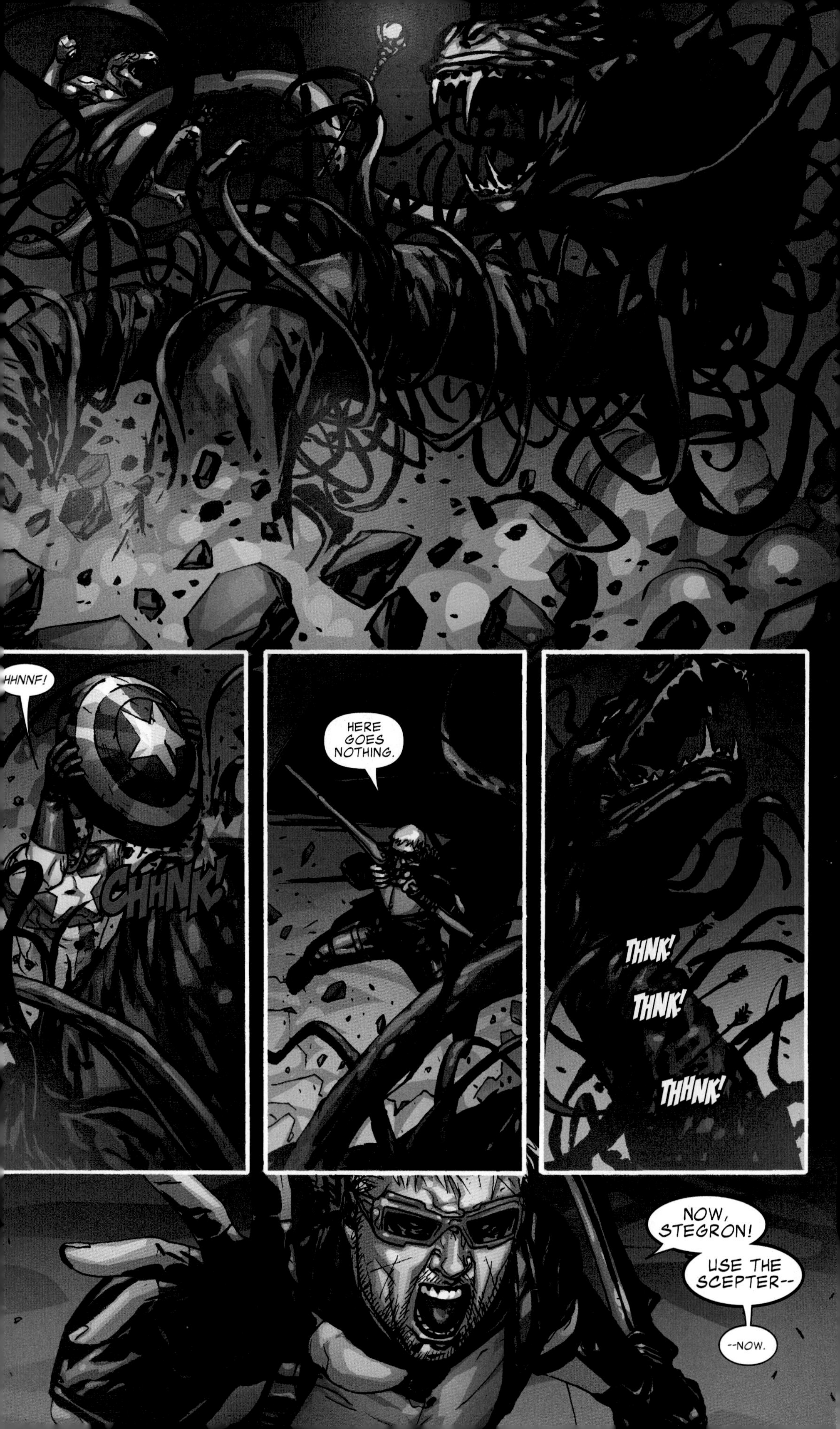
HHNNF!
CHHNK!
HERE GOES NOTHING.
THNK!
THNK!
THHNK!
NOW, STEGRON!
USE THE SCEPTER--
--NOW.

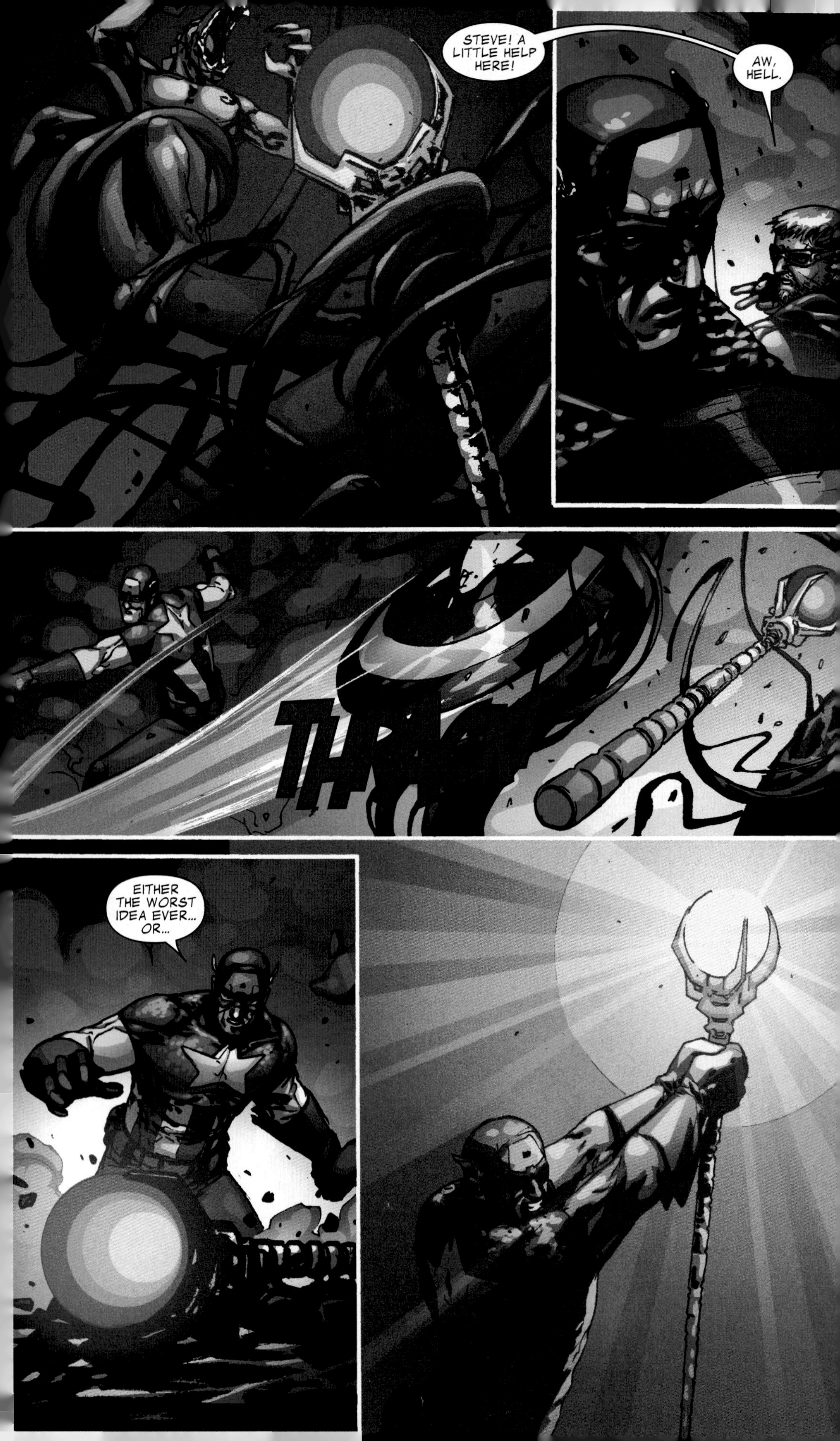

STEVE! A LITTLE HELP HERE!
AW, HELL.
THA
EITHER THE WORST IDEA EVER... OR...

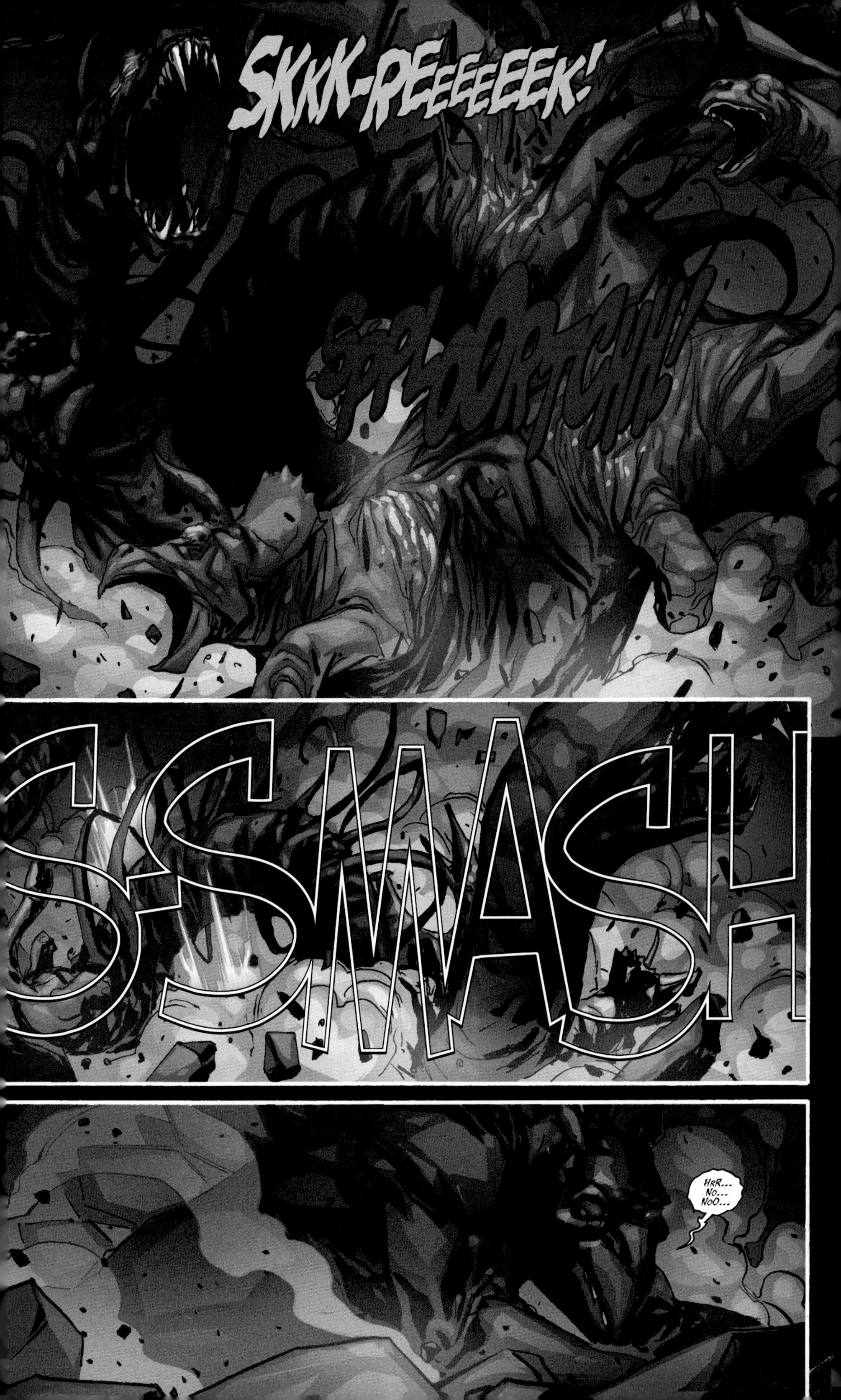
SKKK-REEEEEEK!
SPLOOOTCHH!
S-SMASH
HRR... NO... NOO...

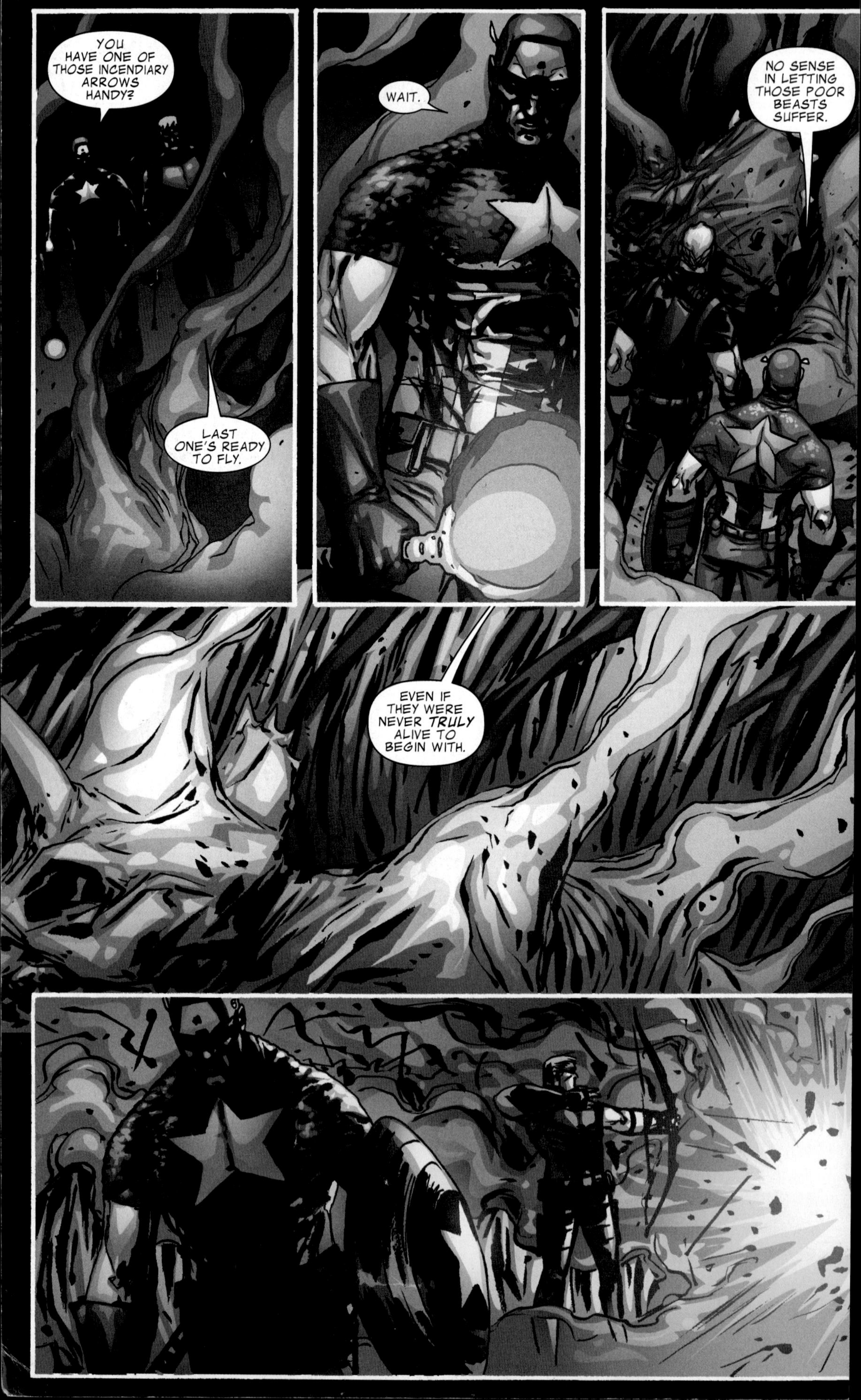

YOU HAVE ONE OF THOSE INCENDIARY ARROWS HANDY?
LAST ONE'S READY TO FLY.
WAIT.
NO SENSE IN LETTING THOSE POOR BEASTS SUFFER.
EVEN IF THEY WERE NEVER *TRULY* ALIVE TO BEGIN WITH.

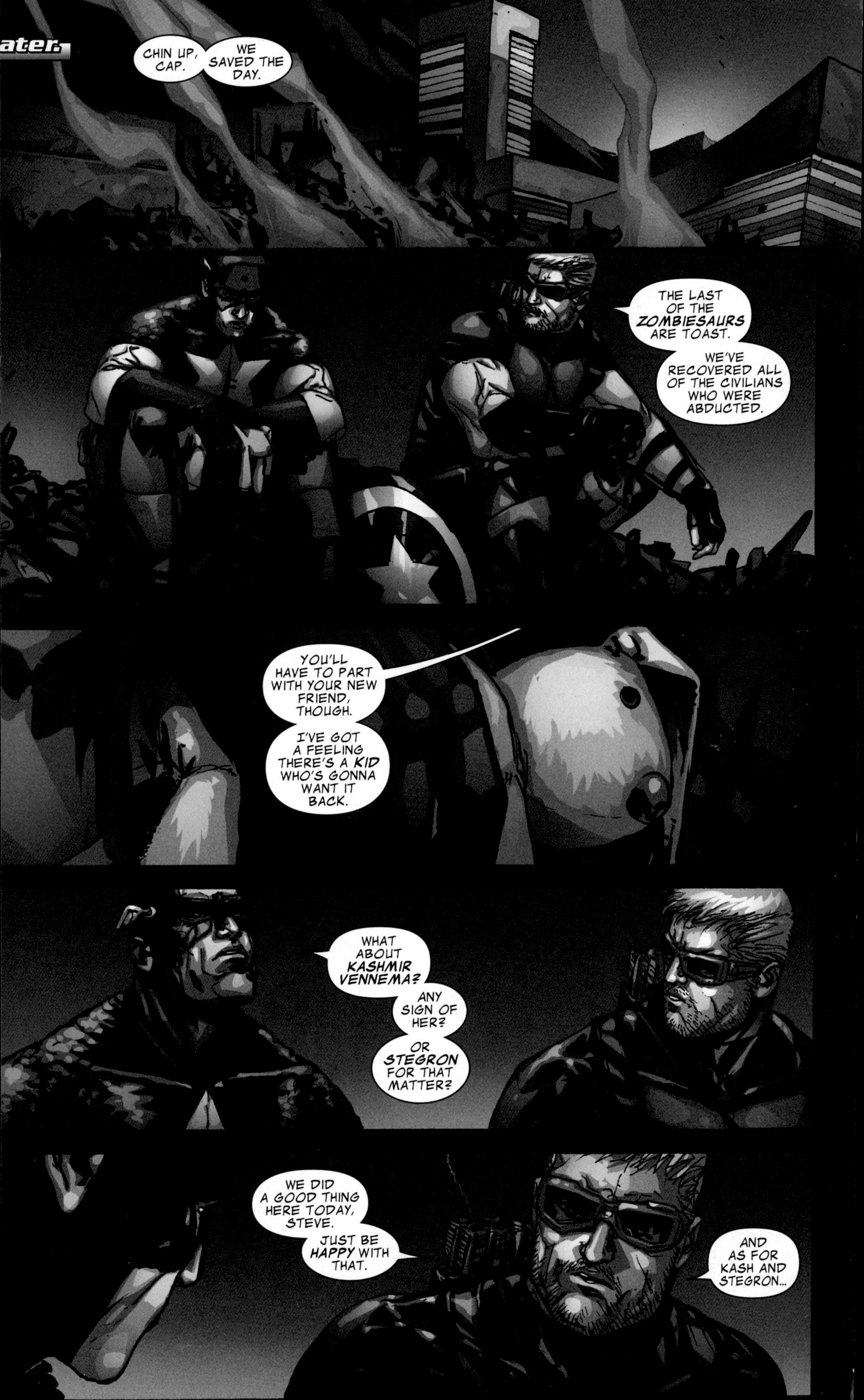
ater.
CHIN UP, CAP.
WE SAVED THE DAY.
THE LAST OF THE ZOMBIESAURS ARE TOAST.
WE'VE RECOVERED ALL OF THE CIVILIANS WHO WERE ABDUCTED.
YOU'LL HAVE TO PART WITH YOUR NEW FRIEND, THOUGH.
I'VE GOT A FEELING THERE'S A KID WHO'S GONNA WANT IT BACK.
WHAT ABOUT KASHMIR VENNEMA?
ANY SIGN OF HER?
OR STEGRON FOR THAT MATTER?
WE DID A GOOD THING HERE TODAY, STEVE.
JUST BE HAPPY WITH THAT.
AND AS FOR KASH AND STEGRON...

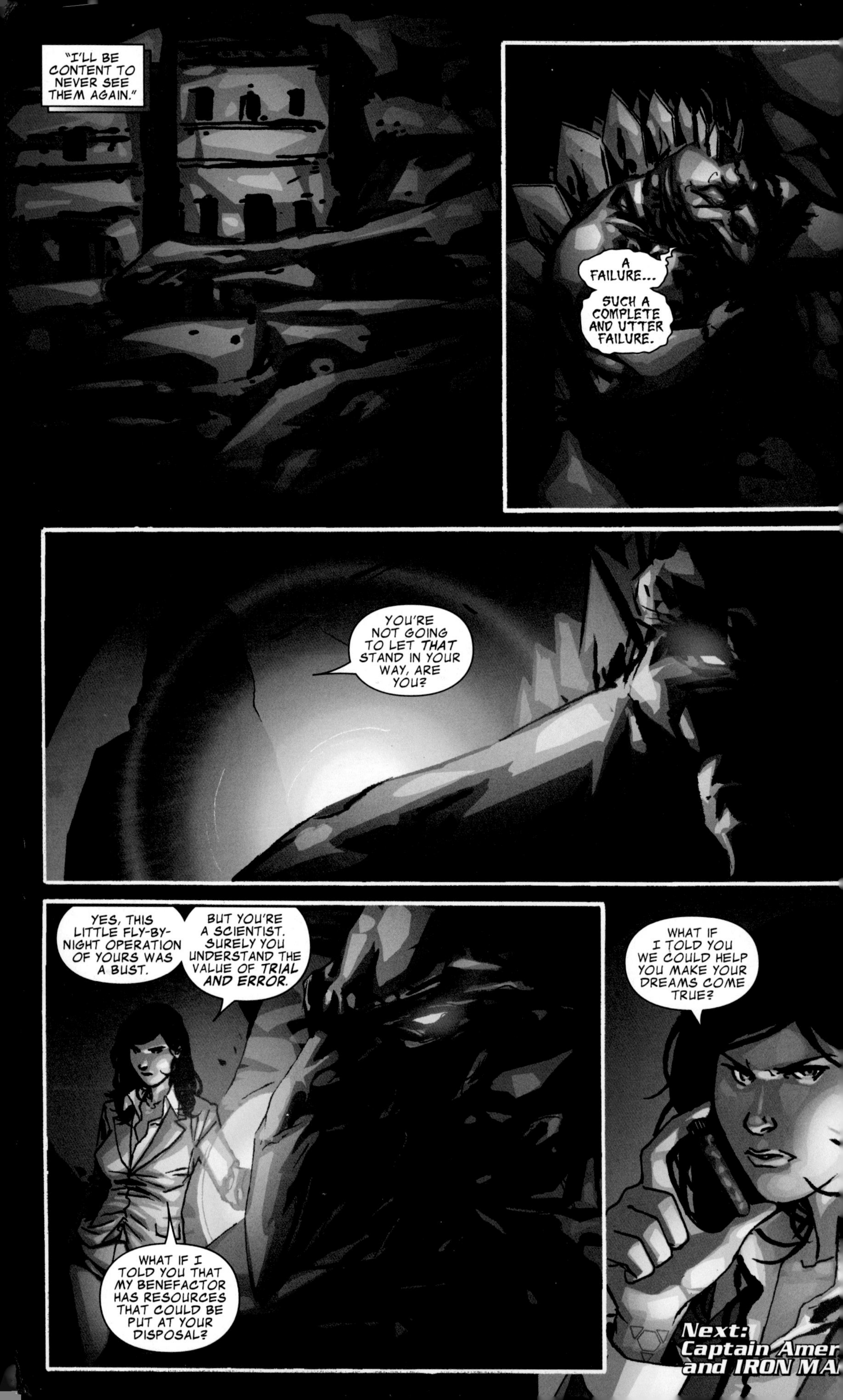
"I'LL BE CONTENT TO NEVER SEE THEM AGAIN."
A FAILURE...
SUCH A COMPLETE AND UTTER FAILURE.
YOU'RE NOT GOING TO LET THAT STAND IN YOUR WAY, ARE YOU?
YES, THIS LITTLE FLY-BY-NIGHT OPERATION OF YOURS WAS A BUST.
BUT YOU'RE A SCIENTIST. SURELY YOU UNDERSTAND THE VALUE OF TRIAL AND ERROR.
WHAT IF I TOLD YOU THAT MY BENEFACTOR HAS RESOURCES THAT COULD BE PUT AT YOUR DISPOSAL?
WHAT IF I TOLD YOU WE COULD HELP YOU MAKE YOUR DREAMS COME TRUE?
Next: Captain Amer
and IRON MA

EXTRAS

PAGE 4

4.1 Hawkeye's arrows hit Cap's shield and bounce off, arcing away and striking four of the soldiers who were approaching from different directions.

> 1/HAWKEYE: Let's not forget that I **could've** had **your** job.

> SFX (Arrows):   Zzzz-twhap! Thwap! Th-thwap! Thwap!

4.2 Cap hurls his shield toward Hawkeye.

> 2/CAP: Don't take this the wrong way, but you would've folded under the **responsibility**.

4.3 Hawkeye ducks his head to the side as the shield streaks past to smash another mercenary.

> 3/HAWKEYE: Yeah, I may not be Captain America.

> 4/HAWKEYE: But I'm not **Bucky**, either, so stop treating me like some **sidekick**.

> SFX (Shield):   Smack!

4.4 Cap and Hawkeye get in each other's faces, snarling. They look like they're about to come to blows with each other.

> 5/CAP: Damn right you're not—

> 6/KASH (Off-panel):   Gentlemen—

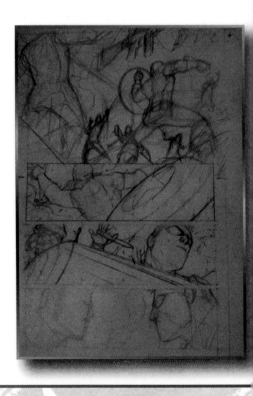

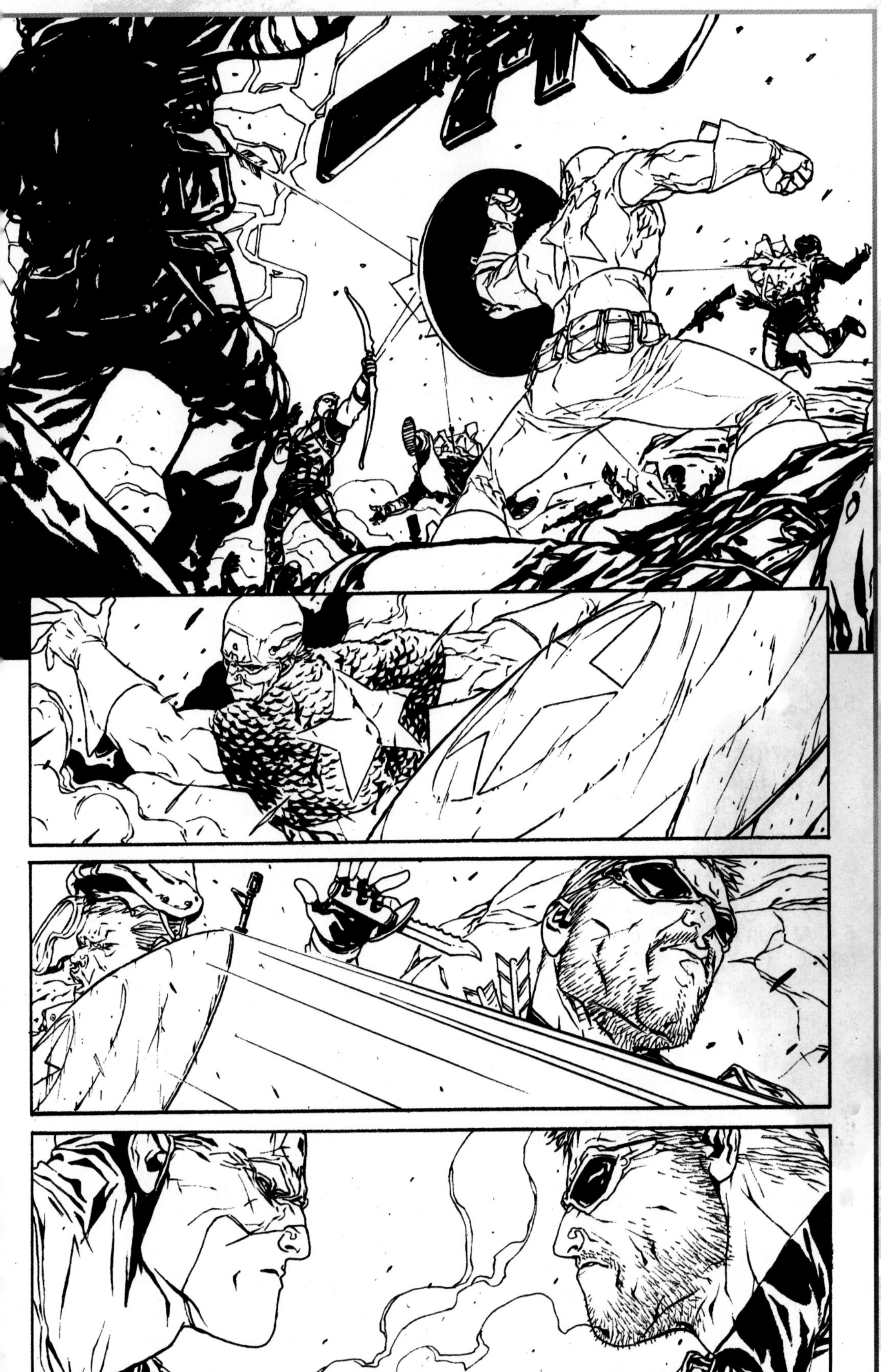

SCRIPT BY CULLEN BUNN, PENCILS AND INKS BY ALESSANDRO VITTI

PAGE 5

5.1 Angle past Cap and Hawkeye as they look across a battlefield littered with unconscious soldiers. KASHMIR VENNEMA stands before them. Kash for short, she is a beautiful woman whose cultural heritage may not be entirely clear. Think Thandie Newton and you're on the right track. Kash is sexy without trying. She's part businesswoman, part Bond girl, part Bond. She's the type of woman who never looks worried. In fact, she almost wears a sly expression that says she's enjoying herself. She is unarmed, and she looks completely comfortable surrounded by fallen soldiers.

1/KASH:	If you're done pummeling my men—and each other—I'd like to introduce myself.
2/KASH:	My name is **Kashmir Vennema**.
3/KASH:	I'm the Director of Operations for the Damocles Research Facility.
4/KASH:	You're **trespassing**.
5/KASH:	You can call me **Kash**.

5.2 Cap and Hawkeye look at each other, puzzled.

6/CAP:	Trespassing?

5.3 Cap turns, looking around the area, and Kash steps a little closer behind him.

7/CAP:	My companion and I are—
8/KASH:	Of course, I **know** who you are, Captain.
9/KASH:	This is New Mexico. We get all the latest news via carrier pigeon.

5.4 At Cap's feet is an unconscious soldier and, oddly, a ratty-looking stuffed bunny rabbit.

10/CAP:	Touché.
11/CAP:	But you may not realize that we're here on official Avengers business.

5.5 Angle past Kash as Cap turns toward her. Cap holds the limp bunny in his hand.

12/CAP:	A group of environmentalists have been reported missing as of three days ago.
13/CAP:	Civilians. People with **families**. People with **children**.
14/CAP:	This is their last reported location.

#629 PAGE 5 PROCESS

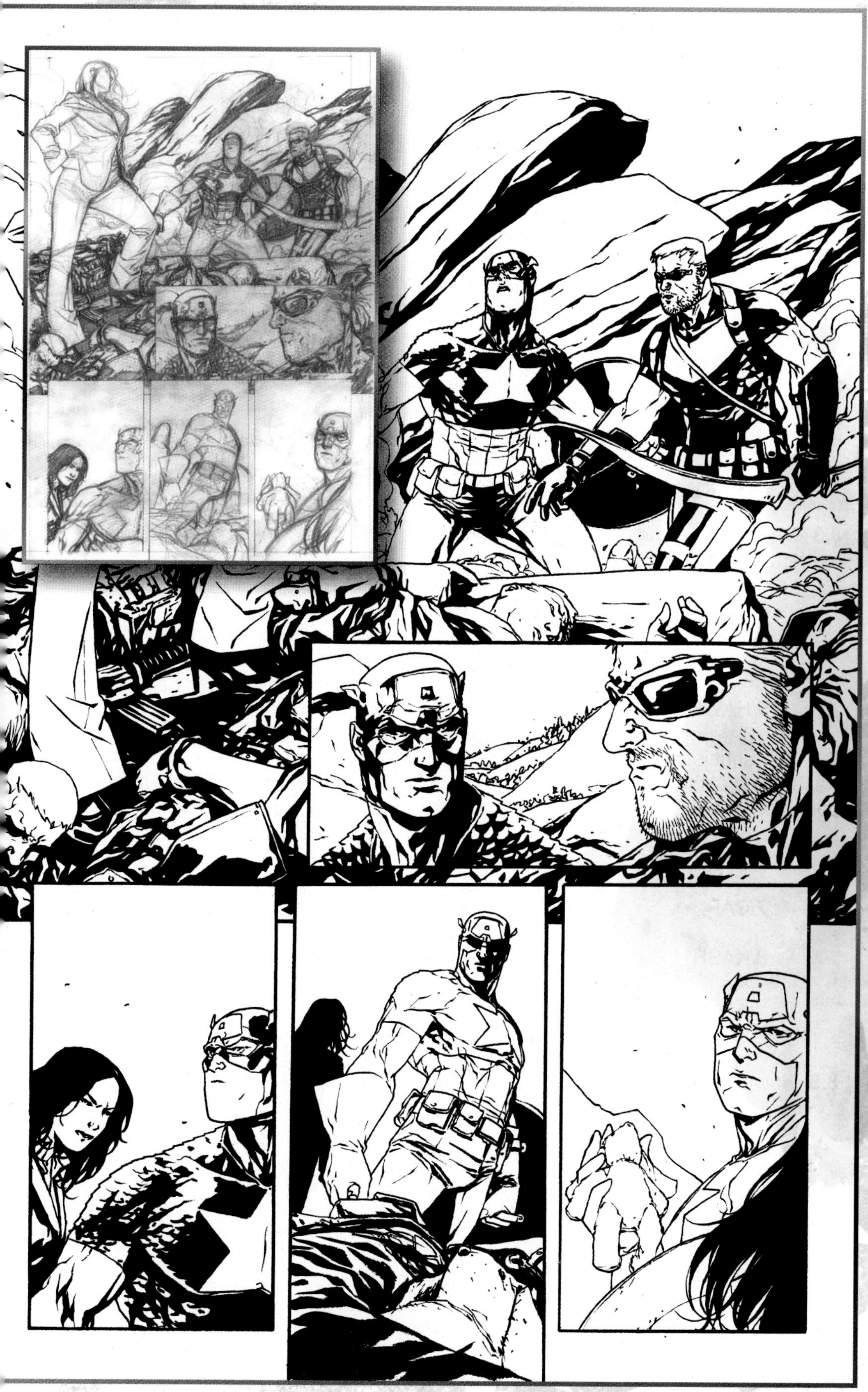

SCRIPT BY CULLEN BUNN, PENCILS AND INKS BY ALESSANDRO VITTI

PAGE 8

8.1 A steel door slides open with a *woosh* of air. Kash, holding a key card and waiting for the door to open, brushes a stray strand of hair from her face as she looks toward Cap and Hawkeye.

1/KASH:	Our charter here is the evaluation of hazardous materials, the development of new propulsion systems, and the advancement of space flight technologies.
2/KASH:	Of course, that means we have our fingers in **several** cookie jars.

8.2 In the foreground, Kash walks down the hallway. The décor is clean and utilitarian. Large windows looking into work areas and labs line either side of the hall. Captain America and Hawkeye walk along a few steps behind her. Grinning smugly, Hawkeye leans in to whisper to Cap.

3/KASH:	Solar energy… cosmic emissions… thermal radiation…

8.3 On Hawkeye and Cap. Cap is looking through one of the windows as Hawkeye mutters under his breath.

4/KASH (Off-panel):	We touch all the same research subjects as **Project: Pegasus**, but we have none of the recognition and a tenth of the budget.
5/HAWKEYE (Small):	Sounds **familiar**.

8.4 This shot is from within one of the labs lining the hallway as Cap, Hawkeye, and Kash stand at the window, looking within. In the lab we see a set of fossilized dinosaur bones on an examination table. The skeleton is incomplete and caked with dirt.

6/CAP:	Ms. Vennema… Uh… Kash…
7/CAP:	What's this?
8/KASH:	Ah. I see you've noticed our "pets."
9/KASH:	We've been unearthing them for years. The mountains are rife with fossilized remains.

8.5 Hawkeye slides in closer to Kash as if letting her in on a joke.

10/HAWKEYE:	You gotta understand…
11/HAWKEYE:	Cap here feels a deep connection to moldering old **relics**

8.6 Angle past Cap as Kash looks at him like a slab of meat.

12/KASH:	Well, who can blame him?
13/KASH:	I've always thought relics have a kind of delicious appeal.

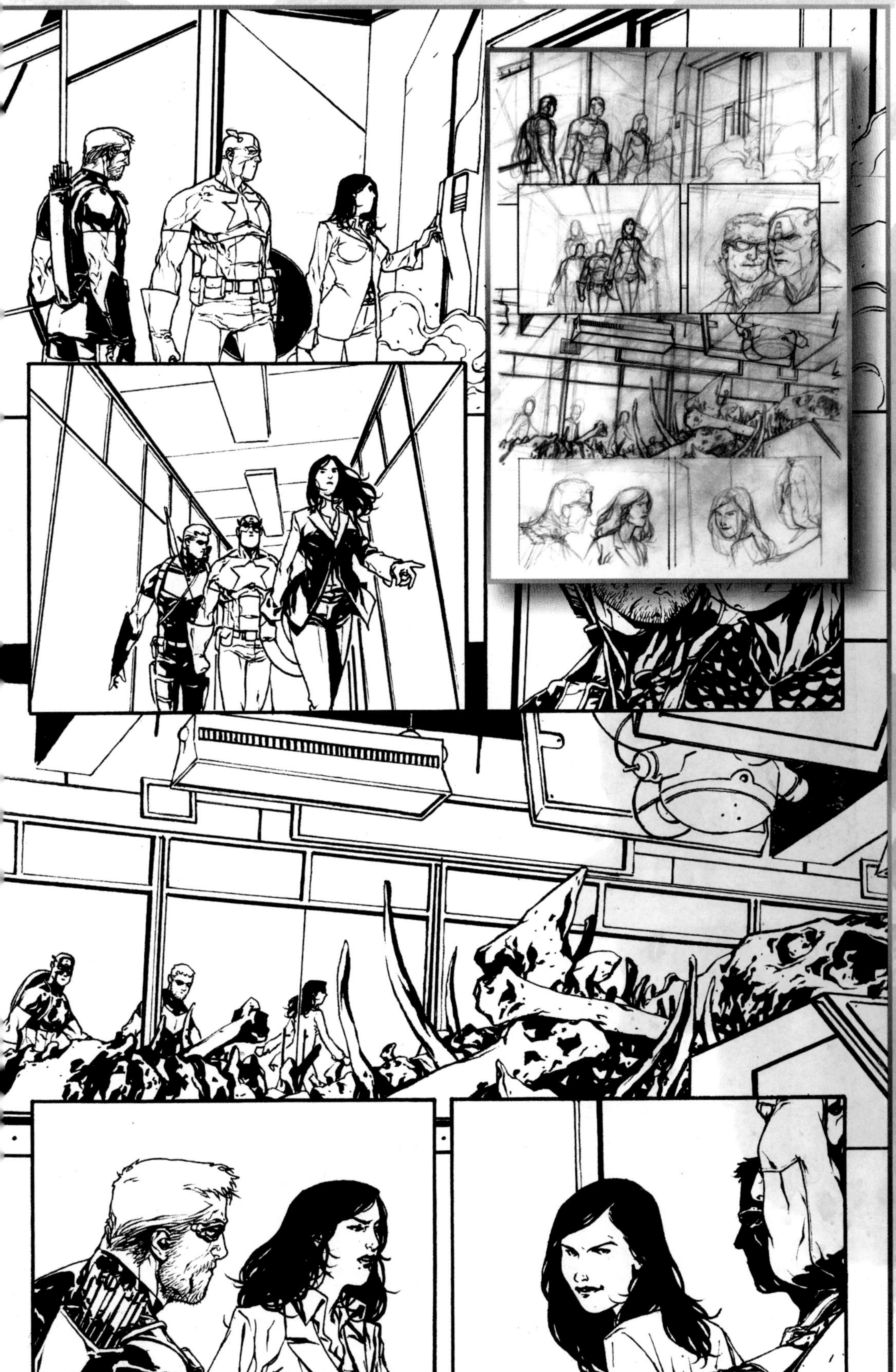

SCRIPT BY CULLEN BUNN, PENCILS AND INKS BY ALESSANDRO VITTI

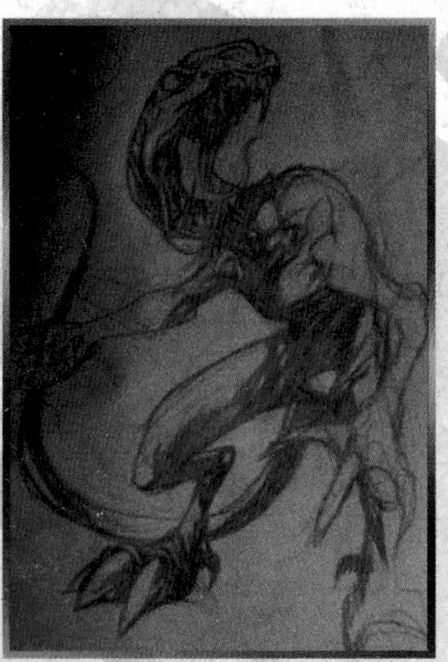

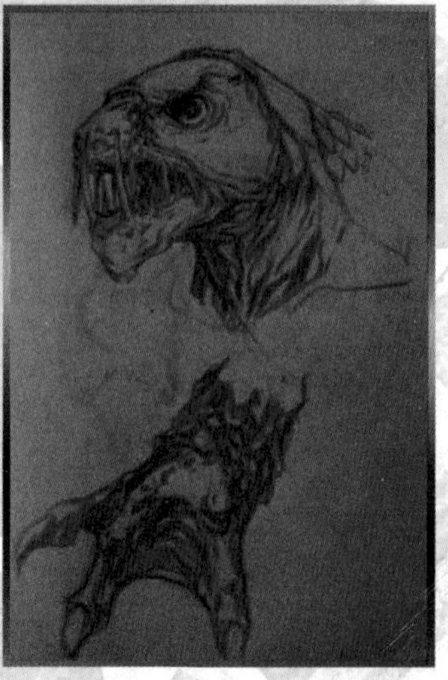

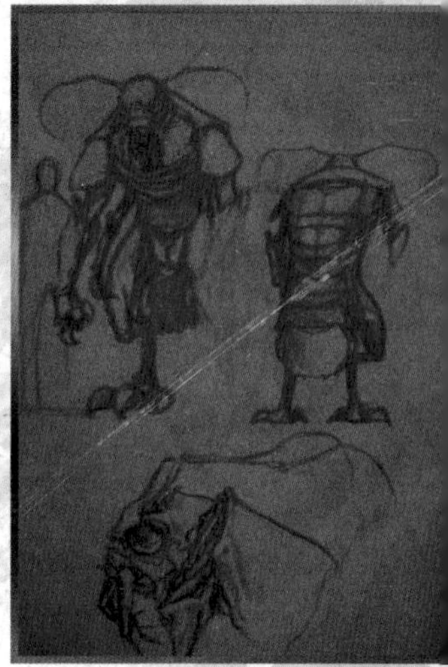

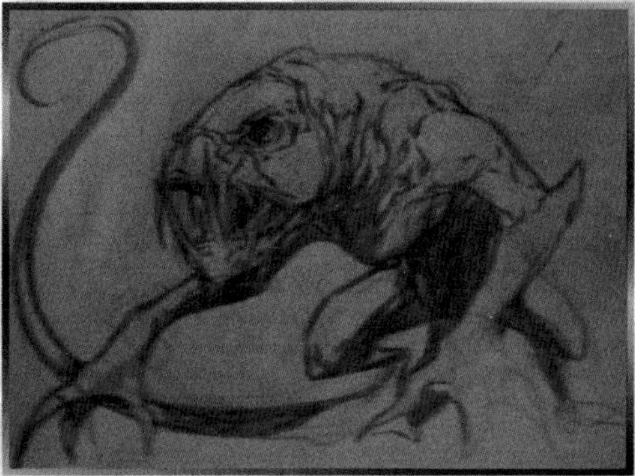

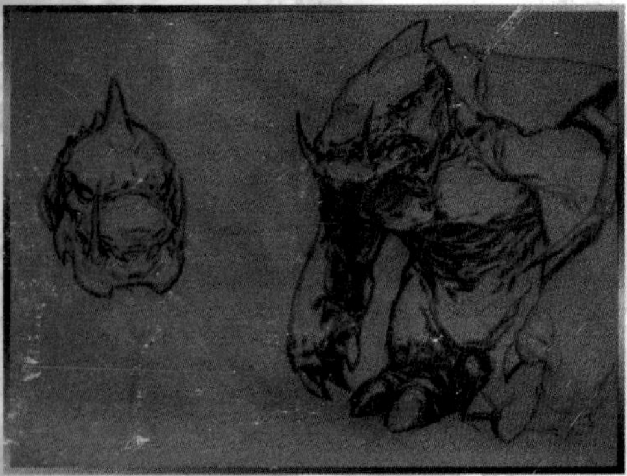

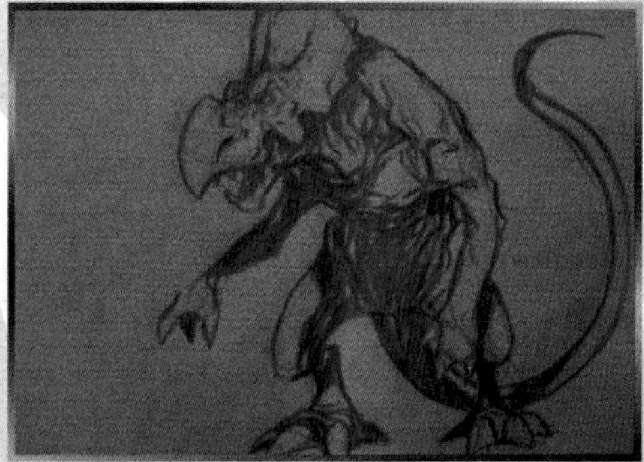

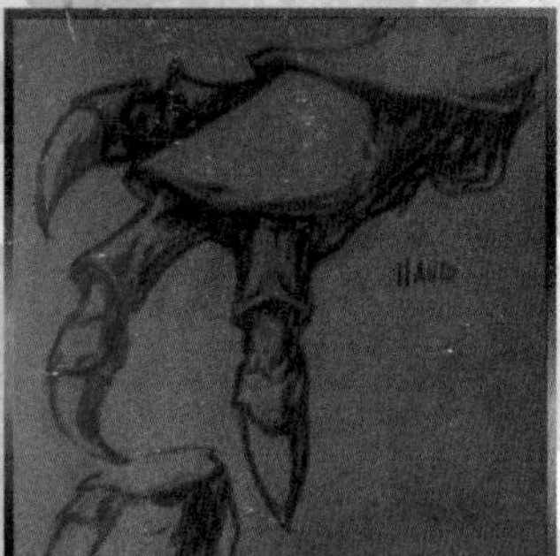
HAND

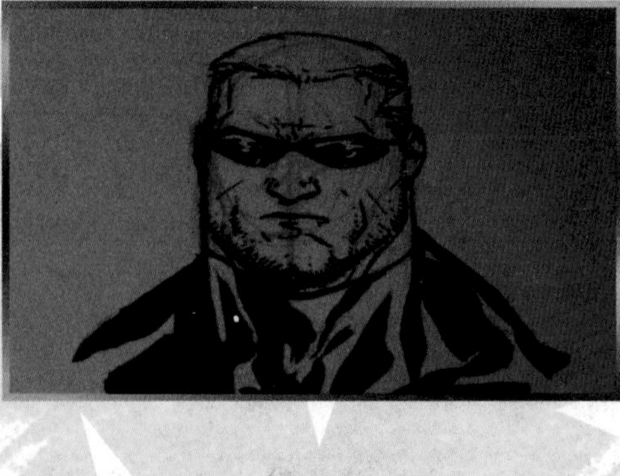

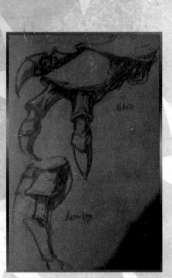

DEVELOPMENT SKETCHES BY ALESSANDRO VITTI